AF556176

TEACHING READING SUCCESSFULLY

ENCYCLOPAEDIA OF TEACHING - III

TEACHING READING SUCCESSFULLY

By

Dr. Marlow Ediger
M.S. Education, Ph.D.
Professor Emeritus in Education
Truman State University
Box 417, 201 W, 22nd St
North Newton KS 67117
United States of America

&

Dr. Digumarti Bhaskara Rao
M.Sc., M.A., M.A., M.Ed., Ph.D.
Reader & Research Director
R.V.R. College of Education
Srinivasa Nagar Colony
Guntur–522 006
(India)

DISCOVERY PUBLISHING HOUSE PVT. LTD.
NEW DELHI-110 002

Reprinted – 2019
First Published - 2000

IISBN: 978-93-5056-516-2 (Set)

ISBN: 978-81-7141-556-4

Teaching Reading Successfully

Published by:
DISCOVERY PUBLISHING HOUSE PVT. LTD.
4383/4B, Ansari Road, Darya Ganj
New Delhi-110 002 (India)
Phone: +91-11-23279245, 23253475; 43596065
E-mail: discoverybooksindia@gmail.com
discoverypublishinghouse@gmail.com
web: www.discoverypublishinggroup.com

Printed at:
Infinity Imaging Systems
Delhi

Preface

Teaching Reading Successfully' is written for pre-service and in-service education of elementary school teachers. We believe that the contents herein possess a scope and sequence which guide teachers to provide for individual differences so that each pupil may achieve as optimally as possible. This work integrates well in reading content in science, social studies, mathematics, language arts and literature. Thus, an inter-disciplinary curriculum might well be in the offing. As teachers need to keep up with the very latest in literature pertaining to teaching reading in the schools, this book will serve well their needs. Also, this book will be of great use to educational planners, administrators and researchers.

Marlow Ediger
Digumarti Bhaskara Rao
September 8, 1999
International Literacy Day

Contents

1
Goals of Reading Instruction

The reading teacher needs to choose goals carefully that pupils are to achieve. Each goal needs to be weighed carefully before implementation in classroom teaching of reading. There are many goals from which to choose. It might well be that a specific pupil needs to attain other goals than what the rest of the class is focused upon. Learners differ one from the other in terms of needs to be emphasized in teaching and learning situations. The first kind of goal to emphasize is cognitive ends. Cognitive ends stress that which emphasizes mental operations, thought, application, comparisons and contrasts made, or use of the mind in general. These kinds of goals can be identified at different levels of complexity. Certainly, the reading teacher wants pupils to be able to remember what has been read. Why ? Otherwise, the teacher cannot have pupils build on what has been retained. This means that a pupil cannot stop with merely being a word caller in reading. He/she must also understand and attach meaning pertaining to words read. Pupils need to be challenged in discussions to reveal quality comprehension from reading. Unless pupils can state what has been read in their very own words and also be able to answer questions covering ideas read, they have not moved higher toward different levels of cognition. Once pupils understand and comprehend what has been read, they are now able to use information acquired. The level of knowledge use is salient in that pupils need to apply what has been learned. Unless ideas gleaned can be applied to a new situation or to problem areas, the act of reading might have limited values.

Higher up in cognition, the pupil needs to be able to analyse subject matter read. This might well mean to separate content into component parts. The analyzing may include separating facts from opinions, accurate from inaccurate ideas, and relevant from irrelevant content. Making contrasts and comparisons also stresses analyzing in the cognitive domain.

Analysed content should be followed with a joining together or fusion of ideas. With fusion, the content is put back together again after selected elements have been omitted, such as inaccurate ideas or irrelevant subject matter. With analysis having been completed, the learner is now ready to use the fused subject matter to solve a problem. The subject matter, however, must be relevant for the problem being solved. Ediger (1997) wrote the following :

A variety of reading materials may be used in a problem solving curriculum. The role of the reading teacher is to motivate students to identify problems within the framework of a stimulating environment. After a problem has been clearly identified, related information is gathered to solve the identified problem. Library books, basal reading text-books, encyclopedias, pamphlets, brochures, among other reading materials, are used to gather data. Audio-visual materials, including software packages, may also be used in data gathering.

Based on the data, a hypothesis is developed in answer to the problem. The hypothesis is tentative and not an absolute. With further reading experiences, as well as use of audio-visual materials, the student with teacher guidance tests the hypothesis.

Fusion may also involve creating new ideas. The novel, the unique, and the original may come about when gaps are perceived in knowledge. For example, in writing poetry, the pupil needs to achieve novel ideas and fuse content resulting in a couplet, triplet, quatrain, limerick, haiku, tanka, and/or a diamante.

Generally, the highest level of the cognitive domain is appraisal. Here, the learner has designed criteria to use in appraising the quality of oral reading, a written folklore, a puppetry presentation, and/or a dramatization.

In the reading curriculum, the teacher needs to guide pupils to move upward and higher on the cognitive level of objectives.

Affective Objectives

Pupils need to achieve well in affective dimension of objectives. The objectives involve the feeling and emotional aspects of learning. Certainly if pupils feel positively about learning, they will attain at a higher rate as compared to having negative beliefs about and pertaining to reading. Pupils who like to read will do more reading and do a better job of accessing information than those having a lack of positive responses. There are numerous ways in helping pupils develop positive attitudes toward the reading curriculum. Among others, the following are important :

1. listening to interesting stories read by the teacher to pupils and discussing in a fascinating manner the inherent subject matter.
2. pupils in a collaborative relationship reading collectively and sharing ideas from content read.
3. learners, individually or in committees, identifying and solving problems from a given reading selection.
4. the pupils selecting a library book to read for enjoyment.
5. pupils in a committee dramatizing content read from a reading selection.
6. learners making and developing a bulletin board display to encourage pupils reading of library books.
7. pupils making a collage or mural pertaining to contents read in a library of text book.
8. pupils doing journal writing and including personal feelings and interests pertaining to the library book read.
9. learners selecting books to read from a learning station whereby there are an adequate number of diverse titles and the books are on diverse reading levels to provide for individual differences.
10. pupils choosing how they wish to be evaluated after reading a specific library book (Ediger, 1997).

Multiple Intelligences

Howard Gardner (1993) identified nine intelligences through which pupils may reveal what has been learned. These are : verbal/linguistic, logical/mathematical, visual/spatial, musical, bodily/kinesthetic, the human condition, nature/science, interpersonal, and intrapersonal.

Gardner recommends harmonizing what is taught with the individual pupil's intelligence. Most of reading instruction has involved verbal/linguistic intelligence. Thus, the printed word and the use of real language makes for verbal/linguistic intelligence. What about bringing in the other eight intelligences so that more pupils may benefit from reading instruction ? How might this be encouraged ?

1. have library books on the interest center pertaining to diverse titles. Thus, there should be library books on mathematics, architecture (visual/spatial intelligence), music such as history of great musicians, athletes and athletic endeavors for bodily/kinesthetic intelligènce, as well as books on the natural sciences for pupils to read.

2. have pupils reveal what has been learned form reading using diverse means. Thus, after having read a given selection, a pupil may report individually in a self-chosen manner such as in intrapersonal intelligence. Pupils in a committee may have read the same selection and wish to report collectively such as in interpersonal intelligence. Additional ways to reveal what has been learned from reading a library book or a selection from a textbook may include (a) making an art scene such as in visual/spatial intelligence, (b) revealing musical content read by writing related words and lyrics of the pupils very own thinking, (c) planning and performing a dance routine pertaining to content read, (d) writing selected mathematics problems for class-mates to solve based on content in the library book . With the eighth intelligence identified by Gardner, namely, nature and the natural world, pupils might develop a diorama based on reading about volcanoes,' as an example.

Multiple intelligence emphasize that pupils may read content based on their interests and strengths as well as show what has been learned through one of more of the intelligences. Thus, evaluation procedures based on standardized or criterion referenced tests is not adequate. These tests tend to evaluate pupil learning in terms of verbal/linguistic intelligences. Their are eight other intelligences then that are not being used. Teachers and tests writers need to be fair to all pupils in that bias needs to be eliminated with the use of standardized and criterion referenced testing. All intelligences identified by Gardner need nurturing and yet, at the same time, pupils need ample opportunities to use their strengths in the reading curriculum (Ediger, 1997).

Philosophy of Reading Instruction

There are different philosophies of education which might assist the reading teacher in the selection of objectives. Philosophy emphasizes looking at values, beliefs, and strands of thought pertaining to the reading curriculum as well as other academic areas.

(1) Idealism is one of the older schools of thought in reading instruction. Idealists tend to believe that one can only receive ideas of the natural/social world and not know the real world as it truly is. Idealism stressed an idea centered world. Thus pupils achieving vital concepts and generalizations pertaining to content read is important. A challenging discussion of ideas read also enhances the concept of "idealism". The idealist teacher emphasizes the abstract more so than the concrete when pupils read and discuss content. The concrete, if used as readiness activities, is to assist pupils to achieve more readily in the abstract with relevant concepts and generalizations.

Idealists tend to believe that the mind is real and needs to be developed with the academic and the intelligible. The teacher then needs to guide pupils to focus upon valid concepts and generalizations in a subject centered reading curriculum. Ediger (1995) wrote :

Idealists tend to be very academic and rigorous in the teaching of subject matter. They emphasize cognitive objectives much more so than affective (attitudinal) or psychomotor (use of muscles and eye-hand coordination) in teaching-learning situations. Meaning, understanding, and depth learning of subject matter are important to idealists. Vital subject matter, carefully selected, needs to be taught to students. The student in acquiring subject matter in ongoing lessons is to move from the finite to the infinite Being. Ideas are important to attain in an idealist's curriculum. The ideal is also important to achieve in terms of moral standards and values.

(2) Somewhat opposite of idealism as a philosophy of teaching is realism. Since one can know the real world in whole or in part as it really is in realism, pupils should focus their attention in choosing library books which stress science and mathematics. Realists then believe the pupil can know the real world as it truly is, in degrees. Thus, the reader can obtain somewhat of a duplicate of the real world in actuality. This is quite different as compared to the idealist who believes the pupil might secure ideas only/largely of the material/social world. Wahlquist (1942) wrote :

Realists generally agree in stressing the need of making philosophy scientific. A major part of the realistic program of reform consists of emphasizing the close relationship of philosophy to the sciences. There are those who think that the proper procedure for philosophy is to use the method of abstraction perfected in mathematics and made the basis of all scientific investigation. Generally, realists are agreed that the method of scientific analysis is the fundamental approach. The ultimate determinate of the truth of an idea is regarded as something beyond mere personal satisfaction, something external to the personality, and no dependent upon it. Consequently, truth must be discovered by objective means, as free as possible from the subjectivity of the experimenter. The realist is interested in the temperature of the room as registered by a gadget, not by the impression of the person in the room.

The realist teacher needs to have an ample supply of library books available for pupils to read about the natural world of science and of mathematics. These two academic discipline are interesting and fascinating to many pupils. Precise information may be read pertaining to each of these two disciplines of knowledge. Realism harmonizes well with the measurably stated objectives movement. Thus, prior to instruction, precise objectives have been developed on the state and/or local levels. The curriculum areas of social studies and literature are also included in developing measurably stated objectives for pupils to achieve. Since precise information is inherent, the teacher might develop criterion reference tests to measure pupil achievement in reading content pertaining to the diverse academic areas. Measurably stated objectives chosen by the teacher or on the state level may be selected for pupils to attain. The objectives are precise so that either the pupil has or has not achieved the stated objectives after instruction. The objectives to be achieved pertaining to each lesson may be announced prior to instruction so that pupils individually know what is expected of them in terms of knowledge to be acquired. After instruction, it can be measured how well each pupil has achieved. The realist teacher of reading might well have the following model to use in teaching:

a) behaviourally stated objectives for pupils to achieve.

b) literature for pupil reading to achieve the precise objectives.

c) criterion referenced test to measure pupil progress.

(3) A third school of thought in educational philosophy which provides guidance to teachers is experimentalism. Experimentalists believe that individuals cannot know the real world as it truly is, nor can individuals know ideas only pertaining to the real world. What can be known are the experiences of the individual(s). We can then only know experiences. With experiences, one experiences change and modification. Thus, problems arise in a changing environment subject to one's own experiences. Problems encountered need identification and clarity in their being stated. After clearly stating a relevant problem, information from a variety of reference sources need to be obtained in answer to the identified problem area. An hypothesis should result. The stated hypothesis is tentative and subject to testing. Again, reference source need to be used to do the testing in a life-like situation. Reading activities are a

useful set of experiences to provide a source for problems, gathering information, developing an hypothesis, testing the hypothesis, and modifying the hypothesis if necessary. Pertaining to John Dewey, a leading philosopher of education embracing experimentalism, Meyer (1949) wrote :

For Dewey.......thinking becomes significant only when applied to life's situations. It is, he has said, "an instrumentality used....in adjusting....to the practical situations in life." Or, to phrase it more simply, human beings think in order to live. Because of this stimulus, which has its basis in biology and sociology, it is impossible—it is absurd—to interpret life in a systematic and abstract way. Since, moreover, Dewey holds that life is in a constant flux, it is impossible to solve problems with any degree of finality for the problems of tomorrow will be different from those of today.

As for the purpose of knowledge, Dewey believes that knowledge is experience and that true knowledge is functional.

(4) As fourth philosophy providing guidance to the teacher in the reading curriculum is existentialism. Existentialists tend to emphasize the human condition with its uncertainties, anxieties, tension, fears and dread.

Existentialists tend to advocate that choices made are subjective. The individual chooses from among alternatives as to what to value, prize, pursue, and achieve. The individual is the chooser. Permitting someone else to make personal decisions for the self makes the latter inhuman. To be human means to choose and select, from among the many decisions possible. Harper (1955) wrote the following pertaining to existentialism:

Existentialism is, as the word implies, a philosophy of human existence it arose early in the nineteenth century in response to a cultural climate in which Soren Kierkegarrd observed that man had forgotten what it means to exist. Men had learned what it means to be one in the crowd, to be a mass-man; they had forgotten what it means to be an individual, that is, what it means to die, to suffer, to decide, to love. They had forgotten what it means to die, to suffer, to decide, to love. They had forgotten what it means to stand apart, as each man is born to stand apart, from the rest of the universe and from one's fellows.....

Individualized reading would work well here since the pupil selects which library book to read, from among alternatives. There should be an ample supply of library books dealing with the human condition from which a pupil may choose one to read. The library books should be on diverse topics and on diverse reading levels to provide for individual differences—fast, average, and slow readers.

After the pupil has completed reading a library book, he/she should have a conference with the teacher to appraise achievement. The conference needs to center on the concerns and situations involving the human being.

(5) A fifth philosophy of teaching reading involves perennialism. Perennialists believe in looking to the past in selecting objectives for reading instruction. Their purpose is to have pupils read ideas that have endured in time and space. Good ideas then remain important in the past as well as continue to possess importance presently. The Great Books represent enduring ideas from the past which are relevant today. Content written presently may not survive in time and space and thus, become obsolete. There are many books which pupils may read that stresses the Great Books philosophy. Mother Goose rhymes is an example of books for young readers which has remained important over the centuries. When briefly outlining selected books for pupil reading emphasizing perennialism as a philosophy of teaching reading, high school juniors and seniors read selected works of Shakespeare such as *Hamlet*, *Romeo and Juliet*, *The Merchant of Venice* and *Julius Caesar*.

Achieving well intellectually is a major goal of Perennialists. Lively discussions are advocated whereby pupils are thoughtfully involved in the ongoing activity. The teacher must be a good leader of discussion groups and not lecture to students. He/she needs to ask challenging questions of pupils when serving as a discussion leader. The teacher needs to be an admirer of classical literature and be well versed therein. Pupils should enjoy reading due to relevant classical content and the interesting related discussions that follow.

In the Junior Great Books Curriculum, students have many opportunities to interact with thought provoking literature as they develop their reading, writing, oral communication, and critical thinking skills. Because of the curriculum's emphasis upon discussion and its focus upon interpretation, all students—whether or not they are reading at grade level—will be able to contribute, and will grow in their ability to read and enjoy challenging literature.

The Junior Great books Curriculum develops student's reading comprehension in the context of thinking about genuine problems of meaning raised by a selection. The curriculum's interpretive activities are designed to help students to become more aware of their reactions as they read, develop a sensitivity to language, and value their own curiosity about a text. Writing—from simple note taking to the composition of elaborated essays—is stressed throughout the Curriculum as an integral part of students' ongoing, personal engagement with the text.

The shared inquiry method of reading and discussion developed by the Great Books foundation enables teachers to create a thoughtful learning environment in the classroom. Through their own curiosity and attentive questioning, teachers serve as partners in inquiry with their students, helping them work together to discover meaning in a selection and build interpretations (The Junior Great Books Foundation, no date).

Pertaining to perennialism, O'Neill (1981) wrote :

Accordingly, educational intellectualism tends to be past oriented and to emphasize stability—the continuity of the great, enduring ideas—over change. In general, the eternal truths are best represented in the abiding masterworks of the world's greatest minds as these ideas are conveyed through the cultural heritage of mankind. The overall goal of education is to identify, preserve and transmit essential Truth (that is, the central principles that govern the underlying meaning and significance of life). More significantly, the intermediate role of the school as a particular social institution is to teach and the students how to think (that is, wisdom) of the past.

(6) A sixth approach in teaching reading is using the Big Book philosophy. Holistic methods of reading instruction are involved here. A large, illustrated book needs to be present for primary grade pupils. This book is large enough for pupils to be able to read the print from their desks. Should the book be smaller in size, pupils can be seated closer to the book in order that all may read the contents together orally. The teacher, first of all, discusses the illustrations that relate to the print with learners. This process builds readiness within pupils for reading the abstract words directly related to the illustrations. The teacher reads the contents orally first to pupils. Pupils and the teacher together then orally read the printed content. Those who have difficulties with word identification may hear the words pronounced as the short selection is read together with pupil-teacher involvement. The contents may also be re-read to practice reading the words and comprehending the subject matter. Re-reading can be an excellent procedure to use in teaching and learning situations. Many pupils love to re-read stories. Pupils than learn to identify words and comprehend syntax in sentences. Sequential big books involving holism may be read together involving pupils and the teacher.

There can be some phonics taught as the need arises, but this is not done in isolation from the context of the story. Enjoyment of reading is a major goal and this is emphasized as a holistic experience. With re-reading, slower learners may also master the identification of words. If there is a refrain that is predicable when the teacher reads orally to pupils, the latter may join in with what is known as echoic reading.

Holistic methods of teaching reading may be compared with a strong phonics approach. A phonics method of teaching young learners stresses sequential lessons in guiding pupils to make associations between graphemes and phonemes that can then be used in reading content in different curriculum areas.

Writing is very closely related to reading in a holistic literature based curriculum. Thus, pupils may write the following, as examples, in journal writing when responding to what was been read :

1. feeling the reader had toward the selection read.

2. modifications to the major character described in the reading selection.
3. revisions to the setting of the story.
4. letter written to the author of the story.
5. elaboration of the plot of the reading selection.

Conclusion

Pupils need to experience a match between their own preferences and learning styles with a specific plan of reading instruction. Too frequently, the basal reading approach is used in teaching pupils. This plan will meet the needs of some pupils. Others will need a different approach. The psychology of learning needs to be used to guide pupils to achieve as optimally as possible in reading. Each plan of reading instruction needs evaluation to determine if a pupil can benefit from it optimally. For all pupils not doing well in reading, we would suggest tape-recording interesting library books. Pupils may then follow along in these library books by looking at the words as the tape plays the related content. Very slow learners then have a chance to read along in the library book with the recorded voice on the tape.

Reading Recovery is an excellent approach for young children who need a one on one approach in reading instruction. Thus, when a pupil is reading from a library book, the teacher is there continuously to offer assistance and help. There is little time then for the pupil to waste time in reading.

References

Ediger, Marlow (1997), "Perspectives in Teaching Reading," *Reading Improvement*, 34 (2), 52.

Ediger, Marlow (1997), "Transcends, Classroom Interaction, and Reading," *Reading Improvement*, 34(1), 31–36.

Ediger, Marlow (1997), "Explicit Teaching in the Language Arts," *The Progress of Education*, 72 (3), 55.

Ediger, Marlow (1995), *Philosophy in Curriculum Development*, Kirksville, Missouri : Simpson Publishing Company, ·22.

Gardner, Howard (1995), *Multiple Intelligences : Theory in Practice*, New York : Basic Books.

Harper, Ralph (1955), "Significance for Existence and Recognition for Education" in *Modern Philosophies of Education*. Chicago : The University of Chicago Press, 215.

The Junior Great Books Foundation (no date), *The Junior Great Books Curriculum*, Chicago, Illinois, 1 and 2.

Meyer, Adolph E. (1949), *The Development of Education in the Twentieth Century*, Englewood Cliffs, New Jersey : Prentice-Hall, Inc., 42–43.

O' Neal, William F. (1981), *Educational Ideologies*, Santa Monica, California : Goodyear Publishing Company, 168.

Rao, Digumarti Bhaskara (1996). *Encyclopaedia of Education for All*. New Delhi : APH Publishing Corporation.

2
Organising for Reading Instruction

The reading teacher needs to be a capable person in organising the classroom for optimal pupil achievement. The classroom should be rich with print materials. Learner should feel free to view and read diverse forms and kinds of printed works. Learners may learn independently as well as in a more structured environment. Small group as well as large group instruction must be in the offing to provide for different learning styles. The opportunities to learn to read in a print rich environment are many. Each pupil is a valuable candidate in becoming a reader who enjoys and wants to increase proficiency in reading. When working with others in the classroom, pupils like interpersonal relations. Social development of each pupil is of utmost importance in the reading curriculum.

John Dewey (1859–1952) strongly emphasized democratic living be it in school or in society. Democracy as a way of life, stressed input from all in the making of decisions by which all would be influenced. Decisions made then should affect involved persons. Decision-makers will be affected by decisions made. This happens in the societal arena and needs to occur also in the school curriculum. Thus, students need to be actively involved in developing standards of conduct by which they will be governed. Student-teacher planning of conduct is a must in a democracy, according to Dewey. Ample input into school government needs to come from those who will experience the consequences of the rules and regulations. Students are citizens presently in the school/societal arena. Education then is not a preparation for the future. Rather, students are presently citizens in identifying and solving problems. The present school should not be separated from the future. Nor should school and society be separate entities. What is vital in society in problem solving is also salient in the identification and solving of relevant problem areas in school... (Ediger, 1995).

Writing is not taught as an isolated curriculum area, but is related to reading. What has been read provides content for writing in using a variety of purposes. The opposite is true also in that what has been written may be read. Authenticity is involved in reading and writing in that both are stressed in context, not in isolation from a life-like situation. A philosophy of constructivism is then being emphasized. The reading teacher needs to be a good organizer of the room environment so that pupils can make optimal use of space in learning to read. Reading materials are there for use and can be obtained readily. Pupils with teacher guidance should be actively involved in making and using reading materials. Intrinsic motivation for learning to read is important in that pupils individually should be accountable for becoming good readers.

Using Space in an Optimal Manner

There should be an area in the classroom designated for large group instruction. Here, pupils may work together as a unit such as when reading from a Big Book in holistic reading. All in the total group should be able to see the illustrations and see the abstract words clearly when the Big Book is used in teaching reading. Discussions of the illustrations, prior to reading, provide background information to pupils. Learners should predict what will be read. The predictions may then be checked as the teacher orally reads a selection first from the Big Book. Pupils may then read it together with the teacher. Re-reading is also good to emphasize with the Big Book in that pupils gain security with the encountered words and comprehend the contents more adequately. In their research study, Dennis and Walter (1996) report good results from pupils when re-reading is being emphasized in the curriculum. Sometimes, the pupils may engage in echoic reading whereby a predictable refrain may be read together, in response to what the teacher has read orally.

Ideas for an experience chart may be presented by pupils to the teacher who in turn prints in neat manuscript letters the content presented. Pupils may then read the contents orally as the teacher points to the words and phrases read by primary grade pupils. The experience charts should be saved and bound so that learners may reread the contents as desired. The following materials should be located at the large group area: chart paper, magnetic board, adequate chalk boards, sentence strips, different kinds of tape such as correction and/or masking tape, diverse colors of markers, among other items.

A second area in the classroom needs to stress committee and small group endeavors. Here, a committee may work collaboratively in discussing a library book read. If there are multiple copies of the library book, each participant will have a paperback to read. A seminar approach may follow with depth discussion of the involved library book.

In most cases, there will be a single copy of a library book. Two or three pupils together may change off reading the book orally. Once it has been read completely, participants may discuss and plan an art project that relates directly to the library book such as developing a mural pertaining to its contents. Adequate space need to be available to display written work of pupils in order to have a print rich environment. To stress a print rich environment, the teacher needs to provide a variety of materials for writing and reading, purposeful to pupils, in the classroom setting. Labels should be placed on familiar objects in the classroom so that pupils may develop a rich set of basic sight words for reading and writing. Thus, the printed word "chair" may be attached to the concrete chair. The room should be so arranged so that the pupil can take care of his/her materials of instruction independently. Pupils' work should be displayed freely in the classroom so all can see and read these products. The reading and writing curriculum need to cut across all curriculum areas. A print rich environment should then be in the offing (Burns, Roe and Ross, 1996).

In the area for independent work, there should be a table and chairs at a suitable place for pupils to read library books. The school furniture here should be comfortable for learners in reading library books quietly to themselves. Another table with chairs should emphasize writing activities for pupils. There are pencils and paper for pupils to engage in writing. Pupils may write journal entries pertaining to the quality of a library book read. Or, the summary of a book may be written for a report. Each pupil should have a container such as a paper box to hold written products. The pupils's name should appear on the box. A word processor needs to be available to pupils so that their written work can be shown on the monitor and a print-out of the content obtained. Learners at an early age need to see the uses of modern technology and its values in the reading curriculum.

Students, teachers, and community members each need access to private communications, general information, and public discussions. These are commonly accomplished with three methods : E-mail, web pages, and discussion forums.....

Electronic mail is the most common type of communication. It serves for direct and private contact and extends office hours to any time the participant decides. But whereas phone calls after school may not be allowed or encouraged, E-mail is non-intrusive. Students, teachers, and parents may choose when to read or respond to any message. Examples of E-mail in a school setting include teachers sending out a message to all students via E-mail to emphasize some point made in class, on the home page, or in a discussion forum.

E-mail can connect teachers and students more intimately than ever before and is fully two way. A student can contact the teacher for further clarification of some class policy or some point left unclear in lectures and discussions. A teacher can contact students directly and confidentially about personal matters such as an unusual number of absences, or learning problems such as a query about an assignment......

Websites are on-line collections of information and can be developed for little or no cost. With servers—the software and hardware that allows access to web pages—can be developed by using current hardware and free web server software. This allows schools to enter the web publishing "business" with minimal monetary investment that can be expanded as demand grows (Gamas and Nordquist, 1997).

Library books need to housed in the independent reading area. These books need to be arranged so that they can be checked out with ease for pupils to read. Thus, they can be arranged by genre such as animal stories in one basket, farm life in another basket, and zoos and circus books in another. Each basket is clearly labeled and pupils should realize how easy it is to locate a book to read. Encyclopedias, dictionaries, reference books, books on poetry, the saurus of synonyms and antonyms, supplementary readers as well as basal readers, word charts, and cassettes, among others, should be readily available to learners. It is good to have a mail box for each pupil so that learners may exchange messages with each other. CD ROMS contain much information for pupil use in browsing and problem solving. All pupils should experience CD ROMS, e-mail, and internet. Rich experiences with technology enhances the reading curriculum.

Learning Stations in Reading

Pupils need to experience choosing tasks at different learning stations while the teacher is working with a small group in the classroom. Each station needs to be rich with concrete (objects and items), semi-concrete (illustrations, audio-visual aids, and slides/snapshots), as well as print materials of instruction. The reading teacher needs to explain each station so that pupils are clear as to what to do at anyone of these stations. Here, learners need to feel responsible for their efforts and behaviour since the reading teacher will be busy with a small group of pupils needing assistance in reading more proficiently. Tasks chosen at the learning stations should possess perceived purpose by pupils. Tasks should be at different levels of complexity so that fast, average and slow readers may benefit from choices made at the learning stations. They are not to emphasize busy work, but rather fulfill a purpose and that being to develop better readers. Concrete and semi-concrete materials are located at the different learning stations to assist pupils to understand background information and be able to read print materials more effectively. There needs to be quality sequence between the background information and what will be read.

Pupils should have ample opportunities to choose which station to work at. No doubt, the teacher may also assign pupils at selected interval to a station. At a station, a pupil may choose to read a library book based on a specific genre. After completion of reading the library book, the pupil may choose how to reveal comprehension such as pantomiming what has been comprehended. At a different learning station, a pupil may choose to play a phonics game with other pupils. At a third station, a pupil may desire to cooperatively read a library book with another pupil and indicate comprehension through making a diorama.

Periodically, pupils and the reading teacher need to evaluate the quality of the classroom as to its encouraging the use and development of print materials. The following statements may be used in the assessment process with rating each item on a five point scale :

1. Is the room inviting for the reading of library books?
2. Do areas for large group, committee work, and individual endeavours serve their purposes well for reading?
3. Is it easy to locate books that you wish to read?
4. Is it easy to return books that have been read?
5. Are the written works of pupils displayed often for others to read?
6. Are there an ample number of books from different genres for pupils to read?
7. Are there ample library books available to read for different levels of reading abilities?
8. Do you feel that doing much reading is encouraged in the classroom?
9. Is the level of the noise in the classroom kept at a level whereby one can concentrate well on the task at hand?
10. Is ample time given for reading and writing in the classroom?

The Need for In-service Education

Reading teachers need to spend an adequate amount of time in in-service education in guiding pupils to read well. Unless teacher motivation is high and recommended trends are stressed in the reading curriculum, pupils may not achieve as well as they should.

In-service education for teachers should be theme orientated. Hopefully from the in-service education program, pupils will learn to read more proficiently through improved quality of teaching by teachers. If whole language approaches are to be used in reading instruction, teachers need to experience objectives which will strengthen teacher knowledge and skills in this area. Learning opportunities need to be available to have teachers achieve the stated ends of whole language instruction. There should be activities whereby teachers see demonstration teaching in whole language instruction. Adequate time for questions needs to be given. Teachers also need to practice with peers whole language instruction using small numbers of pupils. The lesson may be revised after being critiqued with peer teacher involvement. The revised lesson should then be taught. Integrating writing with reading should be strongly stressed. The philosophy and psychology of whole language instruction needs to be understood and implemented by teachers in the in-service program as well as in the regular classroom.

After teaching whole language procedures in the regular classroom, the involved teacher needs to state in the in-service session how the new procedure worked out. The teacher may also state what needs to be done to improve what was taught. A community of learners are there to evaluate and discuss whole language instruction as compared to other plans of reading. In an atmosphere of respect, teachers are participating in appraising whole language philosophy of instruction as well as assessing this plan of instruction when used in the regular classroom.

Video-taping of demonstration teaching in whole language as well as when teachers teach, using this procedure of teaching, in in-service education should be in the offing. There are numerous opportunities for participants in in-service education to diagnose and remedy needed reading instruction pertaining to observations made.

For quality in-service education, the following additional, criteria should be stressed :

1. Classroom teachers should video-tape their teaching performance and have trusted peers provide suggestions on improving performance.
2. Adequate printed resources should be available to read on the study of whole language instruction.
3. Technology can provide many resources for teacher use in using innovative procedures in teaching. These include World-Wide WEb, Internet, CD ROMs, computer packages, among others.
4. Resource personnel should be available for consultation involving in-service education.
5. Comfortable furniture needs to be in the offing for in-service education programs.

The important item in in-service education is to have teachers obtain knowledge, skills, and resources to do a good job of teaching in the regular classroom.

Managing the Classroom in Reading Instruction

Pupils need assistance from the reading teacher in things that can be done during spare time. The teacher needs to refer to this list periodically when pupils are idle and not properly involved in learning to read better. These tasks may include choosing a library book to read from the reading corner. The books should be on a variety of genres and on different reading levels to provide for individual differences.

A second listed task could have pupils reading from their journal entries. With periodic review of these entries, pupils engage in reading and rehearse previously acquired content and skills. Pupils enjoy re-reading subject matter whether in Big Book form, library books, and/or journal entries.

Third, pupils in their spare time may write entries in the journal pertaining to what has just been read. Clearly and precisely, pupils need to write and read these entries.

Fourth, pupils need to be reminded of the diverse genre of books that may be read such as ABC books, fairy tales, and poetry as examples. Reminding pupils of what is available for reading encourages further engagement in learning to read more proficiently.

Fifth, pupils may select a Big Book to read. These books may have been read before and now are being reviewed. Or the Big Book may be entirely new to the learner. Even if a Big Book will be read later by the entire class, the pupil who chose this book for individualized reading may be better prepared for classroom reading when the time comes for the entire class to read this Big Book.

Sixth, a pupil may choose a wordless Big Book to look through and provide possible related sentences. These sentences may be recorded by one who possesses a writing vocabulary. The recorder and the involved pupil may read through the composed sentences.

Seventh, a pupil may select to read a library book whereby the recorded voice is contained in a cassette directly related to the printed words. As the cassette plays the sequential words, the pupil may follow along in his/her own chosen book. The pupil is gaining an increasing number of sight words for reading in this activity, as well as increasing skills in reading.

Eighth, experience charts developed previously may have been bound and pupils may check these out for re-reading. Usually, learners are quite independent in re-reading these experience charts. They were actively involved in providing the content for the experience chart. This provides background information, not only for the initial reading of the chart but also for the re-reading process.

Ninth, pupils may volunteer to watch a video on a famous author. *The Life and Times of Maurice Sendak*, author of *Where the Wild Things Are* fascinates many pupils. Learners have said they understand the content of a story better if more is known about the author. Questions are raised and discussed about the author. Sometimes a letter is written to the author. Usually, a response is received.

Tenth, pupils prepare and give oral reports on a favorite library book read. With each oral report given, pupils are held to higher standards. Pupils need to learn early in life how to organize their time so that optimal progress is made. Too frequently, pupils walk in the classroom aimlessly by sharpening their pencils, getting a drink of water, and going to the bathroom. These tasks might need to be done when purpose is involved; however many pupils waste too much time in doing so.

Selected pupils walk in the room for the sake of doing so or they continue to get drinks of water endlessly. This wastes much time that should be used in learning to read and write effectively. Whispering to pupils and bothering others takes its toll of time. One of my colleagues on the university campus mentioned how he had helped a freshman organize his time. The student was failing in class work and had no concept on how to use his time wisely. So, my colleague assisted the freshman to organize his time so that adequate time could be spent on each course taken. The student promised to live by the worked out schedule. His grades improved and at the end of the school year was doing C+ work. He continued to see my colleague at selected intervals of the school year and the next school year also. The sophomore student realized he could be successful in university course work. At the end of the sophomore year of school, his gpa went up to the B average. My colleague and I discussed how important it is to have good study habits at an early age. This might take care, in part, of the many failures that are experienced in public school and university course work (Ediger).

Time spent with young children in the public schools to stay on task is well spent. It is not easy for teachers to keep healthy young energetic children on task. However, this is an important goal of the teacher.

I visit Old Order Amish schools regularly near Bloomfield, Iowa. In these six one room school houses, pupils seemingly are always on task. The old Order Amish teacher can write assignments on the chalkboard for five to six minutes with the back turned to children in the classroom. All the pupils continue to work on their assignments. With time on task, Old Order Amish children's test scores compare very favourably with those of other pupils. These children are taught by a teacher of their own faith who like all Amish individuals completed eighth grade education only. Parents of Old Order Amish faith are very strong backers of their children behaving well in school (Ediger, 1997).

Here are selected suggestions for young primary grade pupils to use their time well in the reading curriculum: For reading the teacher should use whole class activities. The Big Book approach is very useful in that all can see the illustrations and print clearly. The teacher provides readiness experiences by discussing the related illustrations with pupils. The teacher then orally reads the content to pupils as the latter follow along with the printed words in the Big Book. Pupils together with the teacher then read contents orally from the Big Book. By this time pupils should have developed an addition to their sight vocabulary from the reading of the Big Book. Shared and interactive reading are important for pupils. An experience chart may be developed from the content read. An art project may accompany the written work. The illustration(s) developed should accompany the written work which is directly related to the content read from the Big Book.

The teacher needs to have pupils become very familiar with the different spaces in the classroom such as the areas for large group, committee work, and individual endeavours.

Pupils should realize objectives of teaching reading that encourage writing and reading being integrated, no separate subject areas. Both reading and writing need much emphasis in the language arts as well as in social studies, science, and mathematics. Thus, pupils need to be able to read in order that writing can occur and what is written can be read. The classroom needs to be filled with written work of pupils. Learners need to see their products in print and displayed. The displays in the classroom provide opportunities for all pupils in the classroom to read the works of others and share ideas in an atmosphere of respect.

Pupils should be given directions on how to check out

library books and how to return them after the completion of their reading. The classroom will have an appearance of being busy and orderly at the same time.

The teacher must read orally to pupils each day. This should assist pupils in learning to enjoy literature. The books read by the teacher should fascinate pupils and encourage reading the same library book or other children's books. Pupils need to become as independent as possible in word recognition and study habits. They do need help in developing time on task habits and self-monitoring of reading comprehension.

Lesson and Unit Plans

The reading teacher needs to be well prepared for each day of teaching. Unprepared teachers fail to have a sequence that permits continuous progress for pupils. Pupils know if teachers are ill prepared for teaching in that a lack of preparation is in evidence.

The teacher should start with developing a well constructed unit in teaching reading. The following parts should be inherent in the unit plan.

1. A statement of philosophy of reading instruction. The teacher here needs to state why a plan of teaching reading is being used. This helps a reading teacher to focus upon basic beliefs that are represented within a philosophy of teaching reading. If whole language is being emphasized, the teacher needs to review and rehearse these involved tenets. A teacher is served in teaching reading by having inherent beliefs and ideas pertaining to the teaching of reading.

2. A clear statement of objectives in terms of what pupils are to learn for an entire unit, be it two, three, or four weeks in length. Three categories of objectives should be in evidence. Thus, understandings objectives should indicate which knowledge goals need to be stressed. What do pupils need to know to do a better job of reading ? For example, are there basic sight words that will be taught ? If so, which ones ? Or will these sight words be learned in a pure whole language approach ? If so, then the sight words may be

learned in cooperative oral reading approaches with pupil and teacher involvement. If these sight words are learned along with whole language procedures in reading, will they be taught in isolation, in some manner ?

In addition to understandings objectives, skills goals also need emphasizing. By putting the understandings to use, skills are being stressed in the reading curriculum. Skills such as critical and creative reading and reading to solve problems are important to implement. Additional skills are for pupils to use context clues appropriately and be able to apply relevant phonics sills in reading. The third category of objective to implement in the teaching of reading is to emphasize quality attitudes. What will the teacher do to stress pupil enjoyment of reading so that increased time will be given by learners in learning to read better ? What will the reading teacher do to have pupils experience success in reading so that positive attitudes will prevail ? If pupils experience failure, they will not become good readers. If they fail to perceive purpose in becoming good readers, they no doubt will shun reading activities. Attitudinal objectives need to be clearly stated so that the reading teacher knows what to aim toward when teaching and learning activities are in evidence.

A third part of the unit plan in reading instruction is to emphasize quality evaluation techniques to determine what pupils have learned. The teacher here needs to refer continuously to the statement of objectives when appraising pupil progress. There are numerous procedures to use in appraising pupils progress. Teacher observation is an excellent way. The teacher must have quality standards in mind, as contained in the objectives, when using teacher observation to appraise pupil achievement in reading. Checklists may be used to evaluate pupil achievement. On the checklists are reading behaviours listed after which the teacher will place a check mark if a learner has achieved that goal. A rating scale is a similar evaluation device. The major difference between the checklist and the rating scale is that in the latter each reading behaviour is rated on a five point scale or very good, good, average, below average, and poor.

The teacher may then diagnose which problems are faced by the individual pupil and how to remedy the problematic situation. The results may also be used to improve reading instruction for individual pupils. So often, the teacher does not know what is on a standardized, norm referenced test or even the criterion referenced test taken by pupils. The teacher is at a loss to ascertain what needs to be stressed in terms of diagnosis and remediation. Standardized tests have been used much in the past to assess pupil achievement. Some schools still use them to appraise pupil achievement in treading and the language arts, as well as other curriculum areas. There are no objectives for teachers to use in teaching reading when standardized tests are used to evaluate learner progress. These kinds of tests are used to spread pupils out from high to low, such as from the 99th to the first percentile.

Standardized test are constructed in ways that do spread pupils out on this long continuum. Thus, a pupil may reveal results that indicate being on the 65th percentile in reading, meaning that for every 100 pupils having taken this test, 65 are below and 35 above the percentile rank of the pupil. Percentile ranks are relatively easy for parents to understand. However, on a standardized test, they are not based on pupils achieving the objectives stressed by the teacher.

Criterion referenced tests are also used by the teacher to appraise learner progress. These tests evaluate what pupils have learned in achieving the predetermined measurably stated objectives. The reading teacher then selects learning opportunities that assist pupils to achieve the measurably stated objectives, also called behaviourally stated objectives. The reading teacher generally has much guidance in determining what pupils are to learn with the measurably stated objective being written very precisely and being available prior to instruction.

More recently, portfolios are being advocated for use in ascertaining pupil achievement. Here, the pupil with teacher guidance chooses which products to place into the portfolio. The following items as examples may go into a portfolio to indicate pupil achievement :

1. written poems, stories, plays, and journal writing entries

of the pupil. These papers represent a sample of what a pupil can do in written products.

2. cassette recordings of oral reading, reader's theater, story telling, and involved dramatic activities.
3. video-tapes of being involved in committee work and individual endeavours.
4. teacher comments of the pupil's achievements in reading and the language arts in general.
5. art products as they relate to the area of reading instruction.

The Daily Lesson Plan

From the unit plan, discussed above, the reading teacher may select what is useful in daily lesson planning. The objectives section needs to have understandings, skills, and attitudinal objectives that are relevant for pupils to achieve. These objectives are based on pupil needs and interests. Individual differences are provided for among the fast, average, and slow learners. Learning opportunities are chosen by the reading teacher based on developing and maintaining pupil purpose and motivation to achieve objectives. Evaluation procedures are selected to determine if a pupil has attained the stated objectives.

Careful planning is very necessary when the reading teacher is thinking and implementing a quality program and plan of organisation in helping pupils learn to read.

Grouping Pupils for Reading Instruction

There are many ways to group pupils for the teaching of reading. The plan selected by the reading teacher needs to be flexible so that pupils are in groups that are functional and assist pupils in becoming good readers. One of the older plans to teaching reading is to use ability groups. Here, the teacher has pupils grouped so that they are as uniform as possible within the committee. Pupils may then challenge each other in a wholesome way to achieve as optimally as possible. In a reading lesson being discussed, the teacher has a somewhat uniform achievement group to work with. Extremes in terms of high and low achievers are then not present, but the teacher still needs to make provisions so that all understand and achieve well. This plan of grouping, namely using ability grouping, does not rule out that some achieve more rapidly and better that others.

With ability grouping, there may be a group made up of the highest achievers only, the average achievers only, or the slow learners only. The reading teacher needs to have a definite purpose in using ability grouping to assist pupils to achieve as much as possible. Having a group as homogeneous as possible is the goals in ability grouping for reading instruction.

Second, the reading teacher may use interest grouping in the teaching of reading. Here, pupils are reading a library book or a reading selection that captures the interests of the pupils who have volunteered to be in the interest group. Pupils may then cooperatively read and discuss what has been read. Projects might be developed by pupils within the interest group.

Third, pupils may work together who are friends. These pupils have definite goals to achieve in reading. If a seminar method is used, pupils need to have read the same selection so that depth discussion may come about.

Fourth, peer tutoring may be used as a means of grouping pupils for instruction. With peer tutoring, two to three pupils may assist each other in a small group. The peer group may work on comprehension abilities or on selected problems in word recognition. As is true in all plans of grouping pupils for instruction, time on task is of the utmost importance.

Fifth, skills groups are commonly formed by teachers of reading. Pupils in a skills group lack certain elements that hinder becoming a better reader. Thus, with diagnosis, the reading teacher may place a few pupils in a skills group that need assistance in using syllabication skills. Or, a set of pupils has difficulties in using specific consonant letters to identify unknown words.

Sixth, project groups may be formed. Thus, pupils in a set are working on a mural to show comprehension. Or a set of pupils working on a series of dioramas may work together to show what was learned from a reading selection. Art work and reading correlate well.

Seventh, heterogeneous grouping may be used to provide for individual differences. With heterogeneous grouping, pupils come from mixed achievement levels, from the top to the lowest level. Pupils of diverse ability levels do need to learn to work together well and respect each other. When using the Big Book method of reading instruction, pupils of all ability levels may join in with oral reading of the selection after the reading teacher has provided readiness to read the new selection.

When starting a cooperative learning group in reading, the teacher needs to :

* carefully consider the goals of the task.
* write out all instructions.
* assign no more that four to five students to a group.
* select at least one resource person for each group.
* place children who are academically advanced, developmentally delayed, or socially or linguistically problematic in groups where at least one other child can support their special needs.
* post group assignments.
* select specific roles for every student within each group.
* provide space for each group to work in comfortably.
* provide a central area for supplies.
* set reasonable time limits for completing a task.
* schedule sharing time to provide feedback on group process and the work completed (Templeton, 1995).

Conclusion

To emphasize a quality program of reading instruction, the teacher needs to :

1. make teaching and learning procedures as interesting as

possible for learners. With pupil interest, increased proficiency in reading should be an end result.

2. establish purpose for pupils to participate in ongoing lessons and units of study. Reasons are then in evidence to learners as to why it is important to learn and to achieve.

3. provide for individual differences among pupils in reading instruction. Pupils differ from each other in many ways including achievement in reading. Should the teacher not respect these differences by having pupils read materials at end of different levels of complexity ? Each pupil needs to be respected and assisted to achieve as well as possible in reading.

4. give continuous opportunities for pupils to experience success in learning. This is positive to do so. Successful learners in reading achieve more optimally than those facing failure excessively.

5. assist pupils to attach meaning to what is being learned. If pupils understand that which is being learned, they will retain content and skills longer. Achievement in reading is sequential and needs careful planning by the reading teacher. Pupils also need to be involved in determining sequence such as individualized reading whereby the learner chooses sequential library books to read.

6. show enthusiasm for teaching. Teacher enthusiasm for teaching reading does reflect within pupils when the latter is learning to read at increased levels of complexity.

7. share with pupils what you are reading. Bring the content down to the understanding level of pupils. We believe that even Plato's *The Republic* can be told to pupils in a manner whereby pupils attach meaning to the content.

8. use sustained silent reading to show that you the teacher also like to read. The entire class together with the teacher are reading during the time devoted to sustained silent reading. The reading teacher then is a model for pupils in the classroom.

9. read orally to pupils during story time so that pupils can

enjoy quality literature in a relaxed manner. Look at pupils as the reading is being done. For young children, it is good to show the related illustrations in the library book as you read orally to them.

10. indicate your interest in the welfare of each pupil. This is more necessary than even before when many children come from single parent homes and/or divorce appears to be minimizing the stability of family life. Be aware of child abuse of individual pupils. Pupils are young and vulnerable due to their age and lack of experience. The teacher can definitely be a stabilizing force here (Ediger, 1997).

References

Burns, Paul C., et al (1996), *Teaching Reading in Today's Elementary Schools*, Boston : Houghton Mifflin, 47.

Dennis, Geraldine and Eileen Walter (1995), "The Effects of Repeated Read-Alouds on Story Comprehension as Assessed Through Story Ratellings," *Reading Improvement*, 32(3), 140–49.

Ediger, Marlow (1997), *Teaching Reading and the Language Arts in the Elementary Schools*, Kirksville, Missouri : Simpson Publishing Company, 54–55.

Ediger, Marlow (1995), *Philosophy in Curriculum Development.* Kirksville, Missouri : Simpson Publishing Company, 87–88.

Ediger, Marlow (1997), "Examining the Merits of Old Order Amish Education, *Education*, 117(3), 339–43.

Gammas, Warren, and Neil Nordquist, "Expanding Learning Opportunities through On-line Technology," *Bulletin of the National Association of Secondary School Principals*, 81(592), 19–20.

Templeton, Shane (1995), *Children's Literacy*, Boston : Houghton Mifflin Company, 158–59.

Bhaskara Rao, Digumarti (1989), *Teaching of Biology*. Guntur: Nagarjuna Publishers (in Telugu language).

3
Reading and the Structure of the English Language

The structure of the English language is important for pupils to know about. Knowing structural ideas can assist learners in getting the feeling of what comes next sequentially in oral or silent reading. Having objectives to achieve pertaining to these structural ideas can be quite abstract and difficult. We have observed in classrooms at different grade levels how learning key ideas and these structural ideas can be interesting and useful in reading. During the 1960s and 1970s, the structure of each academic discipline became major objectives for pupil attainment. However, educators must say that careful selection of what to teach is always important. The structure of knowledge emphasizes the selection of what is relevant and important to teach. It is ridiculous to think that the structure of knowledge movement was stressed only in the 1960s and 1970s. Determining key ideas and main ideas to teach is always important. Determining the structure of the English language, and any language for that matter, is very important. Much wasting of time occurs if teachers teach what is irrelevant and unimportant. The structure of knowledge movement also emphasized that pupils learn these ideas inductively. Inductive learning today is very important. Pupils like to discover rather than receive knowledge through lecture or heavy use of explanations. When pupils engage in problem solving, they are learning inductively. Thus, a problem is determined by pupils with teacher guidance in an ongoing lesson or unit of study. The problem is contextual and not outside the present learning activity being pursued. The problem indicates feelings of perplexity and uncertainty as to a course of action. The problem needs to be clear and unambiguous.

Pupils may then obtain information in answer to the problem. A variety of learning opportunities may be involve here when securing needed information or data. Sometimes, much time is needed in the solving of problems. At other times, instant decisions need to be made. Little time is then available to gather information. The information secured is used to develop an answer or hypothesis. The hypothesis is evaluated in a real life situation. Inductive learning then is used in problem solving, be it in literature or any curriculum area. Problem solving is always important in school and in society due to individuals facing problems in many facets of life.

Learning structural ideas can be quite complicated and lack purpose such as application. However, we have come to believe, after observing many student and cooperating teachers in the public schools, that enjoyable ways can be found to have pupils achieve key, major ideas in English as it relates to reading instruction. Listening, speaking, and writing are also involved here.

To emphasize the structure of knowledge approach in teaching, the teacher should :

1. have an excellent knowledge of major generalisations in sentence patterns since these key ideas become objectives for learner attainment.
2. sequence learning opportunities in that individuals experience the enactive (objects and items), the iconic (semi-concrete materials of instruction), and the symbolic (abstract ideas).
3. appraise pupils to ascertain how many of these structural ideas are being attained by pupils in a spiral curriculum. With a spiral curriculum, pupils meet up again and again at increasing levels of complexity the structural ideas which serve as objectives of instruction.
4. ask quality questions of pupils so that they may truly learn in an Inductive manner. Inductive teaching then assist pupils to achieve the structural ideas.
5. use enactive, iconic and symbolic materials in inductive approaches in learning (Ediger, 1997).

Sentence Patterns

There are five sentence patterns, in particular, that pupils should have knowledge about in order to become more proficient in reading. These five patterns will come up again and again in oral or silent reading. Enjoyable, yet scholarly methods may be used to guide pupil achievement in attaining these five sentence patterns. The first pattern is the subject/predicate pattern. The reading teacher may take sentences from the basal reader or a library book read by children to illustrate sentence pattern. Sentence pattern number one—Boys swim. There are just two words here to express a complete thought or idea. Pupils in class can be asked for another word which would replace "Boys". There are numerous correct responses here. One word is "girls". A brain-storming approach can be very interesting for pupils to see how many words would fit in. The sentence pattern stays the same and yet the subject changed from "Boys" to "Girls."

Pupils may wish to do journal writing on different sentence patterns discussed in class. It is good too if learners reflect upon what has been written. Reflecting stresses thinking about diverse sentence patterns and using these win writing sentences in journal writing. Application of what has been learned emphasizes review, practice and use of sentence patterns in a multitude of ways. Pupils may wish to bring pictures to class which illustrate what is shown in an illustration. These illustrations are also good to indicate concepts stressed in sentence patterns, such as "Fish swim" for sentence pattern number one above.

A next sequential question could call for words that replace the predicate part "swim". Responses to be given by pupils might include the most obvious word "swam." Learners need to experiment with different words to take the place of "swims", such as using a singular subject with a singular predicate. Here, pupils could dramatize or use pantomime to illustrate a verb in a sentence. When verbs show action, it is relatively easy to dramatize/pantomime the contents.

A second sentence pattern for pupils to study and experience is the subject/predicate/direct object pattern, such as Bill hit the ball. Here again, pupils may suggest an endless number of words to substitute for the subject "Bill." Substitutions could also be made for the predicate "hit", as well as for the direct object "ball." Substitutions for each of these three words could be the following, as an example—Carl, caught and fish. Most pupils enjoy working with sentence patterns in this way. They also notice how the English language works, even with changes being made.

A third sentence pattern involves the subject/linking verb, predicate adjective pattern, such as "Flowers are beautiful." This sentence pattern brought on diversity of responses from a class of fourth graders when they noticed the many words that may be substituted and yet the sentence pattern stays the same. One pupil brought a vase of flowers to school, a concrete experience, to show the third sentence pattern mentioned. After the class discussed the vase with flowers, pupils added another learning activity not previously mentioned above. The activity emphasized using concrete materials in the classroom to show sentence pattern number three—Flowers are beautiful. What did pupils come up with ? The following materials were used to show this sentence pattern :

1. The eraser was dusty. This sentence stressed what was observed at the chalkboard.
2. The food was delicious. This sentence came from eating in the school lunchroom.
3. The desk was dirty. A pupil observed his own desk in the classroom.

A fourth sentence pattern is represented by the subject/predicate/indirect object/direct object pattern such as, "Sally gave Sue a present. Sally gave "what ?' The answer is "present." "Present" is the direct object whereas to whom was the present given ? The answer is "Sue". "Sue" is the indirect object.

At this point, pupils may be ready to experiment with what makes for a subject of a sentence. The subject will tend to be a noun or pronoun. A noun is a word that can be changed from singular to plural, such as girl/girls and woman/women. Singular refers to one whereas plural indicates two or more of something. This is relatively easy for pupils to access. Pupils may also experiment with the subject doing the acting, such as "caught" the ball. The subject may also receive the action such as the package was wrapped by Alice. Thus, something was done to the subject of the sentence which was "package".

In their journals, pupils listed nouns and checked these with the teacher. Pupils in committees drew pictures of nouns representing those which are singular as compared to those which are plural. Active and passive voice of subjects was dramatized such as—The boy was revived by two classmates. Here, a pupil lay motionless on the floor with two classmates. Applying artificial respiration ! Pupils do like to dramatize and be creative in the language arts involving the study of sentence patterns.

A fifth sentence pattern is the subject/predicate/predicate nominative pattern, such as "Alice is a singer". Alice equals singer in this sentence. It names the same person. "Alice" is singular and needs a singular verb such as "is". "Alice is also the name of a person and thus comes under the traditional definition of what a noun is, such as a person place, or thing. The word "singer" is a noun too since it refers to a person. "Singer" is singular and when comparing that word with 'singers' where more than one person is in evidence.

Pupils can provide many responses as to substitutions that can be made for the words—Alice, is, singer; the sentence pattern of subject/predicate/predicate nominative would stay the same, e.g. Bob was a swimmer (Ediger, 1988).

In studying these five sentence patterns, pupils do not need to memorize content. In fact, when brain-storming, many correct responses are given by learners and they can experience much success inductively. Open-ended answers are given by pupils and these usually harmonize with the many possibilities that are necessary in terms of responses given. Pupils need to be successful learners so that they are increasingly more motivate. Pupils tend to develop knowledge and feelings pertaining to the structure of the English language which assist then to read in a more confident manner. For example, the subject/predicate sentence pattern indicates there are certain words that would fit into this pattern. Pupils then receive cues and clues as to which words should follow in sequence (Ediger, 1997).

Higher levels of cognition might well be an end result when pupils engage in thinking about different sentence patterns. Sternberg (1997) has developed an excellent model for teachers to use when teaching and pupils are assisted to think at a higher cognitive level;

Memory. Remember what a gerund is or what the name of Tom Sawyer's aunt was.

Analysis. Compare the functions of a gerund to that of a participle, or compare the personality of Tom Sawyer to that of Huckleberry Finn.

Creativity. Invent a sentence that effectively uses a gerund, or write a very short story with Tom Sawyer as a character.

Practicality. Find gerunds in newspapers or magazine articles and describe how they are used or say what general lesson about persuasion can be learned from Tom Sawyer's way of persuading his friends to whitewash Aunt Polly's fence.

Let's consider sentence pattern number one—The subject/predicate pattern—"Boys swim." Using the Sternberg model, the lowest level of thinking would be *memory*. Here, pupils could recall "the subject/predicate sentence pattern. They might also recall what a noun is and what verb is. For *analysis*, pupils may be asked to explain the difference between the noun and the verb. To stress *creativity*, the pupils may be asked to write a sentence containing a noun and a verb. For *practically*, pupils might locate nouns and verbs in a very short story.

The Thornberg model provides guidance to teachers in having pupils move upward to higher levels of thought with four levels, namely memory, analysis, creativity and practicality in studying grammar as well as the structure of the English language.

Expanding Sentences

Pupils with teacher guidance enjoy making sentences longer or expanding them. For each of the five sentence patterns discussed above, the sentence can be expanded. If we take the first sentence pattern of subject/predicate—Alice is a singer, the word "Alice" does lend itself to expansion with single words, but it does better with phrases and clauses. One could say "Brave Alice is a singer." The single word "brave" describes "Alice". If the noun "girl" is substituted for "Alice". Then an endless number of single words may be given to describe "girl". The following are provided as examples: small, tall, young, bashful, aggressive and hostile among others. There are many predicate nominatives that can take the place of "singer" such as older, younger, experienced, amateur, beautiful and tall among others.

Phrases are another way to expanding sentences. Generally, pupils learn rather easily that phrases contain more than one word and yet do not contain a subject and predicate. The following are phrases which modify "girl":

1. with a red sweater, such as "The girls with a red sweater was a singer".
2. Feeling well, such as "Feeling well, the girl was a singer".
3. On the pond, such as "The girl on the pond was a singer".

Later on, in sequence and when readiness is in evidence, pupils may study and learn if a phrase is adjective and modifies a noun or is adverb and modifies a verb, adjective or another adverb.

A clause can do much to clarify meanings in a sentence and at the same time the concept of expansion is being emphasized :

The girl *who has black hair* is a singer.

The dependent clause is underlined and contains a subject "who" and a direct object "hair". A clause has a subject and a predicate, but does not express a complete thought.

Pupils may provide words which take the place of the subject "girl" and the predicate nominative "singer". They may also give words that replace the direct object of the dependent clause "hair". Pupils should notice that a dependent clause does not make sense by itself, e.g. "who has black hair". The verb or predicate of the dependent clause "has" may also be changed to "had" and yet the pattern of sentence is the same. The teacher should make lessons interesting and meaningful on sentence patterns and no go beyond what pupils can possibly understand. The goal inherent in sentence patterns is for pupils to feel and understand similarities in a sentence pattern. Pupils will become better readers as a result. Pupils will know that the English language has unique routines which are predictable, such as each of the five sentence patterns. They will understand how to expand sentences and why this is done. When pupils read, they will notice these same patterns of expansion, such as single word adjectives and adverbs; adjective and adverb phrases and adjective, adverb and noun clauses. At the beginning in sequence, pupils will learn about single words modifying the subject and predicate pattern; subject, predicate, direct object pattern; subject, linking verb, predicate nominative pattern; subject linking verb, predicate adjective pattern; and subject, predicate, indirect object, direct object pattern.

What about pupils using technical terminology such as "predicate nominative"? We would say the teacher may use these and other complex terms, but not require pupils to memorize them. Meaning, however, is very important for pupils as to what a predicate nominative is when sequencing learning opportunities (Ediger, 1996).

Evaluation of Pupil Achievement

There are numerous procedures to use in evaluating pupil achievement pertaining to knowledge and skills in the structure or patterns of sentences. Teacher observation can be an excellent approach, providing quality standards are used. With teacher observation, the philosophy of constructivism is in evidence. Thus, within context, pupils are applying what has been learned about sentence patterns. Within the framework of every day lessons, pupils are indicating progressin contextual situations.

Standardized and norm referenced tests may be used to ascertain pupil achievement. However, pupils are showing here how well they have achieved outside the context of learning.

Tests, no doubt, will always be with us and we can use results from these tests to indicate where pupils specifically need help. Diagnosis and remediation would then be involved.

Howard Gardner's (1993) theory of multiple intelligence has much to offer in terms of how to evaluate pupil achievement. As the name indicates, pupils have numerous intelligences, not just one only. Pupils individually may possess one or more of these intelligences:

1. verbal/linguistic such as reading and writing well.
2. logical/mathematical such as in strengths of the left brain hemisphere with its logical thinking as well as the other component parts in mathematical proficiency.
3. visual/spatial such as pupils excelling in art work, geometry and architecture.
4. musical intelligence such as in composing, singing and playing musical instruments.
5. bodily/kinesthetic such as in athletics, dance and pantomime.
6. interpersonal such as pupils doing well when working harmoniously in group settings.
7. intrapersonal whereby pupils achieve well on an individual basis.
8. scientific in which pupils use methods of objectivity in scientific knowledge obtained.
9. the human experience such as in coping well with the everyday problems that come about.

How then does the Theory of Multiple intelligences relate to pupil learning and evaluation in the structure of knowledge in reading and writing ?

First, the heart of knowing about and using sentence patterns emphasizes verbal/linguistic intelligence. Here, pupils reveal their strengths through oral use of and written work in sentence patterns. Using these patterns in oral and silent reading also stresses use of the structure of language. We must remember, pupils with other intelligences may not reveal what has been learned through verbal/linguistic intelligence, although this must always be stressed in ongoing lessons and units of study. With logical intelligence, the pupil needs to realize, for example, that substitutions made for the subject/predicate/ direct objective pattern of sentence need to be logical. We have noticed pupils who make illogical substitutions such as Bill (subject) caught (predicate) the "if". The word "if" does not fit in logically.

Bodily/kinesthetic intelligence may be used frequently since pupils can dramatize content in a sentence pattern and attach meaning in so doing. Interpersonal or intrapersonal intelligence may be used in that the former stresses pupils working in committees whereas the latter emphasizes learners working individual on sentence patterns. We should add musical intelligence here since pupils individually who are talented in music may wish to put sentence patterns to an appropriate rhythm. A pupil even invented a dance to go along with syllabication related to a musical accompaniment. There are many possibilities here when stressing using multiple intelligences. Pupils individually may be able to reveal learning better through multiple intelligences as compared to using verbal/ linguistic approaches only/largely when studying structure in the English language.

Conclusion

Pupils having knowledge and skill pertaining to the structure of the English language should become better readers and writers. There are sentence patterns which hold true again and again. There are ways of expanding sentences which are also very consistent. Learners need to enjoy learning opportunities emphasizing structure in the English language. It certainly need not be boring or dull and dry. Rather there are learning opportunities which fascinate pupils and motivate toward greater achievement.

As pupils study the structure of the English language, they should be better able to predict what will come in sequence in reading as well as in writing. Vocabulary growth and development should also be in the offing since pupils experiment with sentences, words, phrases and clauses. There should be much journal writing on the part of pupils when reading and writing are stressed as being interrelated. When pupils hypothesize as to which words might take the place of others in a sentence, individual differences are provided for and all may be successful learners because each pupil can present possible words in context.

The interests of pupils need to be focused upon structural ideas and their component parts. The teacher needs to be certain that pupils are attaching meaning to these structural ideas. They are not be memorized for purposes of passing a test, but rather to use what has been learned in reading and writing. Thus, the level of application is very important since structural ideas have much use. We believe that teachers need to spend time in having pupils perceive how learning the structure of language is practical in reading and writing across the curriculum

References

Ediger, Marlow (1997), *Teaching Mathematics in the Elementary School.* Kirksville, Missouri : Simpson Publishing Company, 28.

Ediger, Marlow (1988), *Language Arts Curriculum in the Elementary School.* Kirksville, Missouri : Simpson Publishing Company, 8–18.

Ediger, Marlow (1997), *The Modern Elementary School.* Kirksville, Missouri : Simpson Publishing Company, 199.

Ediger, Marlow (1996), *Elementary Education.* Kirksville, Missouri : Simpson Publishing Company, 38–39.

Gardner, Howard (1993), *Multiple Intelligences : The Theory in Practice.* New York : The Basic Books.

Lakshmi, Bhagya L. and Bhaskara Rao, Digumarti (1999). *Reading and Comprehension.* New Delhi : Discovery Publishing House.

Thornberg, Robert J. (1997), "What Does it Means to be Smart ?" *Educational Leadership,* 54 (6), 20–24.

4
Affective Objectives in Reading

Reading teachers need to stress three kinds of objectives in teaching and learning. The first kind—cognitive—does receive major emphasis in the reading curriculum. Here, pupils are to acquire vital facts, concepts and generalizations. Too frequently in educational literature, facts are trivia and not treated in a relevant manner. Facts are the building blocks for developing concepts. Concepts are broader in scope than facts. There usually are many facts in a single concept. Consider the fact, "Many people lived on a manor during the Middle Ages". The word *Manor*, a concept, among others, contains several relevant facts such as:

1. A manor contains a castle, a moat in front of the castle, peasant cottages and a mill to grind grain.
2. The manor was a farm, for its day, in Western Europe.
3. Surrounding the manor was farm land used for tilling and raising grain, pasture land for cattle grazing and fallow land left idle to enrich itself for the next planting season.

Concepts are single words or phrases. The following are additional concepts for pupils to acquire when reading about the Middle Ages—page, squire, knight, tournaments and armor used in battle. In addition to facts and concepts, pupils need to relate concepts to form a generalization (Ediger, 1996). Notice how the following underlined concepts are used to form a generalization—To becomes a master, the young person first becomes an *apprentice* and then a *journeymen*. These three stages emphasize a sequence in moving from the lowest to the highest level in the worker's guild. Pupils need to relate facts to form concepts. The related concepts then may become a generalization.

To achieve cognitive objectives including facts, concepts and generalizations, learners need to acquire affectives. Affective objectives assist pupils to do better in acquiring cognitive ends. The better the affect or attitude of pupils, the more likely it will be that cognitive objectives will be achieved. Negative affect hinders pupils in achieving objectives. Being willing to think critically and creatively on subject matter read and discussed, as well as engaging actively in problem solving, accenturates the need to have an affective dimension in pupils that wishes to acquire relevant skills in the reading curriculum.

Affective Objectives in Reading

Affective objectives involve attitudes, feelings, emotions and beliefs. There are numerous programs of reading instruction that emphasize the affective dimension of objectives. Student teachers and cooperating teachers, whom I supervised in the public schools, have placed much emphasis upon pupils acquiring affective objectives. These teachers stress rather heavy pupil involvement in developing the reading curriculum. In numerous situations, the teachers have established learning centers to involve learners in a curriculum of affect. Pupils may then sequence their very own progress by selecting ordered tasks from these learning centres. We will describe one set of centres we observed when supervising teachers in the public schools. The following centers were in evidence :

1. An individualized reading center. Here, pupils chose sequential library books to read. The library books available were on different genres and on diverse reading levels. A variety of ways were emphasized by the teacher in evaluating pupil achievement in reading. The teacher may have a conference with a pupil after the learner had completing the reading of a book. Pupils individually might also select how to be appraised, such as in word recognition and comprehension of content read.

2. A listening center. The pupil may choose a library book to read which has an accompanying cassette tape. The pupil may then follow along in his/her book while the tape is playing the related abstract words. Questions, located a the center, covering the content read may be answered

by the involved learner. The pupil with teacher guidance might appraise how well the learner comprehended contents read. Each pupil could also select a section from the library book to read orally to the teacher to notice progress in a word recognition skills.

3. An experience chart center. The pupil here may view a set of pictures or objects. Based on observations made, the pupil may dictate story content to the teacher. The teacher writes the dictated ideas on a flip chart or types the resulting ideas into the word processor. With teacher guidance the pupil may read his/her dictated story orally. The teacher then has ample opportunities to appraise word recognition as well as understanding the ideas on the experience chart.

4. An art center. Based on multiple intelligences theory, a pupil may develop an art project on a character in a story read. The art project might also be developed on the setting, plot, theme, and/or irony in the library book read. Content in the art project will indicate pupil understanding of the previously mentioned elements of the story.

5. A drama center. Here pupils individually or in a committee may select content from a library book read to develop a creative or formal dramatics presentation. Content read needs to be divided into different roles for individuals to play. If the play parts are written out, formal dramatics is involved when learners individually read their respective parts. In creative dramatics, the parts are not written down, but presented sequentially as different roles are played by pupils in the presentation. No words might also be stressed in play production such as a pupil in a committee pantomiming content from the selection read.

Pupils may rotate at the different centers so that each pupil has an opportunity to work at the different centers. There should be an adequate number of tasks at the different centers so that pupils individually may omit tasks not possessing perceived purpose. The role of the reading teacher is to motivate and guide pupils to make choices and decisions based on interests and affect possessed. There needs to be chances for pupils to work collaboratively at the different centers. There are pupils who prefer working together with others as well as by themselves. It is important to provide choices to pupils to use their preferred style of learning. The feelings and emotions are involved in a reading curriculum of affect.

Emotional Intelligence

Considering the feeling dimension of learners is vital in teaching and learning situations. Goldman (1995) in his book *Emotional Intelligence* indicates five dimensions of emotional intelligence. The first is self-awareness. Here, the learner realizes his/her strengths and weaknesses and uses these to become decisive in decision making. Self-confidence is vital in order to make choices and act to make decisions.

Second, pupils need to learn to handle their emotions. Impulsive behaviour may make for incorrect decisions. Learners need to develop more of a *wait* approach so that options may be scrutinized in terms of advantages and disadvantages the consequences of each choice needs to be assessed. Third, learners need to feel motivated to achieve objectives. Hope is involved in having these challenging objectives in life. Motivation then comes from the different objectives that individuals aim for. Optimism is necessary to achieve and reach objectives one has in mind. Fourth, empathy is a very important trait for pupils to develop. Feelings of empathy make it possible to sympathize with others. Empathy is learned and a pupil learns to assist others in positive ways. Compassion for others is important. Fifth, the development of social skills enables a pupil to help others in everyday situations in life. Politeness and friendliness enable a person to interact effectively with others in society on a daily basis.

Emotional intelligence harmonizes well with an affective reading curriculum. With teacher/pupil planning of the reading curriculum, self-awareness is developed increasingly so when pupils choose the order of materials to read. Strengths in decision making should be an end result in the choosing of reading materials. When pupils learn to handle emotions effectively, there is persistence and effort put forth in learning. The immediate objective is not what is necessarily good such as impulsive behaviour. Rather, the pupil needs to evaluate the pros and cons in making choices. Motivation is necessary in order that objectives are achieved by pupils in reading. With the absence of objectives in reading, energy levels for learning go downhill.

Feelings of empathy make it possible for pupils individually to get along well with others. In school and in society, it is necessary to have good human relations so that achievement and group efforts are possible. Human beings are feeling individuals, not automations. Social skills need learning by pupils so that a friendly and considerate environment is available for all to achieve more optimally. Committee endeavours in on-going lessons and units of study in réading provide many opportunities for pupils to develop social skills.

In my own experiences as a teacher, school administrator, and university professor, including supervising student teachers and cooperating teachers, we believe affective and cognitive objectives interact. Thus, when we speak at conventions for teacher education and write for publication, we stress that quality emotions and feelings assist pupils to achieve at a more optimal level in the cognitive domain. My observations of pupils in the public schools indicate that individuals who are hostile, negative, have short attention spans and mistreat others in the classroom have a difficult time to achieve what their potential is, more so than other pupils in the class setting. Thus, quality attitudes in the affective domain assist learners to achieve more optimally in the cognitive area in reading.

Open-ended objectives are desired, rather than measurably written or behaviourally stated objectives for pupils to achieve. Why ? Not all pupils, by any means, learn the same things due to individual choices and decisions made in on-going units of study (see leaning centers above for examples). If teachers determine objectives for all pupils to achieve, there is no room for learners to select and omit learning opportunities, based on perceived purposes. If pupils select sequential objectives to achieve, within a flexible framework, a psychological approach is involved as compared to a logical order whereby the teacher arranges the order of objectives for pupil attainment.

Sequence resides within the learner, not within the minds of teachers or textbooks in reading. Formal methods of teaching reading are eliminated and replaced with learner choices and decisions as to what to accomplish and what to omit. The feeling, affective dimension is definitely involved in making choices and decisions (Ediger, 1996).

A pupils centered curriculum might be emphasized, in part, through individualized reading. Thus, instead of using basal readers in ongoing units of study, pupils may choose to read library books that relate directly to the unit being studied presently. In a literature, social studies, or science thematic unit, an adequate number of library books on different reading levels need to be available for pupil choice. We have observed this approach to be very successful in ongoing lessons and units of study. Pupils relate what was read from a library book to the ensuing discussion. There appears to be much discussion and excitement when this approach is used in teaching reading across academic discipline lines. Pupils might then notice different points of view expressed which can lead to analysis and evaluation of subject matter read.

In addition to pupils choosing sequential library books to read and relating the content to ongoing discussions, the reading teacher might also have conferences with individual pupils or several pupils who have read the same book when multiple copies are available. Here, the teacher might observe pupils enthusiasm, interest and quality of comprehension. The reading teacher must always diagnose strengths and weaknesses shown by pupils in the conference setting. What has been diagnosed as weaknesses might then be remediated through additional learning activities (Ediger, 1997).

Conclusion

The emotions, feelings and values are important in an individual's well being. Reading teachers should emphasize an adequate number of objectives stressing the affective domain. If pupils possess quality attitudes, the chances are that cognitive objectives will be achieved well, as much as the individual can be capable of doing.

The teacher needs to emphasize affective objectives in reading instruction. Learning opportunities to achieve objectives should have both affective and cognitive inherent ends. Evaluation procedures do need adequate emphasis placed upon the affective components of learning in the reading arena.

References

Bhaskara Rao, Digumarti (1996). *Educational Psychology.* Guntur : Creative Press (in Telugu language).

Ediger, Marlow (1997), *Teaching Reading and the Language Arts in the Elementary School,* Kirksville, Missouri : Simpson Publishing Company, 32.

Ediger, Marlow (1996), *Elementary Education.* Kirksville, Missouri : Simpson Publishing Company, 134.

Goleman, Daniel (1995), *Emotional Intelligence,* New York : Bantom Books.

5
Reading and Writing in the Curriculum

The reading and writing curriculum correlate well with each other. Why ? Very often, reading experiences provide the springboard for writing. Thus, a variety of kinds of poetry may be written based on content acquired from reading. Diverse kinds of rhymed and unrhymed poems may then be written. Literary elements such as characterization, setting, plot, irony, theme and point of view may be rewritten or elaborated upon by pupils from having read a given story or selection. Creativity should be a major objective of pupil writing, Novelty, uniqueness and originality of content from pupil writing, should be wanted. Written work should emphasize cutting across all academic disciplines. Written work then has no single academic discipline to stress but writing across the curriculum should be the objective of instruction (Ediger, 1997).

There are definite assumptions pertaining to writing. These assumptions are the following :

1. Pupils learn to write by writing.
2. Proficiency in oral language assists the learner to do a better job of writing.
3. Success in writing helps pupils to extend major goals to improve continuously in written work.
4. Writing seemingly is the most difficult of the four areas of vocabulary development—listening, speaking, reading and writing, but each needs to be emphasized to assist pupils to achieve as optimally as possible.

5. Pupils individually learn to write, but each pupil may learn much through collaborative endeavours in writing. Pupils learn from each other in writing.
6. Writing needs to be taught as being interrelated with grammar, punctuation, spelling, vocabulary, syntax, semantics, structure in the English language, handwriting, whole language and phonics.
7. Written work cuts across all academic disciplines whenever print discourse is used.
8. Pupils need to write for a variety of audiences such as the teacher, parents. friends, brothers and sisters among others.
9. Sequence in writing improvement begins with the preschool years, including scribbling and occurs throughout adulthood.
10. Written work should be useful whereby application is made of print discourse, as well as be creative for leisure type and utilitarian activities.

The teacher needs to focus upon the above named objectives in teaching writing and their inter-relationship with the other areas of the language arts. Writing must be related to all academic disciplines when written work is being stressed. These ideas are expressed further in basic goals that pupils need to acquire in on-going lessons and units of study. Pupils are to:

1. write frequently to record ideas in print discourse.
2. experience the relationships among listening, speaking, reading and writing.
3. expand literary experiences to incorporate written expressions.
4. use a variety of purposes to convey meanings in writing.
5. experiment with diverse genres and subject matter when engaged in writing.

6. attend to conventions in writing such as quality punctuation, capitalization and grammar.
7. edit personal work and the work of others in writing by using collaborative endeavours.
8. appreciate writing skills possessed and enjoy what has been written.
9. utilize reading and children's library books as spring-boards in writing in their diverse manifestations.
10. indicate pride in being successful in listening, speaking, reading and writing.

Leadership from the principal is vital. The principal and the teacher need to work together for the good of the child in attaining more optimally in the school setting (Ediger, 1998).

Creative Writing and Poetry

An important source for writing is to use content from basal texts and library books, among other print discourse sources, to engage pupils in written work. Through reading, viewing objects, items, illustrations and audio-visual materials directly related to what is/has been read, might well encourage creative poetry writing by learners. Discussions pertaining to what has been read might also impress pupils to apply what has been learned in poetry writing.

First of all, let's take a look at writing poems which rhyme. Many pupils like to write poetry which contains rhyme. There are numerous patterns in rhyming poetry. Early primary grade pupils who can hear rhyme may wish to write couplets, individually or in a small committee. A couplet contains two lines with ending words rhyming. These young learners may wish to dictate the couplet for the teacher to print in neat manuscript letters. Dictated poems may be saved for re-reading by pupils in class. Later on, and for all pupils, learners may wish to write triplets containing three lines. With a triplet, all ending words rhyme. A slightly more difficult poem to write is the quatrain. Here, with four lines of verse, all ending words need to rhyme or lines one and two as well a lines three and four should rhyme.

The limerick has five lines with lines one, two and five rhyming as well as lines three and four rhyming. Limericks generally begin with "There once was.... The limerick may be written as follows :

There once was a man of great height
He always seemed to be up tight.
He swatted a bee
and landed in the sea
That wonderful man of great light.

There are pupils who cannot hear rhyme or may wish to write unrhymed poetry. The haiku is a favourite of many people to write. The haiku contains three lines with the following sequence : five syllables for the first line, seven for the second line, and five syllables for the third line. The following haiku is an example :

Birds
Birds fly without rest
Where do they get the power ?
I do not know why.

A tanka is a slight variation of the haiku and has a total of five lines with the following number of syllables for each line: five, seven, five, seven, and seven. The following tanka presents a model :

The Arctic in Winter

The blasts of cold air
Keep the polar bear on ice
Whither the young cubs ?
Walking on the tall iceberg
Never mind the cold weather.

The haiku and the tanka above were written by elementary age pupils whom we observed when supervising student teachers and one of us cooperating teachers in the public schools. We find that pupils like to write poetry when background information has been experienced and motivation to write is there.

Free verse has no rhyme and no syllabication involved for writing. One pupils whom one of us observed in the classroom wrote the following free verse :

The horse
gives us rides when wanted.
is fed well in the barn.
exercises much during the day time.
loves to be petted.
wants to be noticed.
desires to be comfortable all year long.
hates flies and gnats in summer.
eats grass in summer and grain/hay in winter.
wants to please others.
may ever be grateful for good care.

In the writing of poetry, pupils need to use elements that poets apply in writing verse creatively. One element is onomatopoeia which stresses words written to make echoic sounds. The following emphasize words making their very own sounds : splish, splash, swoosh and slash. The relationship will not always be sound made in the environment. These words also bring in a second element poets use in writing and that is alliteration. With alliteration, two or more sequential words start with the same sound. In this case, the "s" sound is made. A third element is imagery. Imagery has two dimensions and these are similes and metaphors. Similes connect two phrases, in general, such as in the following example of a poem written by a pupil : The cloud of smoke looked like a billowing lion. Thus, the 'cloud of smoke' is compared with "a billowing lion". The word *like* connects the two phrases. Another word used in similes to make these creative connections is the word *as* e.g. "The crow caws *as* a coughing giant. Metaphors, as a second element of imagery, do not have the words "like" or "as" to make these novel connections. For example, the following imagery pertains to a metaphoric approach : "The egg in the pan bubbles tiger like in the water." There is no connector, such as *like* or *as* between, "The egg in the pan" with "bubbles tiger like in the water".

Writing in Journals

Journal writing is quite popular as an activity for children in the elementary school. There are numerous items that might be written in a journal. Here, many pupils record what they have experienced in a reading lesson such as summaries of content read and discussed in the classroom, vocabulary terms learned in a lesson or unit of study, results discussed from a test taken, and/or impressions acquired from a study of characterization, setting, plot, theme, point of view and/or messages of the writer of stories and literature in general.

Some pupils write journal items each day. Others write once a week or biweekly. We suggest encouraging pupils to write each day, but at least once a week. Pupils need to do much writing in order to become proficient in written work. Practice makes for proficiency in writing. We do much writing of manuscripts for publication and at the beginning, our written work left much to be desired. With effort put forth, we have been quite successful in having our manuscripts published in educational journals. We are convinced that most pupils can communicate effectively in writing if there is adequate practice, assistance from the teacher and from parents in the home setting, encouragement from many, a stimulating environment to provide ideas for writing and a designated place for writing with the necessary materials.

Journal writing should have important purposes such as the following for the writer : to be more observant of happenings in every day life, to keep record of ideas and events, to use models that stress quality writing and to establish meaning in life's endeavours. It is important for the pupil to carry his/her journal and a pencil along, in order to record important things in life. What might go into journal writing ?

1. Happenings in class that were of interest.
2. Content read from library books as well as the basal textbook.
3. A sketch of something that is difficult to write about.
4. Poems that were of personal interest.
5. Letters written and received.
6. Frustrations felt in writing.
7. Descriptions on items and objects that fascinate the writer.
8. A creative description of a modified setting, characteriza-

tion, plot, theme, point of view and other elements of a story read.

9. Statements on what you would like to be or become in the future.
10. Play parts of a story in literature or unit in the social studies.

Writing A Personal Experience

Pupils tend to like telling incidence about their own life and times. The personal experience involves a part of the person's life time. The learner needs to choose what is personally relevant and what might be important to the reader of the essay. Sometimes, pupils have so much to write about that the reader feels overwhelmed in its reading. At the opposite end of the continuum, selected pupils just cannot get started in writing a personal experience. Readers like to know which events truly shaped the history of the writer. The pupil also needs to write how he/she fits into wider social roles in life.

A narrative account of events then needs to be shared with peers. The account actually involves a part of the history of the individual doing the writing. Some important pointers for the writer of the essay are the following :

1. Think of what is truly relevant to write about in your life and times.
2. Select an event that is clear and distinct. The event(s) should be written about in detail.
3. Describe each incidence carefully so that readers may role play selected characters in the story of life. There needs to a character, setting and plot in the historical account.
4. Sequence the order of events in the writing so that it makes sense to the reader.
5. Write details which assist the reader to be an inherent part of the story.
6. Use depth coverage in writing about the major events or characters in the writing.
7. Emphasize dialogue in the writing to breath life into the

personnel experience.

8. Build the major events or incidences of a story up to a climax.
9. Wrıte for a target audience and identify this audience.
10. Give each person in the essay should have a name.

Writing An Outline

Outlining salient subject matter may be a good way to learn about main ideas, subordinate ideas and details. When a person reads, he/she needs to sort out what is of major importance as compared to that which is less salient. To view each sentence as having the worth of others, robs the reader of securing important ideas. With the explosion of knowledge, it behooves the reader all the more to arrange content read in terms of major versus minor ideas. Otherwise, the reader is bombarded with ideas which do not lend themselves to remembering effectively what has been read. The teacher needs to model good outlining habits to pupils. Peers may also assist each other in outlining subject matter read.

When pupils outline content read or the spoken voice listened to, careful attention needs to be paid to major as compared to more minor ideas. Let us suppose we are reading/listening to an essay on *Bears*. The first major division of the presentation is, "Looking for food". The first major division of the presentation is, "Looking for food", is a phrase. A subdivision may indicate the kinds of food being looked for. The pupil doing the outline may write the following kinds of foods—fish, rodents, seals and birds. The latter animals emphasize details. A second major division under the heading *Bears* might be, "Finding shelter". A subdivision here might be the kinds of shelter which are acceptable, such as caves, an old deserted building, the side of a mound of dirt and among intertwined branches.

Questions that might the raised pertaining to outlining include the following :

1. How long should the outline be ? This depends upon the length of the reading selection being outlined. Or a teacher

might assign the length of the outline.

2. How many main major division are there in an outline ? This depends upon how many broad ideas there are in a selection that is being read and outlined. We would say that a reading selection of 250 words will generally have two major divisions. Rules in outlining say that there need to be two major divisions at least under one title or topic. There also need to be two subdivision, at least, under a major division. There also should be a least two details under a subdivision. What if *two of each* (such as main divisions, subdivisions and details) cannot be found ? Then put the data within the statement preceding the two items of lesser value.

3. Should there be a sentence outline or a phrase outline ? This depends upon the teacher and the pupils involved in writing the outline. We prefer the sentence outline since each sentence says something that is complete in meaning. In my thinking, phrases lack the clarity that sentences possess. The above examples emphasized a phrase rather than a sentence outline. We will now write a model sentence outline :

The Holy Land

A. A region that is sacred to Muslims, Jews and Christians.

   1. There are Five Pillars of the Muslim religion.

      a) the Hajj at Mecca, Saudi Arabia is made at least once during the life time of a devout Muslim.

      b) The Holy Book of the Muslims is *The Koran*.

   2. The Pentateuch, the first five books of the Old Testament, is holy to devout Jews.

   3. The Church of the Holy Sepulcher is a holy place to devout Christians inside the walled city of Jerusalem.

B. A region made up of the Mediterranean climate has rainy weather from October to April.

The above outline contains two major divisions, such as in A and B. It has three subdivisions such as the numerals 1, 2 and 3. Two details are in evidence such as a and b under the first subdivision. As more content is read, additions may be made to this outline.

Writing An Opinion

A personal perspective of a writer contains a point of view or an opinion. Generally, the writer wants to be understood in terms of what is believed in the opinion. The writer may challenge his/her own point(s) of view in the writing. Sometimes, through writing, the writer wants to understand the premises better of his/her own ideas. By writing about personal beliefs, the writer may also clarify and critically evaluate thoughts brought forth. The following are selected pointers for the pupil in writing about his/her opinions :

1. Choose something that has been on your mind for a long time.
2. Assist readers to comprehend and understand your beliefs.
3. Be yourself in the written content... Do not write about someone else's opinion.
4. Use your own distinct style in writing.
5. Write in the first person.
6. Use examples and details in your writing to make meaningful the opinions expressed.
7. Write on what "bugs" you.
8. Take a point of view which represents your thinking on an issue.
9. Give your thinking on capital punishment, the creation story or the evolution of the universe or the pros and cons of governmental spending on social projects.
10. Write about your favourite pet peeve.

Proofing your writings provides numerous opportunities for reading ideas and content. The final copy should be one that you are very proud of.

Writing on How Something Should be Done

There are numerous occasions when we are asked to provide information on how something is to be done. Directions need to be given frequently on assembling a mower, repairing a kitchen appliance, installing a door bell and building a deck, among other items. People tend to be curious on how something works as well as why something does not work. We believe children find it interesting and challenging to write about something within their area of readiness involving how to do something. The "how to" essay may also involve providing explanations about an event or reasons for an occurrence or happening. There are a plethora of writings that stress how to do something. We would want pupils individually to be involved in determining content for developing the how to essay. Pupils do need to be ready in terms of subject matter acquired so that writing on how to do something is possible.

We have the following suggestions when pupils write the "How To" paper. The pupil needs to choose a topic that he/she understands well and can explain it to pupils. It is truly frustrating when one is asked to do something that is not conceivable. Second, the content should relate to what others do not understand and need assistance in its doing. Third, the writer should have an audience that needs to have this information conveyed. This means that content needs to be written on the understanding level of the target audience. The writer needs to determine what it is that the reader might lack in understanding. There might be something in the how-to-essays that clarifies that which makes for confusion on the part of the reader. Proper sequence needs to be in offing when writing clearly and distinctly the order of steps involved in how to do something. The ordered steps should not be isolated from each other, but rather follow a related set of ideas. Thus, the sequential steps follow a relationship, not an isolation from each other. Step one is related to step two while step two is related to step three and so on.

The following additional pointers are salient in an How To Do It paper, as well as in all written work :

1. eliminate redundant ideas.

2. modify vague statements that are relevant otherwise, so that the reader may follow directions carefully and implement successfully what was given in the essay.
3. try the steps written in the 'How To" paper to see if they work.
4. proofread very carefully that which was written.
5. have a peer try out what is written in the essay.

Writing and Problem Solving

Developing problem solving skills is important for elementary age pupils presently as well as in the future at the work place. Seemingly, problems are with us continually. Selected problems may be solved rather quickly. Others are much more time consuming in solving. What is important is that pupils learn to identify and solve problems. The first flexible step is to identify the problem. Clarity is involved when identifying problem areas. Data is then gathered in order to offer solutions to the problem area. Information then is available for an hypothesis. The hypothesis is a tentative answer to the problem. The hypothesis is tentative and subject to testing. A real live situation needs to be used for testing the hypothesis. If evidence warrants, the hypothesis is rejected. New data or information then need to be gathered. This results in a new hypothesis which is again subject to testing in a life-like situation. If results indicate, the hypothesis may then be accepted.

There are numerous reasons pupils need to learn to write information essays. New information has come out on a topic and the learner believes others need to be informed of the new content. Perhaps, there is a need to inform individuals about the necessity of selected current events items that have just come off the news network. The major purpose here being to inform learners and others about the newness of the situation. Information then is being shared. There is so much new information coming out that it is difficult to stay abreast of what is new. We certainly do live in an information age and individuals feel so limited when they can only learn to know a small amount what is new content. If we think to internet and all the information that is therein, it baffles the individual who thinks of possible ways to learn as much as possible. Newspapers and news magazines attempt to keep individuals informed as to what is going on. But the amount of information coming therefrom is overwhelming. There are selected pointers that may be provided pupils when writing the information essay. These are the following :

1. Try to be as objective as possible when reporting information. The information does not represent opinions, feelings and subjective thoughts.
2. Remember that the writer is writing for human beings and not automations.
3. Write facts, not opinions, to be presented in an appealing way.
4. Delimit the topic to what can be accurately covered and in detail. Overly broad topics may be too complex to cover as compared to a more delimited approach.
5. Cover your delimited topic in a comprehensive way be discussing the five w's—who, what, where, when and why. Shallow and survey methods of reporting information may not stand up under scrutiny. Depth coverage of information will influence the reader much more so as compared to survey procedures.
6. Be as accurate as possible in reporting information. Sources of information need to be checked for reliability and accuracy.
7. Make certain that the information being reported is new and not something that is a rehash of previously presented ideas.
8. Have pupils perceive the new information being reported as related to what was known previously.
9. Sequence ideas presented effectively so that readers perceive the relationship of new knowledge to what was presented previously.
10. Use drawings, diagrams, figures and illustrations to report information clearly and accurately.

In an information age, pupils need to be able to present content accurately and in depth. The information needs to be as factual as possible and yet it needs to be presented in an appealing manner. It is always important to secure learner attention in reading written work.

Writing to Describe

Descriptive writing is very important to a pupil. Why? Each pupil needs to learn to describe something as accurately as possible. In conversing with others, individuals are asked to describe something such as a car, bicycle, house, and/or a place, among others. When pupils are ready, they should have sample opportunities to describe something that is purposeful in their lives. When going to the doctor's office, we are asked to describe how we feel, what the pain is like and the kinds of foods we like to eat frequently. When engaged in descriptive writing, the writer needs to be as accurate as possible when describing an object a musical performance and/or a delicious meal at a banquet, among other things.

Generally, a good conversationalist can converse well and in conversing, decisions enter in. There are selected excellent pointers that may be given in order that pupils write well in descriptive writing :

1. Have something worthwhile to describe. Worthwhileness is an important concept to stress in writing since pupils do better in writing when a purpose or reasons are involved in written work.
2. Have a peer evaluate the descriptive writing product to notice accuracy, in particular, in the written product.
3. Appraise the sequence of ideas in the descriptive writing. Good sequence or order of sentences can assist to clarify the descriptive writing product.
4. Have major ideas be supported with details, whose ideas are of lesser value but do add emphasis upon the major ideas.
5. Use adjectives wisely in your writing since these words describe nouns used as subjects and objects.

6. Develop pupil interest as much as possible when writing to describe. Due to interest factors, the reader might continue to pay attention to the entire written product.
7. Use adverbs effectively to describe. The descriptive adverbs modify verbs, adjectives and other adverbs within the framework of descriptive writing.
8. Check for meaning within the written product. Meaningful statements assist in improving any descriptive writing product.
9. Pay careful attention to the mechanics of writing such as correct punctuation, capital letters, spelling of words and indentation of paragraphs among other items.
10. Proofread and modify weaknesses in the descriptive writing paper.

Narrative Writing

Narrative writing tells a story. Pupils need to do much reading of narrative stories so that they will understand the elements that go into this type of writing. Thus, there needs to be good models of narrative writing for pupils to emulate. Much interest then might be developed in the writing of narration. Interest is powerful factor in learning. Interest in writing might well propel children to pupil forth effort in narrative writing. Pupils, too, need to perceive reasons for writing narrative content. These reasons should be stated deductively by teachers as well as inductively. There are times when prizes and awards in extrinsic motivation allow a pupil to really buckle down to write narrative forms of stories.

When readiness factors permit, the pupil with teacher guidance may begin using the elements of writing narrative accounts.

There are definite pointers for the teacher to point out to pupils when narrative writing is in the offing :

1. Have pupils understand the important ingredients of narrative writing by reading stories that clearly point out what narrative writing is.

2. Permit pupils to use a familiar story for revision and thus stress, heavily, sequence of happenings in the story.
3. Provide quality continuity when pupils are heavily involved in writing sequential happenings in narration.
4. Read aloud narrative accounts so that pupils understand sequence in narration.
5. Guide pupils to choose a character that will be fully described in the narrative account.
6. Assist learners to write a setting for the character that will interest the reader.
7. Help pupils write a theme for the story. The theme will be the underlying message in narrative writing.
8. Let pupils develop a point of view in terms of someone telling the sequential events in the writing.
9. Have pupils write a plot which tells what actually happened in the story. The plot must keep the reader reading to find out what really happened in the story.
10. Use conversation in the story whereby quotation marks indicate what a character said at a specific time.

As is true of all writing done by pupils, the teacher needs to have conferences with pupils individually and collectively so that optimal progress for each pupil is possible. A writer's workshop might assist individuals to improve in the area of writing.

Writing to Assert

Information written by the learner, at times, will need to be backed up with logic and evidence based upon research. Assertions go beyond opinions, feelings and subjective knowledge. The assertion attempts to prove selected ideas, concepts and generalizations. Quality reasons given by the writer to make these assertions include strong and consistent logic, as well as good research which is accurate and reliable.

Sometimes, a writer believes that too many people have inconsistent ideas that are based on partial truths and poor research. The record then needs to be straightened out. There are selected pointers for pupils to become more proficient in developing written content which does hold water :

1. The central idea of the essay must be the assertion, not opinions, feelings, attitudes and subjective thoughts.
2. Vocabulary terms in the essay should be clear and meaningful. Peers and the teacher who proof-read may need to point out the fallacy in logic used as well as terms that are vague and fail to communicate.
3. With critical thinking, the essay may need to be analyzed into important parts which then make it possible to take out and weaknesses in the assertion.
4. Ample evidence must be given to substantiate the assertion.
5. The evidence presented at diverse places in the essay needs to be sequential and related, not in terms of isolated fragments.
6. Evidence presented needs to be written in a manner readable to the audience or target group.
7. Research information may be presented in terms of graphs, charts, illustrations, tables and figures.
8. The summary of the essay needs to present a generalization which draws conclusions, supporting the assertion.
9. The assertion made will need to be written in a serious manner, but in a way which facilitates the reading thereof.
10. Clarity in writing and direct communication is necessary.

Oral discussions whereby pupils need to defend statements made, could be a pre-requisite in writing assertion essays. These learning opportunities provide background experiences for pupils in being able to defend statements made. Assertions should be backed up with supportive information which is logical and research based.

Evaluation Within an Essay

Individuals seemingly are always evaluating ideas, objects

and statements made. Their worth and accuracy is then being evaluated. Quality criteria need to be used in the evaluation process. Otherwise, the evaluative statements may have little worth. There are definite pointers that may be given to assist the writer in writing an evaluation essay :

1. There needs to be clarity on what is being evaluated.
2. Comparisons need to be made between and among comparable items. Apples and oranges should not be compared since they are different fruits and the comparisons a writer makes depend upon the feelings and subjective ideas of the evaluator.
3. Evaluative statements should be valid in terms of the topic presented in the essay.
4. Clàrity in the criteria used to judge the worth of something is a must.
5. There seems to be an opposite and equal reaction to many statements made in society. The writer must allow for other points of view, presented by listeners, that may have much merit.
6. Statistical devices should be used to support evidence in the evaluation process, such as tables, charts, graphs, figures and research data.
7. Sequential statements should be made to support the evaluation process.
8. Evidence to support an evaluation should be significant, not minor ideas nor trivial content.
9. Bias and prejudice need to be avoided in the evaluative statements.
10. Defend what has been written, based on logic, reason and objective data.

Writing Business and Friendly Letters

Business and friendly letter writing are two kinds of written work which have high utilitarian values. Most people write both kinds of letters to serve personal needs.

The business letter needs to have a heading to show where it came from such as the street and its number, the city and state as to its origin and the present date. Convention indicates these items should be on upper right hand side of the business letter. The inside address should be located on the left hand side of the letter. The inside address indicates to whom the letter is written, street address, city and state with zip code number. The greeting is directly below the inside address. The body is the major part of the business letter and pertains to what is being ordered in terms of merchandise or other requests, followed by the closing and the signature. Thus, a model business letter might look like the following :

Heading

D-43, S.V.N. Colony
Guntur 522006
Andhra Pradesh
India
August 15, 1996

Inside Address

Bowen Book Company
1849 Skyview Hall Drive
Kansas City, Missouri 69981

Greeting

Dear Sir :

Body

I would like to request a price list of current books you have on education. Your prompt attention to this would be greatly appreciated since our class is studying the educational systems of different countries.

Thank You

Closing

Sincerely Yours

Signature

D. Bhaskara Rao

The friendly letter has the same format as the business letter above, except the inside address is not necessary. The reason for this is that in friendly letter needs to contain personal experiences of the writer which would be of interest to the receiver of the letter. I would suggest here that the writer of the friendly letter include such items as the following :

1. hobbies and interests being pursued.
2. vacations that were taken.
3. weekend trips experienced.
4. a new addition to the family.
5. gifts given and received during holidays, birthdays and other special events during the year.
6. an unusual event or happening.

Before a letter is sent, careful proof-reading needs to be in the offing. Politeness is involved when business and friendly letters are carefully and accurately written. Receivers of letters need to be clear as to the meaning of content written. Writing in long hand needs to be proofed in terms of clarity in handwriting. It is difficult to write legibly in long hand. Pupils should have ample experiences in using the word processor when conveying information in business and friendly letters.

Writing to Persuade

There are occasions when individuals need to persuade others in writing as well as orally. Selected educators have stated that persuasion is the most important kind of essay writing. Frequently, there are no right or wrong positions on an issue. Therefore, the individual, having strong feelings about one side of the issue, may use persuasive powers to have others, who initially disagreed, change their minds. When voting for officers at any level of government, the candidates running for office take different positions on an issue. Each candidate attempts to persuade voters to accept his/her position when voting. Liberals versus conservatives, agriculture versus business, pro-choice versus pro-life, as well as pro-labour versus pro-business provide opportunities to hear and determine how each person stands on an issue. The position taken may represent how the candidate will vote in an election.

Some pointers that may assist pupils in being able to persuade others include the following :

1. Select a position on an issue which you agree with wholeheartedly. Write a persuasive essay to support your contention. Attempt to influence others to accept you point of view.

2. Write the essay for a selected audience. The audience should tend to believe the other side of the issue.

3. Do possess clarity in terms of where you stand. Your position should be very clear in the essay.

4. Argue, using logic, to substantiate your thinking on the issue.

5. Focus on the one issue so that your argument will be stronger and more influential.

6. Provide evidence which strengthens your point of view.

7. Appeal to the feelings and emotions of the reader when presenting your argument(s).

8. Establish credibility in your writing so that readers will wish to share your position on the issue.

9. Sequentially, order your statements to support your point of view on the issue. The best supportive statement comes toward the end of the essay. The attention of the reader must be kept so that the most powerful influence comes toward the end of the essay.

10. Clarity in the writing of ideas is important with a variety of vocabulary terms used to convince others. Redundancy in writing makes for less influence over the unconverted reader. Arguments given must be direct, logical, and used to obtain converts from the uncommitted.

Being able to influence others is very important in a

democracy. There are may ideas and points of view on the many issues in society. Peaceful means of resolving these issues is important. Too frequently, violence is resorted to in society to influence others toward a certain position or point of view. The pro-life versus pro-choice issue is a good example. There needs to be rational means with debate and persuasion used to convince others to join a particular group having a specific point of view. Democracy in society emphasizes the freedom to express and listen to diverse sides of an issue. The atmosphere here must be such that listeners and readers might make up their own minds, after hearing the different points of view on an issue.

Finding Time to Write

If pupils are to become proficient writers, when will there be time to do much teaching of writing ? I have noticed student teachers and cooperating teachers use different time schedules to permit increased time for writing. Numerous elementary school teachers indicate that there needs to be a scheduled period of time to have pupils be actively involved in writing for different purposes. Perhaps, two to three thirty minute periods are then given to teaching writing each week. Here, pupils are provided guidance and direction in writing. A definite type of writing might then be emphasized such as narrative or expository writing.

A second approach in finding time to teach writing is to relate writing with all curriculum areas in the elementary school. For example, there are many writing activities then that can be stressed in the social studies. Poetry writing might then be correlated with a thematic unit in the social studies (Ediger, 1997).

Third, before the school day begins, there could be writing instruction as well as writing projects for pupils. Pupils may write collaboratively or individually. It is good to provide choices for pupils as frequently as possible.

Fourth, pupils need to be encouraged to write in the home setting. Through parent/teacher conferences, a way may be worked out whereby the home setting becomes conducive to pupil writing. Definite goals in writing for pupils to achieve might be discussed with parents.

Fifth, writing clubs have been successful in many schools. These clubs meet after school. The Writing Club has specific goals for learners to attain in writing. Sharing of written products might be an end goal to stress. Pupils may learn from each other and challenge learners to achieve at a more optimal level in writing.

Sixth, pupils should definitely be encouraged to write when assignments and tasks have been completed. Some of the finest writing comes from pupils when they write in their spare time during the school day !

Conclusion

There are many kinds of writing activities for pupils. Pupils need to develop proficiency for a variety of types of writing. Hopefully, pupils individually will achieve more optimally in writing. With writing experiences, pupils engage in reading also. Writing and reading cannot be separated. What is written will be read. Sometimes the re-reading is done many times since the end product needs to be proofed and become a quality written product.

We would like to end the writing and reading connection by indicating ways to motivate writers to increase proficiency in print discourse. How might pupils then be motivated to increase writing skills and products ?

1. Developing a classroom that is very rich with materials which encourage writing by pupils.
2. Encouraging pupils to write content pertaining to their very own interests and purposes. The content then for writing comes from the learner.
3. Providing rich experiences from which pupils enjoy writing in their diverse manifestations.
4. Showing interest and respect for pupil's writings.
5. Building on the interests of pupils to encourage participation in many purposes in writing.

6. Building a classroom environment for writing that is free from ridicule, embarrassment and fear.
7. Giving adequate time before, during and after the school day for pupils to truly become proficient in writing.
8. Assisting pupils to use the mechanics of writing well without losing out on quality ideas for written expression.
9. Helping pupils to feel confident when sharing ideas from writing.
10. Evaluating pupils progress in writing which encourages, but does not destroy interest in written work (Tiedt, 1983).

A quality program of evaluation needs to be in evidence to appraise pupil progress in the language arts and reading. This is true also in appraising pupil achievement in motivation. The teacher needs to evaluate, continuously, pupil progress in motivation. Motivation needs to be there to have pupils attain worthwhile objectives in the language arts/reading curriculum (Ediger, 1996).

References

Ediger, Marlow (1997), Teaching Reading and the Language Arts in the Elementary School. Kirksville, Missouri : Simpson Publishing Company, 135–44.

Ediger, Marlow (1997), Social Studies Curriculum in the Elementary School, Fourth edition. Kirksville, Missouri : Simpson Publishing Company, 168–83.

Ediger, Marlow (1996), Elementary Education. Kirksville, Missouri : Simpson Publishing Company, 107–17.

Ediger, Marlow and Bhaskara Rao, Digumarti (1996). Science Curriculum. New Delhi : Discovery Publishing House.

Ediger, Marlow (1998), "The Principal of the School", Reading Improvement, 35 : 45–48.

Tiedt, Iris M. (19983), The Language Arts Handbook. Englewood Cliffs, New Jersey : Prentice-Hall, 184.

6
Speaking Activities and Reading

Pupils who are far along in their speaking vocabularies tend to do well in reading. These pupils speak clearly and have a large vocabulary for their age levels. Each pupil needs to receive guidance and assistance to achieve as optimally as possible in oral communication. Hopefully, achievement in oral use of language will also assist pupils to do well in reading.

The oral communication curriculum needs to have clearly stated, worthwhile objectives of instruction. Pupils individually need to be encouraged to take part in formal and informal experiences involving oral use of language. Learners need to attain as optimally as possible. Expectations should be high, but feasible, for goal achievement. Those who are deficient in oral communication are at a disadvantage in school and in society where there are expectations for each learner to be able communicate needs, wants and wishes. To be successful in society, especially at the work place, individuals need to be able to express themselves in an efficient manner. Promotions at the work place depends upon many factors, including the ability to communicate well orally.

The teacher must be creative and think of diverse ways and approaches in helping pupils do well in speaking effectively with others. Literacy and oracy skills are complimentary. With oral communication, there needs to be a listener. What is said orally and listened to, can be recorded in written discourse. The recording here involves reading and attaching meaning to abstract symbols making for words, sentences, paragraphs and larger units of written expression.

.....research on typical reading acquisition shows that reading is built on a foundation of oral language competence—in other words, not just on phonology but also on vocabulary, grammar and so on. The idea that reading can be taught exclusively or even primarily through the visual modality, without regard to these foundational linguistic skills, is not consistent with what is known about the process of reading development (Spear-Swerling and Sternberg, 1996).

Critical Listening to the Spoken Voice

Speaking involves a listener to ideas expressed. Critical listening to a speaker is important. Ideas need to be analyzed into component parts to become meaningful. Ideas may be expressed to manipulate individuals in numerous ways.

First, the glittering generalities approach might be used by a speaker. Here, the positive aspects of a topic are covered only. The information presented by the speaker leaves many loopholes that need to be filled. If a speaker states that "we need to become more democratic", but does not define "democratic" nor is it said how this goal of being "more democratic" is to be fulfilled, facets of content are lacking. The speaker merely states how wonderful a life can be with increasing emphasis placed upon democracy as a way of life. Over generalizing is in evidence and the positive side is mentioned only with vague statements.

Second, a bandwagon approach is used by a speaker. The speaker indicates that everyone agrees with him/her and needs to join the crowd, be it in buying of cereal, a specific car, a type or brand name of clothing, or of a personal computer. Others are joining the crowd and the listener needs to do the same. Charisma and a persuasive tone of voice with appealing content may be in the offing with the band wagon approach.

Third, a testimonial procedure may be used. Thus, a famous personality may endorse a product wholeheartedly, meaning the listener also needs to buy the product endorsed by the testimonial.

Fourth, deck stacking approaches are used. Thus, a product is advertised as being very nutritious with multiply vitamins. The speaker does not say which vitamins and how many are involved.

Fifth, a positive association approach is to entice consumers. Thus, a soft drink is advertised with an attractive woman nearby as well a luxury house in the background. The soft drink advertisement has nothing to do with the unusually pleasant surroundings. An association is to be made by the reader between the soft drink to be consumed and the beautiful surroundings. The speaker/advertiser hopes that the soft drink will be purchased increasingly so, due to the appealing environment, even though it is unrelated.

Sixth, a plain folks setting is provided with the product being emphasized, which is to be sold. The ordinary people concept is stressed due to the thinking that most individuals are common in society and not ivy league college/university graduates. Historically, the common man (or woman) has been glorified in being able to rise through the ranks from poverty to riches and fame. Thus, if plain folks like and support a product, then the majority of individuals in a nation should also prize the product highly.

Seventh, an upper class appeal can be enticing to some people. An appeal in a commercial is then made to going higher on the socio-economic level. A new product being advertised then needs to be purchased to rise on the socio-economic ladder in order to compare with wealthier individuals who have larger, spacious homes.

Eighth, name calling is used by some when the other person or side disagrees with the personal ideas being presented (Templeton, 1997). A person then might be called a "leftist" with communist connotations. Or an individual may be labelled a Nazi. I (Ediger) was called a Nazi, during my junior and senior high school years—1940–1946, before and during World War Two by a few persons. We had German services in church and being a General Conference Mennonite, I was a conscientious objector toward participation in war. These two traits, German services in church and being a conscientious objector, made a person a Nazi. Another name used here was to call a person a "Hitlerite", referring to Adolph Hitler, Germany's dictator from 1933–1945.

Pupils need to be aware of the dangers of name calling,

not only to the receiver of the negative name, but also what it does to have hatred within the caller of these names. Both lose here in that the self concept of the individual might be lowered due to being on the receiving end of the name calling as well as being the name caller. Respecting and being a caring person are so necessary for the welfare of all in society. Being filled with hatred, psychologically, seemingly is not good for anyone in society. In the oral communications curriculum, there are basic criteria which need to be followed so that all feel valued and prized. These criteria are the following :

1. each person needs to be treated with respect in school and in society.
2. all need to participate actively in developing rules and regulations for classroom conduct.
3. pupils individually should be involved in appraising student conduct in terms of these standards.
4. standards for pupils in the classroom to abide by may be modified and changed as the needs arises.
5. safety, security, belonging and esteem needs should be met for each learner.

Teaching and learning should be based on the best theories available in education (Ediger, 1996). We will now discuss learning opportunities in oral communication for pupils to achieve the five objectives above.

Using Puppets

The use of puppets can be a good way to assist pupils to express themselves more proficiently when using oral communication. Shy, withdrawn learners tend to feel more relaxed in speaking when puppets are used. We recommend, if at all possible, that pupils make these puppets, bit sack puppets, sock puppets and/or stick puppets. The puppets may be used in different units of study in an integrated curriculum. Thus, if pupils are studying a farm unit, they may make stick puppets pertaining to different kinds of livestock. Speaking parts may be developed, based on pupil background knowledge, for a committee presentation to the rest of the class members or within a neighbouring classroom of learners. Or, in studying life on an assembly line in a factory, pupils may develop speaking parts for the different roles of involved workers. Assembly lines have fewer and fewer workers due to automation. Here, pupils may do research using needed reference sources to discuss how the role of the worker has changed due to automation. Effective oral use of language should be in the offing. Puppets may be made and used to play different roles of participants in the discussion. There is novelty and newness involved in the use of puppetry. Individual pupils tend to forget their shyness and reservations when participating in role playing with puppet use. We would like to suggest the following pointers when stressing puppetry as a part of the learning activities provided in ongoing lessons and units of study :

1. emphasize quality art work when puppets are being made. Multiple intelligences emphasizes that talents in art work should be prized highly by all in the learning community.
2. an integrated curriculum in reading and the language arts may be emphasized when art work receives its due emphasis in worth and value.
3. speaking activities need to be carefully developed in an ongoing lesson or unit of study.
4. pupils need to practice their speaking parts after the role of each has been decided upon by pupils, with teacher guidance.
5. standards and goals for oral communication need to be carefully defined. Each pupil should be challenged to achieve as optimally as possible.

Speaking parts may be recorded by cassette or videotape to be reviewed by participants in the puppetry activity as well as by those who were observers. May be, there are parts in speaking that will result in being revised and modified. The new approach, as modified by feedback from the audio-visual presentation, might be tried out in the classroom. Developing interest in puppetry use should be an end result and not to destroy interest in learning. It is so very important to develop and maintain a powerful factor in learning and that is pupil interest.

Using Role Play Activities

Pupils at a very young age love to play different roles in the pre-school years. What child does not like to put on the parents' shoes and role play the parent ? These kinds of activities are very excellent to emphasize on the elementary school and higher years of schooling. Thus, high school students love to have roles in plays which are put on for the public as well as for students. Adults try out for parts in local play performances. It is motivator to perform in front of others. Those who participate in plays also have made lasting friendships from these performances.

We believe all should have opportunities to be in plays, if they so desire. Elementary and secondary school pupils seemingly feel quite relaxed while performing in front of groups. As Adults, more seem to have fear in getting up in front of others. In the elementary school years, performing within a classroom can be very rewarding. The threat a criticism should not be used when role playing is used as a learning opportunity. The teacher needs to develop standards for pupils to follow in classroom role playing so that positive attitudes toward others is developed. Role playing may stress a story from literature or a biography in history.

With creative dramatics, no speaking parts are written down. Pupils decide cooperatively upon who will play which role. It is good to give everyone a chance for role playing. Each person in the creative dramatics activity needs to have the content well in mind when playing a specific role representing an individual in literature or in history. This is especially important since no play parts are written, but rather individuals play their respective role and orally provide the speaking parts when sequence demands it.

In formal dramatics, pupils collaboratively in a committee write play parts for each person in the literary or historical context. The parts may be memorized or read to the class or audience. Listening, speaking, reading and writing are stressed in this learning experience.

In addition to creative and formal dramatics, pupils may engage in socio-drama. With socio-drama, pupils play the role of another person to see how it feels to be in someone else's shoes. For example, if a pupil has been ridiculed, that individual and the one who did the ridiculing change roles. Thus, each person may attempt to feel how it feels to be ridiculed as well as the one who did the ridiculing. Feelings experienced need to be discussed. Hopefully, pupils will learn the consequences of belittling others.

Pointers for pupils to remember in role play activities are the following :

1. try to feel the role that is being played.
2. use voice inflection with stress, pitch and juncture when communicating orally.
3. use gestures and facial expressions as non-verbal factors in communication.
4. speak clearly and accurately when oral communication is in progress.
5. use feedback from the observers and from video-tape to improve the next dramatization.

Committees in the Classroom

There are many occasions in school and outside the school setting whereby pupils need to be capable in a discussion setting. Relevant decisions are made when working together with others to discuss important ideas. Discussions may break down if involved people do not stay on the topic, but digress to the irrelevant. Ideas need to circulate within the committee doing the discussing and not between the chairperson and one other person and back to the chairperson in that repeated sequence. All need to participate and no one dominate the discussion. If content is not presented clearly and accurately, there will be wasted time in obtaining meaning from what is being said. Respect for the ideas of others needs to be in the offing.

Pupils may change off in terms of being leaders within the committee endeavours. The teacher may appoint different leaders or the committee itself may select leaders. The leader needs to try to secure comments from all members. Hardly might one consider it a committee decision if one or two members do all the deliberating. Leadership qualities also stress a desire for all to participate, but no one dominating also stress a desire for all to participate, but no one dominating the discussion within the committee settling. A pleasant tone of voice needs to be used by discussants with clarity of ideas presented for the discussion. Questions need to arise by participants when comments and problem areas are not clear and distinct.

Children's literature provides excellent opportunities for interesting topics to discuss. The following, among others, are fascinating areas from children's literature for pupils to discuss:

1. Character, What are the clues to characters suggested in the writing? From what is said or the action taking place, what inferences can be made about the individual? Why does the character act the way he does? What are his values? Did anyone change in the story? Why?

2. Setting. Can you see where the story is happening? How do those in the story act because of the setting? Is there a basic struggle between the people in the story and the nature of the place where they live?

3. Mood—feeling—tone. What words are used to tell you how the writer feels? What is the tone of voice of the storyteller? Is it serious? Humorous? Is this a true experience?

4. Story Pattern. What would you tell it you had only the first paragraph to guide you? Can you tell what happened by reading only the first paragraph? Is there a theme or lesson that the writer is illustrating? Who is telling the story? What differences does it make? (Anderson and Lapp, 1979).

The voice plays a major role in holding listeners' attention. Good speakers change the speed of their voices. Vary loudness, pitch their voices attractively, and avoid mannerisms that affect listeners negatively.

Young persons need to experiment with variations in speed, pitch, loudness and tone. Probably, the best way to do experiment is to record an oral report on tape. This technique is especially good if the presentation is a team endeavour, for group members can listen to themselves in playback, assessing their vocal expression, the overall organization and clarity of their presentation and their general knowledge of the topic....

Effective communication is as dependent on the body as it is on the dynamic use of the voice. The use of visuals is one way to encourage gesturing and movement of the body in oral reporting. The student who uses a time line to show relationships will point to each entry on the line as he/she talks; the student who works from the map will point to locations on it. Pointing, moving forward and holding up are all non-verbal devices necessary when using a visual. These gestures add action and force to a presentation.

If the school or community owns a cam corder, it can be used to videotape presentations for eventual self study. Each student views his/her contributions to a program and evaluates it in terms of questions as : Did I make eye contact with my audience? Did I gesture automatically? Did I change my facial expressions as required? In viewing a videotape, young people often can spot their problems and without prompting improve on them during future reporting sessions (Hennings, 1994).

Pointers to stress for committee endeavours to function well include the following :

1. Listening carefully to ideas expressed is salient and provides the background information so necessary for a discussion group to function well.
2. Developing a sense of community is vital so that group cohesion is possible.
3. Quality sequencing in ideas expressed makes it easier for all to follow the discussion.
4. Evaluating periodically of what has been covered assists the group to notice achievement.
5. Respecting each other's ideas helps release the creative thoughts of committee members.

Giving Oral Reports

Pupils should have ample opportunities to present oral reports in front of the classroom. To give quality reports, pupils need to have the subject matter well in mind pertaining to what will be reported. An outline continuing the salient points of the oral report provides assistance to the speaker. Video-taping the oral report provides ample opportunities pertaining to securing feedback on the presentation. The reporter needs to observe the speed with which ideas can be presented so that all listeners may obtain the contents as readily as possibly. Quality stress helps the speaker to get ideas across to peers. Stress emphasizes saying words louder or softer in oral communication. To say a word louder tends to place emphasis upon that word. It draws attention to that word with louder stress. Pitch emphasizes pitching words higher or lower so less of a monotone voice is in evidence when speaking. In music, there are notes that are higher or lower on a scale and the reader of music needs to pay attention to the pitch of each note in order to read music accurately. The speaker also needs to raise and lower the voice to use it effectively in oral communication. A third factor that is relevant in speaking is to emphasize juncture. With quality juncture, pauses are indicated at the proper place in ongoing subject matter. If a reader or reporter does not pay careful attention to commas, periods and question marks, among other punctuation marks, there will be misinterpretation and run on sentences and words may result. Pupils with teacher guidance need to practice giving reports using the concepts of stress, pitch and juncture.

Some pointers to emphasize when giving oral reports are the following :

1. Go over oral reports with pupils to determine what makes for an effective presentation.

2. Assist pupils in working on quality presentations in reporting orally to the class.

3. Have pupils work in dyads, two working together, to refine methodology in giving oral reports.

4. Have pupils present oral reports in small groups of three

to four pupils to develop confidence and poise in the given of these reports.

5. Let pupils appraise their own videotape results of oral reporting in terms of desired criteria.

Oral Reading to Classmates

Pupils need to have ample opportunities to read orally to others in the school setting. Too frequently, oral reading has stressed the round robin approach whereby pupils in a class have been placed into three different ability levels in reading. The teacher works with one of the three groups at a time. One facet of instruction here is pupils taking turns reading orally to the teacher. The teacher then may evaluate reading skills possessed by each learner and those needing more assistance for improvement. This approach is used somewhat routinely each sequential day of instruction. Boredom and the routine set in. Pupils here do not have a chance to practice oral reading skills in terms of desired criteria.

Oral reading to an audience has a different goal. Here, each pupil may practice reading a selection until it is suitable to read to a larger audience including pupils in the classroom, other classrooms and to parents. Peers in practice sessions may listen to the oral reading and provide suggestions, in terms of desirable criteria, for improvement. There may be five or six pupils who have modified/refined a selection for oral reading.

Reader's theater is very similar to the oral reading experience just discussed. In reader's theater, five or six pupils may practice reading play parts written out, as is true of formal dramatics. Each person accepts his/her role in the play and reads with voice inflection, stress, pitch and juncture. The play parts are practiced in oral reading by the respective reader until they are good enough to present in front of an audience, such as classmates, parents and others interested in the presentation. Pupils individually may hold their very own book as they take their respective turn in reading orally. Generally, pupils in reader's theater sit in a semicircle on tall stools so they are clearly visible to listeners. A reader then role plays the part being read. The oral reading experience then has elements of the traditional round robin approach as well as dramatic qualities. Thus, the involved pupil needs to play the character in the story as if he/she is an alive person making decisions.

There are definite pointers that may be used by teachers in having pupils read well orally :

1. Learners need ample time to practice reading a selection orally until it has been refined and mastered.
2. Guidance needs to be given pupils in using proper enunciation and pronunciation.
3. Content must be conveyed clearly and accurately to observes.
4. Each pupil's presentation needs to be evaluated in terms of making progress over that of previous performances.
5. Self evaluation is important and, especially, if video-taping of a performance is being emphasized.
6. Pupils should be encouraged to enjoy oral reading and read more literature as a result.
7. Teachers need to model good oral reading of stories and other print discourse to pupils (Ediger, 1997).

Giving and Following Directions

In society, people are asked to give directions when going to a specific place. We think it is frustrating to a person when asking where a place is located and there is vagueness or a lack of knowledge in the response. We believe individuals can become better observers of landmarks so that helpful answers may be given to those asking for directions. Pupils should be given much time to practice giving directions in order to reach a specific destination. Pupil/teacher planning may be used to indicate which landmarks are important to know in a community or area. The following landmarks are important and were brain stormed by a class of fifth graders :

1. parks and school buildings.
2. selected stores and offices.
3. major highways and streets.

4. museums and libraries.
5. the train depot and airport.
6. important bus stops.
7. selected churches and governmental buildings.

To assist pupils in becoming more conscious of following directions, the following projects were completed by pupils with teacher guidance in an ongoing unit of study :

1. making a relief map.
2. developing a diorama.
3. working a written exercise.
4. completing a test.
5. developing a selected dish of food.
6. learning to play a game.
7. making a simple musical instrument.
8. providing a set of directions for others to locate or find a specific object.
9. performing a folk dance.

Quality listening needs to be practiced by pupils in all curriculum areas. The integrated curriculum is then in evidence. In the reading curriculum, pupils need to distinguish between letters and sounds when analyzing words for proficient reading. Thus, reading emphasizes good listening by pupils, not only to hear diverse phonemes clearly, but also to develop much background information for reading different selections. Comprehension of content in reading comes from diverse sources such as listening to a related discussion covering content read or new subject matter to be read.

Extemporaneous Speaking

When readiness permits, pupils tend to enjoy extemporaneous speaking. Here, pupils may be given at random a topic to speak on. A topic from the current unit being studied in reading may suffice. The involved learners are given three minutes, or more, to prepare a talk on the topic. If pupils have been reading on the topic "Animals of the Arctic", a learner may be given the topic of "Polar Bears", at random. The involved pupils then prepares a talk in the allotted time given. Recall of information is necessary. The pupil needs to think quickly on foods eaten, habitat, raising of offspring and dealing with enemies. The pupil then must arrange the items sequentially to report orally to the class. The talk may be videotaped and critiqued by a group of classmates. The pupil realizes that knowledge needs to be recalled rather quickly and thinking on one's toes is important. The talk needs to be given clearly and sequentially.

Pointers that may be given to aid pupils to achieve more optimally in speaking include the following.

1. The teacher needs to be a model in quality speaking activities.
2. Pupils should have numerous opportunities to choose their very own topics for oral communication endeavours in the classroom.
3. Learners need chances to appraise their progress in oral communication.
4. Diagnosis of pupil deficiencies is necessary so that remediation may occur.
5. Peers working together may assist each other to achieve in oral communication endeavours.

Using the Telephone

Much use is made of telephones in society. Messages may be given clearly and effectively. With answering machines, the receiver of calls may return each when convenient. The answering machine is handy for school personnel since messages may be left on the voice recorder to be returned at a more opportune time. Cellular phones has expanded opportunities for the making of phone calls. With cellular phones, calls can be made and responded to, outside the home setting. I believe it is the school's responsibility to develop within pupil's knowledge, skills and attitudes to use telephones successfully. One of my student teachers together with the cooperating teacher wrote and implemented the use of the following criteria pertaining to telephone use :

1. be polite in all telephone conversation.
2. speak at a rate where optimal communication may take place.
3. communicate loudly enough so that the receiver may hear the message clearly.
4. clarify contents where this is needed.
5. be a good listener !

Conclusion

How does quality oral communication assist pupils to become good readers? With oral communication, pupils practice using words, phrases, sentences, and paragraphs. There should be good sequence in what is said (Ediger, 1997). Meaning needs to be inherent in messages conveyed. What is said might be written down and read by the listener. These features are inherent in all reading that is done. Oral communication requires a listener. The listener provides feedback to the speaker in terms of quality communication. There is oral communication that is directly related to reading such as oral reading and reader's theater. There are numerous speaking activities that pupils should become proficient in. These include use of puppets, role playing, committee endeavours, oral reports, oral reading, extemporaneous speaking and giving directions. Additional experiences for pupils to engage in within the speaking and oral communication arena include engaging in discussions, interviewing and making introductions. Speaking and listening are integrated and, in reality, not separate areas of communication. For convenience of instruction, speaking and listening may be separated to emphasize what can be done in each area to assist teachers in guiding more optimal pupil progress.

The section on oral communication may be ended by listing salient objectives for pupils to achieve. These are :

1. to converse with others courteously and easily.

2. to take part in discussions, sticking to the topic and accepting the thinking of others.
3. to sequence information properly and use it effectively.
4. to plan, develop and carry out an interview effectively and courteously.
5. to be competent in the use of the telephone.
6. to use parliamentary procedure appropriately when participating in meetings.
7. to provide clear directions, announcements and explanations.
8. to tell stories with quality sequence and in an enthusiastic manner.
9. to introduce individuals properly to each other.
10. to participate actively in choric reading.
11. to take part in dramatic experiences in ongoing lessons an units of study (Greene and Petty, 1975).

References

Anderson, Paul S. and Diane Lapp (1979), Language Skills in Elementary Education, 296.

Ediger, Marlow (1996), Essays in School Administration. Kirksville, Missouri : Simpson Publishing Company, 136–41.

Ediger, Marlow (1997), The Modern Elementary School. Kirksville, Missouri : Simpson Publishing Company, 192–93.

Ediger, Marlow (1997), Teaching Reading and the Language Arts in the Elementary School. Kirksville, Missouri : Simpson Publishing Company, 158–59.

Greene, Harry A. and Walter T. Petty (1975), Developing Language Skills in the Elementary Schools. Boston : Allyn and Bacon, Inc., 172.

Hennings, Dorothy Grant (1994), Communication in Action. Boston: Houghton Mifflin Company, 224.

Spear-Swerling, Louise and Robert J. Sternberg (1996), Off Track—When Poor Readers Become "Learning Disabled". Westview Press, 46.

Templeton, Shane 91997), Teaching the Integrated Language Arts. Second edition. Boston : Houghton-Mifflin, 349–50.

7
Reading in the Primary Grades

Primary grades teachers need to be certain that pupils are off to a good start in reading. These early years of instruction are crucial in guiding pupils to have a positive altitude toward reading. Pupils should learn to enjoy reading and realize that many benefits accrue from the act of reading. The teacher needs to communicate to pupils that he/she loves to read and communicates these feelings to learners. An attitude of reading is a good endeavour which needs to be communicated to pupils. Not only should reading be enjoyable to pupils but also useful in its many manifestations. There are numerous things that a teacher can do to stimulate young children in becoming lovers of library books.

Strommen and Mates (1997) conducted research into young children's ideas about the nature of reading and wrote the following :

Our observations confirm that learning to read is a developmental process but show that a young child's age, word and later-level decoding skills, are not necessarily reliable indicators of what he/she understands reading to be, and, therefore, of what intervention may be useful.

It is important for teachers to realize that a child's growth in ideas about what readers do an his/her growth in reading itself are interdependent. A fundamental goal of beginning reading instruction should be to move each child toward the understanding that readers reconstruct texts by using multiple strategies to interpret the language encoded by print and at the same time, to make it possible for the child to do this by providing information that will enable construction of appropriate strategies. With this is mind we make the following recommendations regarding children early literacy instruction.

1. Teachers of young children should initially stress a child's ideas about the nature of reading, written language and the written code, as well as his/her reading strategies and tailor reading experiences to the child's ideas about what readers do.
2. Teaches should ask themselves what new information could cause a child to rethink or interpret what he or she believes and challenge each child's non-conventional ideas through demonstrations that contradict his/her current thinking. For example, frequent re-readings of a particular text help to build a child's knowledge of written language, but may also promote the idea that reading is memorizing texts. If a child believes this is what readers do, then demonstrating that readers can and do read a variety of unfamiliar texts may contribute to a shift in the child's thinking.
3. Teachers should set expectations for a child's reading performance that always take into account the child's ideas about how readers read.

Developing a Love for Reading

The act of reading means that pupils are reading enjoyable and useful materials. Reading does not mean a study of phonics, nor lessons on syllabication. Rather, reading involves securing ideas, content and subject matter. Thus, reading stresses a form of holism in that concepts and generalizations are obtained from print materials. An immersed reader find few distractions and is actively engaged in what is being read. The interest factor in reading propels pupils to reach toward higher levels in reading subject matter. Thus, the pupil and the content to be read become one, not separate entities.

With active involvement in reading, the pupil should attach meaning to ongoing concepts and generalisations. Meaning is attached to what is being read. The abstract print then makes sense to the reader. Understanding of print materials assists pupils to like reading in its diverse purposes. Pupils learn to predict what comes sequentially in ongoing reading tasks. This helps the pupil to overcome difficulties in recognizing individual words when predicting in a contextual situation. Further reading will provide the pupil with clues as to the predictions being correct or incorrect. Holism is involved in reading ideas, not fragmented sounds or syllables. Learners need to feel they have control over what is being read. In other words, they are able to understand in a meaningful way that which is being read. Pupils have control over their own reading when they can break the code involving abstract symbols. Does this mean that phonics needs to be taught in beginning reading ? Good teachers have always brought in phonics instruction when stressing a holistic reading curriculum. The phonics is brought in contextually, not within isolated word analysis lessons.

Pupils need to develop a basic sight vocabulary of relevant words as they progress through the early primary grades. The sight vocabulary for reading needs to be developed within a viable context, not within isolated words presented by the teacher. A more meaningful procedure is then in evidence when contextually pupils achieve a vocabulary for reading whereby words are recognized at sight. In addition to a basic sight vocabulary, pupils need to attain basic learnings in phonics. Phonics has its many values when a pupil cannot determine an unknown word, but can identify this word through analysis such as in phonics. Thus, the pupil associates individual sounds with their related symbols. It does not take long before pupils can apply relevant phonics principles when unlocking unknown words in a contextual situation. Interest in reading should never be destroyed through the development of a basic sight vocabulary of words whereby these are known by immediate observation. Nor should phonics instruction in which pupils truly enjoy learning phonics within a contextual situation as the need arises. In have supervised many student teachers and cooperating teachers who have devised games to assist pupils to enjoy mastering new words which then are recognized at once through observation.

As the young child progresses in reading, he/she develops concepts pertaining to what a word is when seeing it in print. Usually, pupils individually also learn the letters within a word and the related sounds inherent in the word. There are words which contain letters that have a one to one correspondence with the related sounds. Other sounds need two letters such as the "th" sound in words such as "the", "this" and "that". Pupils need to do much reading with teacher guidance as well as by themselves so that increased skills in word recognition occur. The teacher also needs to read aloud to pupils so that the latter obtains concepts pertaining to content, sequence of ideas presented, punctuation, stress, pitch and structure of sentence patterns. Selections read aloud by the teacher should be interesting, understandable and purposeful. These reading selections might well serve as a basis for pupils liking or disliking reading instruction.

The Experience Chart

Experience charts are an excellent way for pupils to enjoy reading as well as extend their skills in this area. Here, the classroom of pupils or a smaller group has had an interesting experience such as looking outside the classroom window to notice the rain falling. After an ample period of time for observing the rain fall, pupils may dictate ideas to the teacher in developing an experience chart. These learners should understand the content presented to the teacher since a concrete situation was provided to children to think about. The teacher records subject matter on the chalkboard, when presented by pupils. As the ideas are given, pupils can see talk written down. A word processor may also be used to record pupil's ideas for the experience chart.

Once the ideas have been presented, the teacher guides pupils in reading the recorded ideas from the experience chart. Pupils read the content orally with the teacher as he/she points to each word or phrase. Here, pupils have opportunities to develop a basic sight vocabulary of words for reading. The contents of the experience chart may be read over again as pupils desire. With re-reading, pupils are aided in identifying more and more words by sight. Also, pupils notice that talk is written down. These can be considered as written experiences for young pupils when they see talk written down. Thus, there are individual letters, words, phrases and sentences. Whatever is said by pupils can be recorded on the chalk-board or by using the word processor. Learners usually begin to make statement such as the following pertaining to the recorded contents in the experience chart :

1. Here are two words that begin or end with the same letter.
2. These two words rhyme.
3. These are long words or these are short in length.
4. These are the same letters in the two words but they make different sounds.
5. This word has taller letters as compared to that word.

It is quite obvious that pupils are making discoveries within the experience chart and appear to be interested in this activity at the same time. We have personally observed much enthusiasm when pupils engage in making discoveries by examining words and sentences.

When making comparisons among different experience charts with content provided by young children and recorded by the teacher, it is quite obvious that more sophistication is involved on the learner's part when sequentially experiences of this nature are provided. Ediger (1988) lists the following assumptions involving experience charts :

1. Pupils are actively involved in experiences which provide content for an experience chart.
2. Learners present ideas for the experience chart.
3. Pupils with teacher help read content pertaining to their very own experiences.
4. Learners may notice how ideas are written down using abstract letters and words.
5. The content in the experience chart is familiar to learners since it relates to their own personal lives.
6. The experience chart method may assist pupils to develop interest in reading.
7. Individualization is inherent in using experience charts

since each child has unique experiences. Each child may then present content for a group or individual experience chart.

Pupils soon select library books to read and practice reading those same words that were experienced on the experience chart. Pupils should experience many reading activities so that learning to read is pleasurable and progress is made sequentially. Fountas and Pinnell (1996) wrote the following objectives for guided reading which serve well in all reading programs :

- It gives children the opportunity to develop as individual readers while participating in a socially supported activity.
- It gives teachers the opportunity to observe individuals as they process new texts.
- It gives individual readers the opportunity to develop strategies so that they can read increasingly difficult texts independently.
- It gives children enjoyable, successful experiences in reading for meaning.
- It develops the abilities needed for independent reading.
- It helps children learn how to introduce texts to themselves.

Young children need to achieve these broad objectives in reading sequentially. Success in each sequential step is important. Interesting and purposeful reading materials need to be in the offing. The reading teacher needs to know each pupil well so that a quality reading curriculum may be continuous and ongoing.

Guided Listening Thinking Activity

The Guided Listening Thinking Activity (GLTA) emphasizes the teacher choosing a library book which children would love to participate in. A large picture book for young children would suffice. The teacher asks the children to predict what the book would be about as the title and illustrations therein are viewed. The teacher then reads aloud to pupils a short section in which the height of action in the story is involved. Pupils then need to evaluate their original prediction or hypothesis. Each hypothesis must be respected and further hypothesizing encouraged for the rest of the story. Then the teacher may read to find out what did happen in the picture book. Higher levels of cognition need to be emphasized already on the early primary grade levels. Pupils should be encouraged to do critical and creative thinking as well as problem solving as early as possible in life. Higher levels of cognition are necessary in every day life with its many perplexities and difficulties.

After the reading of the picture book has been completed, the teacher may raise additional questions about the contents. It is salient to obtain pupil reaction to the contents. Pupils should be able to provide reasons for their answers given. Learners should also ask questions covering what was read from the picture book.

The GLTA is teacher directed. The teacher chooses the book to be read. He/she determines questions to be answered by pupils. The teacher stimulates pupils to make predictions, develop hypotheses, think at higher levels of cognition, set the classroom climate for the activity and provide support for each pupil. This does not mean that pupils are left out of the reading curriculum when the GLTA is being stressed. Rather, the teacher encourages pupils responses and is the leader in setting the stage and implementing the reading lesson. It is also child centered in that pupils are encouraged to make predictions and hypothesize. Pupils have opportunities to raise questions, especially at the end of reading the selection from the picture book. We believe with a teacher directed reading lesson, the pupil needs to be as actively involved as possible in responding to the questions of the teacher as well as the child raise questions of his/her own. Listening carefully and well is an important goal to stress in GLTA.

The Shared Book Experience

The shared book experience emphasizes more pupil participation in the actual reading of content as compared to the Guided Listening Thinking Activity in which the teacher does the oral reading and pupils follow along in their own books to achieve in word recognition and other elements in reading. The shared books experiences stresses the use of a Big Book. With the Big Book, all pupils in the group can clearly see the illustrations and print from where they are seated. Examples of two Big Book are *When the King Rides By* (Mahy, 1986) and *The Greedy Goat* (Bolton, 1986).

Contents in Big Books should have predictable subject matter for pupils so that they can rather readily determine what will come next in the story in sequence. The teacher introduces the Big Book to pupils by looking together at the illustrations therein. These illustrations are discussed and provide pupils with background information in order to understand Big Book contents more effectively. The pupils with the background information will be better able to read along with the classroom teacher from the Big Book. Predictions may be made by pupils in terms of outcomes of the story. These predictions may be checked at an appropriate point when reading the Big Book cooperatively. Higher levels of cognition is definitely a goal here, including critical and creative thinking as well as problem solving. These higher cognitive goals are to be encouraged and based upon the present developmental level of each pupil. Respect for the learner and his/her abilities is always important. Good citizenship and democracy need to be practiced continuously in the classroom.

When pupils read along together with the teacher from the Big Book, they learn to identify words which present problems in the teaching of reading. The experience chart approach made it so that pupils presented ideas for the chart with the teacher then reading together with the pupils the contents therein. The Big Book philosophy of reading instruction also emphasizes pupils learning to recognize words contextually while reading together with the teacher. At the end of the reading experience, the teacher may ask questions such as the following to provide interest in phonics :

1. Which words did you notice that started with the same letter or sound ?

2. Which words end with the same letter and sound?
3. Which vowel letters in words make the same sound?
4. Which vowel letters makes a different sound when comparing two or more words?
5. Do you see words whereby two letters make a single sound?

Each of the above learning activities needs to be emphasized or adjusted to the present achievement level of pupils. Pupils should enjoy phonics activities. These experiences need to be positive for pupils and assist in developing word recognition skills. Phonics should not be taught for its own sake, but rather to assist learners to unlock unknown words. Phonics then has practical and utilitarian values and is not taught for its own sake.

When pupils and the teacher orally read together the contents from a Big Book, a type of choral reading is being emphasized. Learners may perceive sentence patterns which provide structure for the English language. Re-reading of a Big Book, especially if desired by pupils, is to be encouraged. We think most of us had our favourite books a children which we re-read many times, in my case *The Little Red Hen* was read over and over again as a child ! A major objective here is to guide pupils to want to read more literature and at a more complex level as optimal progress is being made by individual pupils. With re-reading, comprehension appears to increase, meaning that more complex questions may be discussed with pupils. Familiarity with words is important when assisting pupils in developing a basic sight vocabulary. Choral reading and re-reading assists pupils in achieving a core of functional words, necessary in becoming a good reader.

Word Banks and the Young Reader

One way to assist pupils to master words in reading is to stress the word bank concept. With the word bank, each pupil prints on a three by five inch card a word that has been mastered in reading. With the addition of new cards, each card having a word printed thereon, the pupil must alphabetize the set of words and rehearse the correct identification of each word. The reward to the pupil is to see the stack of cards get larger due to having mastered more words as sight words. The teacher could place an interesting sticker on each card as reinforcement.

There are pupils who enjoy making sentences from words in the word bank. Pupils could work in teams doing this. The point is to have pupils read words within context frequently and thus become better readers.

Peers may also work together by providing drill and practice experiences from the use of these word bank cards.

Word bank cards could also be grouped in terms of

1. those having the same beginning sounds.
2. those having the same ending sounds.
3. those having the same vowel sounds.
4. those having grave irregularities in spelling between symbol and sound.

As many uses as possible should be made of word bank cards. Games may be devised, sentences expanded and stories written with the use of these cards.

Story book Time with Children

The teacher needs to read orally to pupils each day. Why ? Here, pupils learn about a story, about vocabulary terms, about sequential ideas in a story, about sentence patterns, about characterization, about the setting of a story, about the plot, about the theme and messages presented by the author. Pupils also may learn to enjoy good literature for their developmental level. Perhaps, an individual child desires to read the same book during spare time or at home. Background information for the child's time to read has then come from the teacher's oral reading. There should be familiarity when the pupil reads the same book as compared to not having heard the contents read by the teacher. The teacher needs to become very familiar with children's literature so that pupils perceive a model to emulate. A few years ago while supervising a student teacher and cooperating teacher, we noticed how knowledgeable the latter was about library books for pupils. This teacher related library books with the books being read to children. We believe young children here were fascinated with the knowledge the teacher had about library books when integrating different sources. Thus, a good characteristic of a teacher who reads orally to pupils is that he/she likes children's literature. The horizons of the primary grade teacher need to be expanded in knowing about recent books that have come out in children's literature as well as remaining informed about older books of high quality, the latter being important to Perennialists. Perennialism, as a philosophy of education, believes that the enduring ideas in time and space are important and not recently published books.

The primary grade teacher should also read enthusiastically to pupils. Learners are very attentive to these read aloud sessions if the teacher shows love and enjoyment of oral reading of library books. As the oral reading progresses, the teacher needs to show related illustrations in the book to pupils. There should be adequate time for pupil to comment about the illustrations and content. If the comments from pupils seem endless, the teacher may politely say that we have time for one more pupil. Otherwise, it is wholesome and good for children to react to what is contained in a library book.

The teacher needs to observe pupils when reading aloud to notice the pace at which learners can understand the content. I have observed teachers read too rapidly whereby pupils seemingly cannot understand the contents. The opposite has been true also in which the content was read too slowly by the teacher. Remember, pupils can listen to and comprehend content more rapidly as compared to the reading that they do. Thus, pupils read more slowly as compared to comprehending content listened to. With practice and feedback from pupils being read to, the teacher can adjust the speed of reading aloud to what pupils can process in terms of subject matter listened to.

Voice inflection which includes stress, pitch and juncture is very important in oral reading to pupils. Certain words need to be stressed more than others so that proper interpretation is an end result. A monotone says all words with the same stress, but a dynamic speaker places more stress on specific words as compared to others so that meaning in interpretation is in evidence. Proper pitch is important also when reading aloud. Thus, selected words are pitched higher or lower than others. Why ? Whatever is said involves interpretation by the speaker as well as by the listener. If all words are pitched on the same level, a monotone results. By pitching words properly, there are better chances for appropriate communication. It is much easier to secure the attention of others with proper pitch of words as compared to a monotone voice. And by pitching words appropriately, the reader of library books to pupils emphasizes what he/she wishes to communicate. Proper pauses or juncture needs to be in evidence in oral reading of children's literature. Juncture then indicates that the reader pause where commas, periods and other punctuation marks are located. By omitting or slighting punctuation marks, distortion in meaning of content read certainly can be an end result.

In our teacher education classes, we do emphasize university students reading well orally to peers, according to quality criteria and also that they received practice in the schools in reading orally to pupils at different age and achievement levels. This is vital for a good teacher.

The teacher should have good eye contact with each pupil as the read aloud continues. This indicates that a teacher is communicating with all pupils and watches the attention span of pupils. Pupils do need to be attentive and engaged when the teacher reads aloud content from sequential library books. Literature read to children needs to be carefully chosen by the teacher. Hopefully, the contents will be interesting and enjoyable to pupils whereby these learners will have an inward desire to achieve in reading skills and attitudes. The teacher needs to choose a variety of genres in literature so that the diverse interests of pupils is met. Teachers usually tend to become knowledgeable about which library books would fascinate learners when being read aloud to pupils.

It is good teaching practice for a teacher to read privately the library book which will be read aloud to pupils later. A definite strategy should then be developed by the teacher as to how the library book should be introduced to pupils. Here, readiness factors enter in as to what to do to assist pupils to like the new book to be read aloud. Certainly, the teacher should discuss the illustrations at the beginning of the books with children, prior to reading, so that there is more familiarity of learners with the content to be read aloud sequentially. By thinking of procedures to use when reading each library book, the teacher soon develops a repertoire of skills which assist in gaining the attention of pupils in desiring to read children's literature. I think it is good procedure too for a teacher to read aloud these library books he/she enjoys. After all, the positive attitudes should have their affects within listeners. A special time needs to be set aside each day for oral reading of children's literature so that pupils realize the importance of this activity. Primary teachers always set aside time after the one hour noon recess for oral reading of children's literature to pupils. The read aloud had a tendency to make for a relaxed feelings and we believe, provided readiness for studying in the next curriculum area.

Where should the teacher be when reading aloud to pupils? We have noticed teachers for read aloud at different places when supervising student teachers in the public school, such as

1. being seated in front of the classroom.
2. being seated in a chair while pupils are nearby seated on the carpet.
3. being seated on the floor on an even level with the pupils.
4. being seated in the middle of the classroom.
5. being in a standing position and moving around the classroom while reading aloud to pupils.

Individualized Reading

Once children have developed an adequate number of basic sight words for reading, they may become involved in individualized reading. Here, there needs to be an appropriate number of library books for pupils to select from in choosing a book to read. The titles need to indicate different genres to provide for the interest needs of individual pupils. Also, the library books must be written on diverse achievement levels so that each pupil may choose a book which harmonizes with his/her present achievement level in reading. Content which is too complex to read frustrates the reader. Subject matter that is too easy might well become boring to the reader. Thus, there are library books which are on the reading level, not frustration nor boring level, for pupils to select from for individualized reading.

These library books should be displayed at a learning center in an interesting manner to capture pupil attention. A bulletin board with neatly displayed book jackets of new library books should also assist pupils to develop interest in individualized reading. The teacher should tell a few interesting things about a library books as it is held up for learner viewing. Hopefully, this will also assist in whetting the appetites of pupils for individualized reading. The primary grade teacher needs to think of different strategies in developing within pupils a desire to select and read sequential library books. The pupil is the chooser, not the teacher, as to which library book a pupil is to read. The teacher offers assistance if pupils are hesitant in choosing or if they do not find an appropriate library book to read.

The individual pupil then chooses a library book to read at the learning center. Usually, a learner will select a book that refers to a preferable genre and is on his/her reading level. Sometimes, a pupil needs to select a different library book to read due to the complexity of the original book selected. Once a pupil has settled down to read silently, the library book chosen, a good reader or teacher aide may assist pupils with word identification Each pupil should be given adequate chances to determine an unknown word before assistance is given in word recognition. Primary age pupils need to become as independent in identifying words as possible. Sometimes, a few pupils become too dependent upon the teacher for word identification. Through the use of content clues and phonics, a pupil can identify many words which generally would be unknown to the reader (Ediger, 1997).

Following the completion of silent reading of a library book, the pupil should have a brief conference with the teacher. Here, the involved pupil reads a short selection to the teacher from the library book. The teacher may also choose the selection to be read orally by the pupil in the conference. The primary grade teacher may then observe errors made by the pupil in oral reading and assist in remedying the problems areas. Which problems do pupils reveal on oral reading on the primary grade levels ? Student teachers and cooperating teachers whom we supervised have enumerated the following :

1. Omitting words. This can be a major problem if meaning is distorted when reading the selection. Sometimes when "a", "an", and "the" are omitted by learners in reading in the conference setting, the meaning may not change any.
2. Adding words. When the young child adds words that are not in the reading selection, the resulting meaning may or may not change. Pupils do add the article "the" with no change in meaning of the sentence. Other words added may really distort the meaning of what is read.
3. Disregarding punctuation marks. If commas are omitted when words are in a series, the meaning will be greatly distorted. The same is true if a period is omitted and a run on sentence is an end result. Errors made by pupils provide a basis for determining objectives to stress in the reading curriculum.
4. Hesitating too long before pronouncing words. Frequent hesitations, lasting each five seconds or longer, do hinder pupils in reading with understanding. Generally, a library book is too complex for reading if hesitating before word pronunciation hinders pupils in attaching meaning to what is being read.
5. Repeating what has been read correctly.

Teachers of individualized reading need to record the types of errors made by pupils in reading aloud in a conference setting after the letter has completed the reading of a library book. These reading errors should be examined and then noticed if remediation instruction is necessary. As was indicated, some types of errors may not be important enough to stress in remediation work. Thus inserting or omitting articles, among other kinds of errors, might be quite minimal in a holistic approach of reading instruction whereby learners may become skillful in predicting what will follow in sequence in reading.

In the conference within the individualized reading program, pupils and the teacher need to appraise comprehension of the learner. We would suggest that the teacher stress higher levels of cognition in individualized reading. Thus critical and creative thinking, and problem solving need adequate emphasis in the conference involving pupil and teacher. The teacher needs to have a good working knowledge of children's literature when an individualized reading program is in evidence.

We would suggest that the teacher read children's literature, keeping a file on each book read as to its contents, as well as reading reviews of new library books for pupils to read. There are excellent reviews of children's literature in *The Language Arts* (See bibliography entry of the National Council Teachers of English) as well as in *The Reading Teacher* (See bibliography entry of the International Reading Association). The teacher should become very familiar with Caldecott and Newbery Award winning library books. The Caldecott Award is given to the author of the best illustrated library book written for children whereas the Newbery Award is given to the author, also annually, who wrote the best judged content. There are other awards given annually to the best judged content. There are other awards given annually to the best writer of the year in children's literature such as in Missouri the Mark Twain Award is given for writing the best judged children's library book.

Every year, a Children's Literature Festival is held on the Truman State University Campus I (Ediger) have served as a member of the Children's Literature Festival Committee for several year. Live authors speak to children and show their written works. At this Festival, children are divided into small groups of ten so that there are ample opportunities for pupils to ask questions of the authors. Children make some very positive informal comments about the festival during its sessions. Some of these comments which I heard in passing were the following :

1. I didn't know good authors were living individuals. I

thought they had to have died sometime ago to be called an author.

2. I am thrilled to see and listen to an author.

3. One author even signed his signature to a library book I now have !

4. I like to ask questions of live authors that I could never have asked before.

5. I have written letters to authors but never listened to one talk to us.

In a questionnaire provide pupils directly after the Children's Literature Festival, the following were rated high with a 4 to 5 average rating, as marked by pupils in the questionnaire:

1. the Festival was truly worth attending.

2. the pupils listened carefully to authors as they talked about writing their books.

3. I learned much about the children's books discussed.

The lowest rating was given to one author speaking in too quiet a manner when presenting his library book to children.

A Children's Literature Festival seemingly does much to interest pupils in the reading of library books. This observation was confirmed by teachers of pupils attending the Festival. Seemingly, pupils did more reading that previously. Motivation to read had increased. Many pupils read library books written by the authors who appeared at the Festival. Apparently, the authors had provided readiness or an introduction to reading the library books. It does help pupils in wanting to read a book if they have become familiar with it in one way or another. Modelling by authors at the Festival is a powerful factor in encouraging pupil reading of books.

We have observed to how Sustained Silent Reading (SSR) can offer to children a positive model for reading. In one school I visited, everyone in the elementary school building read during a certain time of the day, usually twenty minutes in length. When the word "everyone" is mentioned, this included the custodian and cafeteria workers. Pupils can then notice that people do read and there must be something enjoyable and valuable in doing so. One very important model for pupils in reading is the primary grade teacher. This teacher needs to be enthusiastic about reading and what has been read. One of us noticed a second grade teacher tell about Plato's *The Republic* she had read the previous summer in a university graduate class. She told pupils of how Plato had divided people into three class—the rulers of the nation, the military personnel and the artisans or workers. This teacher showed pictures of present day adults and asked pupils which of the three categories of Plato's Republic they would come under. Pupils were fascinated with the discussion and were actively engaged in the activity. We do believe pupils will remember sessions such as these and consume more literature now as well as wher they progress through the different levels of schooling.

Conclusion

Primary grade reading teachers need to provide a variety of concrete, semi-concrete and abstract experiences for pupils so that a solid foundation is laid for successful reading. The instruction should be as holistic as possible so that pupils read content, not work on isolated sound/symbol relationships. The act of reading is holistic whereby learners need to perceive the whole of the selection read. This leaves room for the teaching of phonics as needed. Some children will need much less phonics as compared to others. How much phonics is to be taught depends upon the needs of individual pupils.

To identify unknown words, contexts clues are important for pupils to use. Further help for pupils in unlocking unknown words is to use phonics. Teachers and pupils need to realize the upper limits of phonics use. There are letters which are rather consistent between symbol and sound. However, there are many weaknesses or limits in phonics use, such as in the following words : phone, through, rough, flight, among others. Here, the relationships between individual sounds and symbols do not harmonize in most cases.

The primary grade reading teacher needs to have all pupils experience initial successes with continual optimal progress emphasized for each child. No child should be permitted to fall through the cracks to be a failure (Ediger, 1998).

References

Bolton, F. (19986), *The Greedy Goat.* New York : Scholastic Book Services.

Ediger, Marlow (1988), *Language Arts Curriculum in the Elementary School.* Kirksville, Missouri : Simpson Publishing Company, 19.

Ediger, Marlow (1998), "Goals of Reading Instruction", *Experi-ments in Education.* 26(1), 11–18.

Ediger, Marlow (1997), "Reading and the Psychology of Teaching", *The Educational Review.* 103(3), 41–45.

Fountas, Irene C. and Gay Su Pinnell (1996), *Guided Reading Good First Choice for all Children.* Portsmouth, New Hampshire : Heinemann, 1 and 2.

International Reading Association, *The Reading Teacher.* 800 Barksdale Road, Newark, Delaware 19714.

Mahy, M. (1986), *When the King Rides By.* Bothel, Washington: The Wright Group.

National Council Teachers of English, *The Language Arts,* 1111 Kenyon Road, Urbana, Illinois 61801.

Strommen, Linda Teran, and Barbara Fowles Mates (1997), "What readers do : Young Children's Ideas about the nature of reading", *The Reading Teacher.* 51(2), 106.

8
Reading on the Intermediate Grade Level

With good sequence in reading achievement on the primary grade levels, pupils should be increasingly ready to attain well on the intermediate levels of instruction. If achievement has not been good for selected pupils, then more of remedial methods will need to be used in teaching reading. Primary grade teachers provide the foundation for success or lack of it in reading. Pupils should have confidence in themselves to achieve well. They need to possess esteem which propels them to higher levels of attainment. Confidence tends to come from success in reading. Pupils here have mastered phonics skills either through whole language or through a more structured procedure. These skills assist pupils to identify and unlock unknown words in reading. Learners have also learned to use diverse purposes in reading to some extent. All of these skills will need to be refined more on the intermediate grade levels as well as achieve new abilities in the reading curriculum.

The most important item when pupils leave the primary grade levels is that they possess a love for reading, an attitudinal goal. A love for reading can hurdle many difficulties in reading and textbooks. There is so much that can be enjoyed through reading. We truly feel privileged to be able to enjoy and do much reading, largely now on the research level in education.

Using Textbooks in Reading

We believe that basals in reading have their important roles to play in reading instruction. When a speaker or writer indicates that he/she no longer is using a basal and therefore is teaching well says nothing to me. We would have to know about the quality of the reading curriculum then without basal text use. Thus, there is a need to have many alternative objectives, learning opportunities and evaluation procedures that stress sequential success for pupils in reading. To be sure, there are many excellent programs of reading instruction, other than the basal textbook in reading. We will at this point only address the use of basal texts in the teaching of reading. Where the class/course was deficient, the instructor probably lacked the necessary teaching skills rather than the textbook being deficient. The text is not a self-teaching device.

Textbooks in reading need to be selected with great care. They should be on the reading level of involved pupils, not the frustrational nor the too easy to read level. New vocabulary terms should be brought in gradually and the meaning kept intact in reading. There was a time when the controlled vocabulary was used much in writing textbooks in reading. Thus, pupils on the first grade level might read, "Bill run, run, run; run Bill run". No doubt in this sentence the words were controlled excessively with the word "run" being in the writing excessively. The controlled vocabulary has basically been done away with, but it did have some merits if not overdone. The merits pertained to pupils being able to see and hear selected words again and again. The purpose involved was to help pupils develop a basic sight vocabulary so that more interesting sentences might be used. The complaint was that pupils now, presently, needed to read interesting sentences so that enjoyment and liking of reading was in evidence.

Whole language approaches for pupils today have taken the place of the controlled vocabulary. Learners then re-read selections with teacher involvement so that more words become a part of the sight vocabulary and increasingly more complex materials may be read.

There should be an ample number of illustrations in the basals; so that if a pupil does not identify a word or attach meaning to the abstract words, the illustration will provide needed meanings. A glossary needs to be a part of the basal so that a pupil may look up the meaning of a word as used in context. If pupils can use context clues adequately, they can determine identification, pronunciation and meaning of words without the glossary. However, it is good to have a glossary to check periodically, as the need arises, on the pronunciation and meaning of words.

In the selection of basals, we believe that pupils should have opportunities to read content therein to indicate the quality of comprehension involved. Certainly, the content needs to be interesting so that pupils pursue and achieve in reading. If interest is not there, the chances are that the act of reading cannot move forward the way it should. The teacher needs to do the best job possible to stimulate interest within pupils in reading a given selection. There interest factor may be developed through discussion and use of illustrations contained in the basal. Good questions raised here might well encourage pupil interest in reading. These questions raised by the teacher or pupils read, we would also suggest the learners see new words in print on the chalkboard before the oral or silent reading activity. The teacher needs to go over these new words before pupils read the content. By pointing to each word and discussing a meaning as used in the text provides additional readiness for reading, beyond that of elaborating on the illustrations contained in an directly related to the print in the text.

When pupils read aloud or silently, they may need to have words pronounced to them by the teacher, an aide, or a pupil in the classroom. Pupils should be given adequate time to try to identify unknown words before they are pronounced to the reader. The pupils needs to become as independent as possible in reading be it in unlocking unknown words or in comprehension. Time is short before individuals need to think of what will happen beyond the public school years.

Continual efforts need to be in the offing by the learner to become the best reader possible. Time is too valuable to waste. Why not rather use time wisely, instead of wasting the teacher's and the pupil's time during reading instruction? Teachers should try to have pupils feel what it might mean if time is continually wasted during instructional periods. Where will each pupil be in achievement after the school years have ended ? Goals need to be set high and each pupil should attempt to achieve these objectives. The teaching of reading is no exception with its expectations so that the pupil achieves as much as possible in reading.

After silent or oral reading, the pupil may respond to the purposes (questions) that were identified as a result of studying the illustrations in the basal reader. These purposes amounted to questions raised by pupils and the teacher covering subject matter to be read. The reading experience then should provide some possible answers to questions raised. Additional reference sources may be used to answer the identified questions. The teacher may also ask pupils to read specific parts of the reading selection to check skills and comprehension.

There are some points to remember in using basal readers in the reading curriculum. One is that the manual section provides suggestions for objectives, learning opportunities and appraisal procedures for teaching pupils. These are suggestions, not absolutes. The teacher might have better ideas on how to provide for individual differences among pupils. Second, the basal is a neutral material in reading instruction; it is up to the teacher to make it relevant and interesting. Third, higher levels of cognition such as critical and creative thinking, as well as problem solving, can be emphasized as much in basal reader use as compared to other forms of reading instruction. Fourth, the basal may be adjusted to pupils of diverse ability levels in reading. Fifth, quality specialists in reading have been involved who have developed reputable basal series. The basal may be used with other approaches in teaching reading, such as library books.

Library Books

Enough library books should be placed on the classroom interest center to meet interest and ability needs of pupils. These books should pertain to diverse genres so that pupils truly find and read what is interesting. With library books on different reading levels available for pupils to read, there should be ample chances for a child to locate a book that is on his/her reading level. If a library book is too complex to read, the pupil might be wasting his/her time as well as become frustrated. If the library book is too easy for the pupil to read, he/she may put too little effort in reading.

Library books read may make a nice project for pupils to complete as well as relate the project to a story contained in the basal reader. If pupils, for example, have read a story on farming in the basal reader, they may read library books on the same genre and make a mural that relates subject matter read. Four pupils who have read the content on farming may make the mural. Cooperative planning is a must! Following the planning, learners may proceed with their individual designated responsibilities. One pupil, for example, may develop the section dealing with egg and poultry production. Rows of caged layers may be drawn with eggs coming down the sides of the cages. Automated equipment brings the feed and water down the troughs for each row of cage layers. A second pupil may develop the milking parlor for dairy cows. Here, a pipeline milker takes the milk, untouched by human hands, from the cows to the bulk milk tank. Other items may be shown pertaining to dairy farming such as bulk milk truck coming to pick up the milk twice a week. A third pupil may develop the beef production center whereas the fourth pupil may portray the pork production facilities. After the completion of the mural, the involved learners may tell about the project to others in the classroom setting as well as to other pupils in school. We have observed a project made just as was discussed. Pupils working on the project enjoyed reading about farming as well as making the art project.

An important point here is to have pupils read and do more reading. With practicing the skills of reading, they become increasingly proficient in using print materials. The project method, such as developing a mural and reading relate well together and promote objectives of pupils doing more reading. There are numerous ways for pupils to indicate what was learned from reading basals or library books in addition to the project method. These include conferences for pupils to reveal comprehension and progress, seminar methods for depth discussions, construction activities to indicate meanings acquired from reading, art work relating to what was read and dramatic endeavours.

Journal Writing

It is salient for pupils to do much writing which relates to the reading of the basal text and library books. Here, the pupil may write about his/her impressions about the print materials consumed. Thus the learner may write impressions pertaining to the character of the story or the setting of the story. Suggestions for revision of either the characters or the setting may be written about. The pupil may also wish to elaborate on the theme of the story. There are so many ideas for the pupil to write about in the journal that it truly becomes endless. The goal is to have the pupil write each day in the journal and read print materials as much as possible. Content for reading and writing may also come from social studies, science, mathematics, art, music and physical education classes.

As pupils write, they need to read what was written. Additional practice in reading is then in the offing. The skills of writing too are being stressed as revisions are being made in journal entries. The first two R's—reading and writing which are so functional in the lives of all—are being stressed here in a related manner. Each is complementing the other.

Vocabulary Development

Pupils need to achieve rich and diverse listening, speaking, reading and writing vocabularies. There are numerous opportunities for pupils to develop each vocabulary. The listening vocabulary may be emphasized when large group instruction is involved in discussing content read from basal readers and library books. Careful listening is vital here. The level of listening may involve receiving relevant facts. Pupils, however, need to do something with the facts. Thus, they might put the facts into a larger context and discuss their meanings. Learners need to understand facts and not merely commit them to memory. If acts are discussed, meaningful interpretation might well be a by product. These meaningful understandings might then be used in a new situation. Pupils can certainly think of the many uses that can be made of understandings acquired. Problems need to be solved and thus the needed understandings become valuable as possible solutions. When applying information in problem solving situations, the contents therein need to be appraised in terms of being relevant versus irrelevant, logical versus illogical, real versus fantasy and accurate versus inaccurate. Critical thinking is then in evidence. This is a higher level of cognition and all pupils need to develop high levels of proficiency in thinking critically. When thinking of new ideas which need to be used in solving a problem, the old as well as the tried and true may not work as solutions, creative thought then should be emphasized. The unique, the novel and the original stress creative thinking. We sincerely hope all teachers emphasize higher levels of cognition when discussing subject matter with children. Thought and thinking are very useful objectives to stress in the reading curriculum. Functional listening should stress the use of higher cognitive objectives.

In addition to careful listening skills to be developed by pupils, the reading teacher also needs to stress quality speaking activities. In fact, listening and speaking become one in a discussion setting involving content read from basals and library books. Many reading teachers work with pupils to speak loud enough so all can hear and yet not so loudly that it is offensive to others. There seems to be that right rate of volume when speaking be it in a large or small group discussion, book reports given or peer interaction.

The rate of speed in speaking should be such that the listener can understand the contents readily. We have heard individuals that speak too slowly or too rapidly. This hinders quality communication. The speaker always needs to observe listeners to notice if the rate of speaking is appropriate to the involved situation. Pupils need to remember that speaking is to communicate with others and not to say things for the sake of doing so.

In speaking, proper pitch is necessary. We say words and pitch them at higher and lower levels. Why ? Effective communication does not come about due to monotones speaking, but rather due to voice inflection which pitches individual words at different levels to make a point or to gain someone's attention. Voice inflection has as its goal more effective oral communication. Proper stress is also important in speaking. We say words individually louder or softer within a sentence. Why do we stress a word more so than others, that is say it louder or softer? The purpose is to get across to others what was intended. When we become excited, we really stress certain words in a louder manner than would otherwise be the case. The excitement indicates that we have something to say that is of utmost importance. Compare this situation with saying words very quietly. The urgency of the message is not there. Nor do we want to shout something in terms of content when it is not urgent to do so. There is a reason for saying a word or several words very quietly and that is to communicate in a manner that conveys thoughts, feelings and ideas. How a word is to be stressed depends upon what the learner has to say and the context of the situation. For example, when expressing sympathy or sorrow hardly would one want to say ideas in an excited manner. Teachers sometimes have said things very quietly to obtain learner attention. Pupils then need to listen carefully, very carefully, to the quiet voice of the teacher.

Pupils need to be cassette recorded or video-taped frequently to notice progress in listening and speaking activities. There are selected purposes in listening that might cause more problems to pupils as compared to others. Thus, listening to directions may be difficult for some pupils, in particular. Perhaps, more learning in listening to follow directions should be in the offing. Or, a pupil has more difficulties speaking, involving giving book reports, as compared other kinds of speaking activities. The teacher than needs to assist pupils individually as well as in groups to overcome problem areas. In the case of books reports, criteria need to be in the offing which when followed can make for quality oral reports. The listening and speaking vocabularies need optimal development for each pupil.

The reading vocabulary complements the listening and speaking vocabularies. Developing well in the listening and speaking vocabularies definitely assists in achieving more fully in an increased proficiency level of the reading vocabulary. Readiness for reading to acquire background information before the child is to read a given selection includes improved listening and speaking vocabularies. Intermediate grade pupils may do their very own writing when an experience chart is being developed. Thus, from an experience, the pupil, instead of the teacher as it true of the early primary grade levels, does his/ her own write-up of these experiences. When proofing the content, the involved pupils are doing more reading. The more practice pupils receive in purposeful reading, the sooner they will indicate proficiency in learning to read. With the experience chart, the pupil is familiar with the words and ideas since he/ she wrote about what was experienced. Vocabulary development is certainly in the offing. Pupils need to enjoy the concrete experiences....as well as abstract ideas such as in seeing ideas in writing and reading the related content. Interest makes for contributions to the chart in a committee setting. Learners seem to like working collaboratively in listening, speaking, reading and writing activities (Ediger, 1997).

There are many kinds of reading programs which can assist pupils to become better readers. Thus basal readers, experience charts or language experience approaches (LEA), and individualised reading, among others, can provide for individual differences among pupils. Each pupil needs to achieve as optimally as possible in reading so that school success and success at the work place might be in the offing.

The fourth vocabulary for intermediate grade pupils to develop is the writing vocabulary. Here, the pupil integrates vocabulary terms from listening, speaking and reading to place items and entries into the writing vocabulary. There are many purposes for writing including the writing of journal entries, book reports diaries, summaries, conclusions and generalization, log entries, outlines and dictionary items for personal use. As pupils write, they also read content such as proof reading. With writing, there are numerous mechanics that need to be addressed such as proper paragraphs, indentation, capitalization, punctuation, direct address and legible handwriting, among others. The teacher needs to decide in developing pupils' writing skills such as which objectives to stress on a given day and how writing can be integrated with the listening, speaking and reading vocabularies. Also, the inter-disciplinary curriculum needs to be implemented where feasible and possible.

We would like to describe learning opportunities whereby pupils may develop each of the four vocabularies more thoroughly.

1. Listen to discussions, reports, cassettes and video-tapes pertaining to content in ongoing lessons and units of study.
2. Bring in a variety of rich vocabulary terms in your teaching. The vocabulary terms are directly related to topics in the ongoing lesson and units of study.
3. Read subject matter on a variety of genres which are related to the lessons and units being studied.
4. Write with a variety of purposes or reasons involved. Work on improving writing skills within the framework of unit teaching.

Problems in Spelling

As pupils practice diverse writing skills in the reading curriculum, there will be learners experiencing difficulties in writing content. The correct spelling was usually whispered into the writer's ear as the need arose. Sometimes, the words needed in correct spelling were printed on slips of paper for the young writer.

There has been a considerable amount of research done on invented spelling. Primary and intermediate grade pupils cannot recall the correct spelling of a word to be used in writing, then the pupil invents a spelling for that word to the best of his/her abilities. Sometimes the invented spelling is so close to the actual spelling that little effort is needed for the pupil later to spell the word correctly. If the invented spelling does differ much from the actual spelling, the pupil may need to explain the pronunciation of the word used. In no way is the pupil to be embarrassed or minimized here; rather the teacher wants to be certain as to which word is intended in being spelled. Generally, most invented spellings are close enough for the teacher to ascertain which word was actually intended in the writing. The following are actual examples of invented spelling of words by elementary age pupils :

1. Nite tim is for sleeping. The first two words should be spelled "night" and "time". The third grade pupil writing these words did go strongly by phonetic elements when writing words with invented spellings.

2. The elefent drank much watter. The "elefent" is spelled quite phonetic in invented spelling, whereas the word spelled "watter" might have been pronounced as "wat ter", by the fourth grader. I find that many pupils are quite logical in invented spelling by using sound/symbol relationships.

It is good for pupils to invented spelling when writing so that there is continuity and sequence in writing. Learners should write as fluently as possible. Having to wait for someone to spell the word correctly when writing does take time and the writer may lose the trend of thought in the meantime. As pupils mature in correct spelling of words, they will use actual spelling of words rather than invented spelling. Spelling of words should be made as easy as possible for pupils so that they learn to enjoy writing with its inherent spelling of words. The teacher can only expect what is reasonable from pupils in terms of spelling achievement.

The spelling curriculum should be aligned as much as possible with writing activities. Sometimes, there is no relationship between the words pupils are attempting to master in spelling from a textbook and what is being written. Many procedure are being tried by teachers to have the spelling curriculum align with writing.

First, words that a pupil misspells become a part of the list for the involved pupil to master. A reasonable number of days are given the pupil to master these spellings. The number to be mastered should also be reasonable in number and achievable by the learner. As much as possible, pupils should learn to enjoy and appreciate the correct spelling of words. Can all learning by pupils be enjoyable and interesting? Probably not. In society, many people seemingly do not like their jobs as means of earning a living. But, the teacher needs to try to make spelling as interesting and meaningful as possible so that pupils achieve, grow and develop. A colleague of one of us who believes all learning is painful and takes sheer effort regardless of the feelings involved. Another colleague feels that some of the learnings needed are like a stack of dirty dishes, they need to be washed regardless of how pleasant or unpleasant the tasks may be. Other learnings might be quite enjoyable depending upon one's personal interests and the methods of teaching used. Thus, this colleague believes that teaching the writing of four kinds of sentences, normally considered dull and uninspiring, can be made interesting to pupils with good methods of teaching. For example, in learning about declarative sentences, pupils would describe a simple dramatization in the classroom such as, "Bill is writing at his desk". This event is actually occurring in the classroom. It behooves the teacher to attempt to make all learnings interesting through appropriate methodology. Additional sentences written in the classroom by pupils also need to be based on concrete experiences in writing interrogative, exclamatory and imperative sentences.

Certainly, sequence in teaching methodology is of utmost importance. There is a logical sequence whereby the teacher orders or sequences experiences for pupils. The teacher selects the goals in learning and chooses which to stress first, second, third and so forth. Learning opportunities may also be sequenced for pupils to achieve objectives such as emphasizing activities first, second, third and so forth. Appraisal procedures too need sequencing to ascertain if pupils have achieved objectives. Thus, appraisal procedures may be used first, second, third and so on depending upon which one(s) relate directly to objectives that have been emphasized in teaching. In these examples, we have noticed that the teacher directly sequences, as an example, the objectives, learning opportunities and appraisal procedures. Usually, even with teacher directed philosophies of language arts instruction, there will be room for pupil participation with questions and problems raised in classes.

Toward the other end of the continuum, pupils with teacher guidance may sequence their own activities in learning. Thus, with an open-ended philosophy of teaching, there may be ten learning centers in the classroom. The teacher initiates learning centers in the classroom. The teacher initiates learning centers use by introducing each center. Pupils then work at the centers of their choice and sequence their very own learning activities. Staying actively involved is important here. The pupil then chooses which task to complete first, second, third and so on. Individual or committee endeavours may be selected.

Hopefully, the learner will choose tasks that are on his/her optimal level of achievement and contain diversity in terms of goals to be attained. The teacher is an observer, a helper, a motivator and an evaluator of learner achievement in the language arts. The teacher her definitely is not a lecturer, nor an assigner of what each pupil is to do individually or on a team. Rather the responsibility is placed entirely into the hands of pupils in the classroom for learning. Thus, the pupil is the sequencer of his/her very own learning opportunities. Sequence resides within the learner not the teacher nor within textbooks or other instructional materials. Sequence here is opposite of the previous example whereby the teacher is the decision-maker and implements the order of experiences for pupils. The teacher attempts to determine what should come first, second, third and so on in teaching and learning situations. This is quite different in philosophical orientation whereby the pupil is largely responsible for sequencing his/her tasks in a learner centered approach. Usually, language arts/reading teachers use strands of both philosophies in teaching. The teacher also needs to look at personal learning styles of pupils when ascertaining what kind of sequence of use in teaching pupils in reading and the language arts.

Reading in the Content Areas

A literature based curriculum in reading may differ in emphasis as compared to a subject centered curriculum, such as in social studies, science and mathematics. Each academic discipline has its own vocabulary as well as a vocabulary which cuts across diverse subject matter areas. In geography, for example, the following vocabulary terms are salient : parallels, meridians, latitude, longitude, degrees, time zones, equator, Tropic of Cancer, Topic of Capricorn, north pole, south pole, among others. In meaningful ways and through a variety of learning opportunities, pupils need to attach meaning to these terms and concepts. Pupils should learn to think as professional geographers do when acquiring and interpreting knowledge. History, anthropology, sociology, political science, economics and psychology also have their unique terms in vocabulary that pupils need to master.

In attaching meaning to new vocabulary terms, pupils should experience concrete situations first. Thus, in geography when pupils are studying the vocabulary terms "parallels" and "meridians", the teacher could ask, "Who am I thinking of when the pupil is seated in the front row?" Pupils may respond with the names of five pupils, not one, since five pupils are seated in the front row. Supposing the teacher now says, "I am thinking of the person seated in the middle of the front row". Now, it is easy for all pupils to identify the name of the pupil the teacher is thinking of. The front row may be considered as a line of reference such as a "parallel". The second line of reference is the "meridian", or the pupil seated in the middle of the front row. The teacher might give several examples of using the two reference lines in thinking of where a pupil is seated.

After the concrete phase of learning has been used, the teacher may now stress the semi-concrete or a model of the planet earth which is a globe. A large wall map may also be used in teaching about parallels and meridians. By using the large wall map, for example, pupils may locate a place thereon when the degrees in longitude (east or west of the Prime Meridian) and the degrees of latitude (north or south of the equator) are given by the teacher. Map and globe reading do take time in teaching and the writer here is merely scratching the surface.

After the semi-concrete phase of learning has been stressed in learning about maps and globes, pupils may enter the abstract and most difficult phase of achieving in map and globe use. Here, pupils may draw a map, for example and as accurately as possible, draw the equator, lines of parallel and meridians. Pupils should also tell how they will measure the number of degrees east and west of the Prime Meridian, as well as the number of degrees north and south of the equator which has zero degrees. Meaning theory in teaching stresses that the teacher move from the use of concrete materials or realia to the semi-concrete (illustrations, drawings, models and pictures of reality) to the abstract (print materials, discussions, listening experiences on cassette recordings) for example and written work directly related to the ongoing lesson or unit of study.

Pupils then need to learn to read in diverse academic disciplines. This should be true for the primary grade pupil as well as for the graduate student. There will be continual expansion then for vocabulary terms be it for young children or students working on their doctorates in different fields of endeavour. There needs to be a continual emphasis placed upon reading with its vocabulary and knowledge to be developed as well as skills to become independent readers.

Scope and Sequence in Reading

An early attempt at sequencing what is taught in the reading curriculum was worked out by Joseph Lancaster in 1806 in his book *Manual of Instruction* (Ediger, 1974). Lancaster developed a way to teach large groups of boys in one building, as many as one thousand depending upon the size of the city in which the school building was located. Generally, the number of pupils taught by a monitor was ten which filled a benchful of young learners. The monitor taught his ten boys from charts located at different places in the large, single room. Each monitor took his ten boys to the chart as the room for doing so was available. One group needed to follow the other since a large number had to file past these charts for teaching purposes.

Each set of ten boys was kept together on a lesson, but individual promotion was possible if a boy had mastered what was on the designated charts, ahead of the others. There were eight levels of achievement in reading. In class one, pupils mastered the letters of the alphabet through memorization. After these letters were clearly identified and committed to memory, pupils in class two were drilled on syllables of two letters untill these were mastered. These syllables could be quite difficult to learn since they did not refer to any meaningful term or concept. Class three stressed pupils memorizing words and syllables made up of three letters. Class four pupils memorized words and syllables of four letters. The syllables part for four letters must have been very difficult to learn since these also were not meaningful. In class five, pupils mastered words of five and six letters whereas in class six pupils learned to read the Old Testament and the New Testament. In class seven pupils read form the entire Bible whereas in class eight books were read "to improve the mind". Books read "to improve the mind" included the classics in literature which stood the test of time and place as far as important literature was concerned.

Joseph Lancaster and his Monitorial System of Instruction did emphasize a definite scope and sequence as written in *The Manual of Instruction.* In most succeeding classes, levels one through eight, a letter was added to a syllable or word to make the next level of achievement more difficult as compared to the previous level. Much emphasis was placed upon pupils memorizing content, such as the individual letters of the alphabet for class one. It took until class six for pupils to actually read, such as the *Old Testament* or *New Testament.* Ideas have to be written down, such as was true of Joseph Lancaster's *Manual of Instruction* in order that improvements may be made for later generations in reading instruction (Ediger, 1974).

Two ideas that Lancaster stressed which are still important today are :

1. Sequence in reading instruction whereby the individual class levels stated what pupils are to learn and when.
2. Individual differences among pupils were provided for with individual promotion from one class level to the next.

Lancaster emphasized a logical sequence whereby the adult spelled out what pupils were to learn in reading on the different class levels. There are reading specialists today who advocate a logical sequence in which the teacher spells out specifically what a pupils is to learn in a lesson, such as from a basal reader. Then toward the other end of the continuum, pupils with teacher guidance sequence their very own experiences, such as when library books are read.

Presently, there are several procedures in teaching intermediate grade pupils which stress a logical approach. We will discuss a few of these approaches. The use of basal reader stresses a logical approach. Here, the teacher chooses objectives sequentially for pupil achievement. The objectives may or may not come from the manual section. Learning opportunities are also chosen by the intermediate grade teacher. These, too, are sequenced by the teacher. The manual section of the basal also suggests teaching procedures for the teacher to use. The evaluation procedures in the manual may or may not be used by the teacher. We have found that good teachers can do a better job of selecting objectives, learning opportunities and evaluation procedures as compared to what the manual has to offer. With much knowledge pertaining to each child taught, the teacher is then able to adjust the difficulty level of teaching to the individual child.

The quality of learning, in my own thinking, from basal reader use depends upon the quality of teaching provided by the teacher, as well as the quality of attitudes possessed by pupils. The basal is a neutral device, neither good nor bad and the quality coming forth in teaching comes from the teacher. We have observed teachers doing a good job of teaching reading from basal use. Critical and creative thinking as well as problem solving were emphasized. A logical procedure in determining sequence was usually in evidence. Ediger (1997) wrote the following :

The debate on explicit versus implicit teaching has had a rather long history in education. During the last two decades, in particular, much emphasis is being placed on implicit learning. There are pros and cons pertaining to each procedure. It appears that the inherent quality of instruction is more important than the either/or thinking in implicit versus explicit teaching dichotomy. Characteristics of good teaching include meaningful content for pupils is in the offing, interests of pupils are developed and maintained, pupils purpose or reasons for learning are inherent, appropriate sequence in pupil learning is in evidence, as well as balance among knowledge, skills and attitudinal objectives are emphasized in the curriculum. Quality teaching stresses using a variety of procedures so that individual differences among pupils are adequately provided for. Pupils possess diverse learning styles; teachers need to match the possible learning opportunities to the styles possessed by individual learners. Explicit teaching may, in many cases, possess too much structure with its accompanying drill and practice tasks. Rote learning might then be an end result. Holism is preferred to segmented learning. The whole of something has more meaning for pupils then do isolated parts. Direct teaching (explicit teaching) provides fewer opportunities for creativity. Critical and creative thinking as well as problem solving harmonize more with implicit as compared to explicit teaching.

In contrast, consider the psychological sequence which many advocate in the teaching of reading. With individualized reading, the pupil selects a library book to read. He/she reads the library book and then has a conference with the teacher. The pupil may identify questions to discuss as well as the teacher choosing questions for the conference. The learner may select a section to read orally to the teacher to indicate progress in reading. Thus, the entire procedure in individualized reading stresses that the learner be actively involved in determining the reading curriculum. Sequence then resides within the pupil since he/she is actively involved in decision making procedures (See Ediger, 1996).

No doubt, the logical and psychological sequences can be integrated. Certainly, in the basal reading approach, pupils can assist in identifying questions for discussion purposes. A psychological sequence is then more and more in operation. Learners might also help in deciding upon the evaluation procedures to be used. For example, after reading a basal story, pupils with teacher assistance may decide upon making a mural, diorama, model or do a dramatization covering content read to indicate comprehension. Sequence here resides within the pupil in making these numerous decisions.

As a further example, the teacher may ask most if not all of the questions when pupils have finished reading a library book and this is in a conference setting in individualized reading. There probably is nothing like an absolute logical sequence nor an absolute psychological sequence. The teacher is there as an instructional leader and the pupils is there as a learner. The two—the teacher and the pupil—need to be brought together as a unit. Both are working together to achieve a goal and that is to have the pupil learn as much as possible. We need to use the logical sequence when appropriate and the psychological sequence when beneficial to the learner. There are no magical formulas for doing this in reading. We are dealing with the whole child who is a complicated being. We think that the late A. H. Maslow (Shepherd and Ragan, 1982) provided an excellent set of guidelines for all teachers and administrators to follow in terms of needs which pupils have. The first need is physiological in that pupils need adequate and proper nutrition, sleep and rest, as well as to take care of basic needs of the human body. Second, pupils need a secure environment free from harm and danger. Third, pupils need to have feelings of belonging in that partners, brothers and sisters, as well as other human beings care for and accept the child as a belonging member. Fourth, esteem needs of pupils need to be met. Pupils desire to be recognised for competencies possessed, major or minor. In the curriculum, the talents of pupils need to be used and recognised. Fifth, pupils desire to satisfy their potential and be what is possible of being.

If a society or school fails in any area, pupils will not do as well as possible in reading and in the other curriculum areas.

Conclusion

Emerging literacy is a mutual product of the home and school environment acting together with common interests. It does appear that literacy provides parents and teachers as supporting each other in an eclectic system to learning. Parents and teachers can feel free to use practices and strategies that draw from traditional practices as well as from emerging new approaches. Instruction in phonics can be blended with invented spelling, story telling can be integrated with oral reading and creative writing can be matched with learning correct manuscript. It appears that teachers and parents are far more eclectic in their perceptions on how to develop literacy than they are married to a specific approach. This liberal awareness is probably a healthy occurrence that signals professionalism on the part of teachers and involvement on the part of parents (Ediger, 1997).

How reading should be taught appears to be an individual matter, according to that which is beneficial to the learner. Even if research results would indicate that one procedure is better than the other—phonics versus whole language—there still are individuals who may not benefit adequately within that statistically significant group. It behooves the teacher to study individual pupils and attempt to find the procedure that best assists a pupil to achieve as well as possible in reading.

In addition to phonics and context clue use, there still are other methods of word recognition techniques that may be taught to learners. Thus, use of picture clues, syllabication, structural analysis and configuration clues may guide pupils to attain more adequately in reading. Pupils are individuals, not masses, which can be taught the same way and expect the same rate of achievement from each. Reading teachers need to be highly knowledgeable of each pupil's learning style as well as knowledgeable about how each pupil learns best in reading. The focal point is the learner, not the group nor the teacher, in guiding optimal pupil achievement in reading.

There are older pupils, beyond the elementary level of schooling, who need teaching in word recognition skills. There are pupils who may not try or waste time in school and thus do not achieve well. Parents may not support the teacher or the school resulting in a pupil going through the different levels of schooling and not becoming adequately literate. A pupil may even graduate from high school, under these conditions and not have gained needed literacy to be employable Ediger, 1997.

In summarizing diverse plans for teaching reading on the intermediate grade levels, the following procedures are salient:

1. Use of basal readers.
2. Individualized reading using library books.
3. Free time for reading when all in a classroom read. This provides a model for pupils indicating that reading in enjoyable. Print may be tape recorded so that those not reading well enough may follow along in the library book as the tape plays the recorded contents.
4. The experiences chart whereby pupils do their own writing pertaining to personal experiences acquired. Reading and writing interact here since both are involved in developing the experience chart, also called the language experience approach (LEA).

5. Reference books, including encyclopedias and CD ROMS, to secure information for a written or oral report.
6. Computer packages containing drill and practice, tutorial, gaming and simulation programs of reading instruction.

What is important in reading is that the interests and abilities of pupils are matched with the right reading materials so that the pupil may achieve as optimally as possible.

References

Ediger, Marlow (1974), *Issues in Developing the Relevant Elementary School.* Kirksville, Missouri : Simpson Publishing Company, 32–33.

Ediger, Marlow (Summer, 1997), "Personalized Reading; A Place Where Whole Language and Phonics Play Well Together", *The Journal of the English Language Arts*, 38(1), 88.

Ediger, Marlow (1996), Elementary Education, Kirksville, Missouri : Simpson Publishing Company, 46.

Ediger, Marlow (1997), "Explicit Teaching in the Language Arts", *The Progress of Education*, 72(3), 56.

Ediger, Marlow (1997), "Which Word Recognition Techniques Should be Taught?" *The Progress of Education*, 72(1), 4 and 5.

Shepherd, Gene and William Ragan (1982). *Modern Elementary Curriculum*. New York : Holt, Rinehart and Winston, 15.

9
Phonics in the Teaching of Reading

Word recognition skills help readers identify words while reading. One skill is sight word recognition, the development of a store of words a person can recognise immediately on sight. Use of context clues to help in word identification involves using the surrounding words to decode an unfamiliar word. Both semantic and syntactic clues can be helpful. Phonics, the association of speech sounds (phonemes) with printed symbols (graphemes), is very helpful in identifying unfamiliar words, even thought the sound-symbol associations in English are not completely consistent. Structural analysis skills enable readers to decode unfamiliar words using units larger than single graphemes. The process of structural analysis involves recognition of prefixes, suffixes inflectional endings, contradictions and compound words, as well as syllabication and accent. Dictionaries can also be used for word identification. The dictionary re-spelling that appears in parentheses after the word supplies the word's pronunciation, but the reader has to know how to use the dictionary's pronunciation key to interpret the re-spellings appropriately.

Children need to learn to use all of the word recognition skills. Because they will need different skills for different situations, they must also learn to use the skills appropriately.

An overall strategy for decoding unfamiliar words is useful. The following five step strategy is a good one to teach :

(1) use context clues;

(2) try the sound of the initial consonant, vowel, or blend in

addition to context clues;

(3) check for structural clues;

(4) use phonics generalizations to sound out as much of the word as necessary; and

(5) consult the dictionary (Burns, Roe and Ross, 1996, 152–53).

There is considerable debate pertaining to how much phonics should be taught in the reading curriculum. Whole language approaches tend to minimize the teaching of phonics. Advocates of whole language believe that pupils will learn to read well when holism in content read is emphasized. For example, pupils together with the teacher here look at a Big Book that all can see clearly to discuss the illustrations. This activity assists pupils to obtain background information so that the resulting print will be understood better. Pupils also speculate on what the print material in the Big Book will be about. The pulls and the teacher then read aloud the contents in the Big Book. Pupils may see the printed words as the oral reading activity progresses. If they do know them or they don't, pulls can determine what each word is through reading aloud together and follow along in the print material. Re-reading is recommended since all pupils have their favourite stories and like to hear them again. Before I was able to read to myself, I liked to hear the Katzenjammer Kids comic strip read over and over again. The contents therein were quite predictable since the Katzenjammer Kids always did something mischievous; the father and the captain never liked to work while mama did all the work.

Big Books read with children should contain predictable content in that pupils have security in knowing something about what will happen in the story. With re-reading and predicable content, pupils learn to identify many words. These identified words become sight words. With a core of sight words in the repertoire, pupils may then read content at a more sophisticated level. With the Big Book approach, pupils are not hindered in sequential thinking when attempting to recognize an unknown word. Enjoyment of the story being read should then be in the offing. If pupils are stumbling along with word recognition, they may learn to dislike the act of reading. Rather, pupils need to focus upon interesting content contained in the Big Book. There are teachers who teach some phonics along with Big Book use. Thus, there may be games that pupils play in phonics related directly to the content read. Pupils then study words which have the same beginning letter and sound. They may compare short and long vowel sounds in words following a pattern such as : cap—cape, hat—hate, fat—, nap—nape and can, cane, among others. Teachers in whole language also stress words that end alike and words that rhyme. By having pupils find which word, for example, starts like 'bat', pupils may enjoy the phonics learning activity. It is not drill in a complete scope and sequence program of phonics, but rather learners locate words with a pattern and these words came from print materials read.

Phonics Integrated with Content from Reading

The view that reading consists of its simultaneous application of many different skills has important implications for our understanding of the successes and failures that readers experience as well as the kinds of educational programs that we should implement. The reason for this is that in reading, as in all cognitive activities, there are many roads that lead to Rome. There are many paths to successful reading and hence many paths to successful reading instruction. On the one hand, failure to read may result from deficiencies in any of the subskills of literacy. On the other hand, readers with strong skills in one facet of reading are bound to be able to compensate for possible weaknesses in other skills. We already have seen, for example, how second language readers use their comprehension and inferential skills to compensate for a lack of vocabulary and word identification skills. Thus, it is true that readers not only can fail to accomplish literacy for many different reasons, but also can succeed for different reasons (Van Den Broek, 1996).

We do not agree with a phonics program that has a scope and sequence of its own whereby lesson after lesson emphasizes phonics. Why? 1. The lessons become much too abstract for young pulls on the primary grade levels. 2. Phonics is separated from the act of reading whereby reading for ideas should be the key component of a quality reading program. 3. Pupils experience much drill when phonics becomes a separate subject area. 4. teachers find it difficult to obtain pupil interests in sequential lessons in phonics. 5. learners have a difficult time to determine reasons for all the emphasis upon "How" to read.

An approach in the teaching of phonics needs to stress reading for content and ideas as well as mastering key concepts pertaining to word recognition. There needs to be rational balance between whole language and phonics. Now we are left with the problem of what makes for balance between whole language and phonics. Now, we are left with the problem of what makes for balance between the two—phonics and whole language. We would give much more importance to reading for ideas as compared to phonics. Why ? We read to secure ideas, not to associate sounds with symbols. Relating sounds to symbols emphasizes keys to unlocking unknown words. It is not an end in and of itself. Phonics should never be taught as an end, but it is a means to an end. If phonics knowledge and use is more important than being a tool to unlock unknown words, then we are stuck with a strong scope and sequence program in phonics. Phonics then may be taught for its own sake. Here, we believe a mistake is made when phonics is conceived to be good for its own sake whether it assists pupils in reading well or not. Compare that line of thought with phonics being a tool to use when needed to determine the word that is not being identified.

Sometimes, even with strong context clues, a pupil cannot identify an unknown word. Perhaps, in these cases, a pupil may unlock an unknown word through identifying the initial consonant and then using context clues. A strong case can be made for emphasizing phonics as needed. If a pupil then cannot identify a word after being given adequate opportunity to do so, the teacher may need to stress selective facets of phonics which are useful here, such as the initial consonant "m" when the word "modify" is encountered and not identified. There is that teachable moment when the teacher needs to emphasize what is salient and in this case, a phonetic element. Phonics also may be taught in the context of basal reader use. Thus, when pupils are to read a story or selection from the basal, the teacher may print on the chalkboard in neat manuscript style the new words pupils will encounter when they are to read silently or orally. Generally, these new words will come from the manual section of the basal. The teacher points to each new word as he/she and the pupils pronounce them. This procedure may be used more than once per lesson if the need exists. The point is that pupils should be able to recognize these same words when reading. It still will be necessary as the act of reading is in evidence for the teacher or a good reader to pronounce words not known to the teacher. The pupil needs to be helped after allowing not known to the reader. The pupil needs to be helped after allowing five seconds, in general, before the unknown word is pronounced. Pupils not knowing a word should attempt to the best possible to determine it during these approximate five seconds. When pupils have ample opportunities to see the new words in near manuscript print, prior to oral or silent reading, the chances are they will identify many of these in the ongoing reading experience.

What about a phonics program that has a scope and sequence of its very own ? Pupils should realize that a consonant sound is made with an obstruction by the speaker between the throat and the lips. This is true of all consonant sounds. When thinking about the teaching of single consonants, the teacher or committee of teachers need to decide when these should be taught. There are individual consonant letters that are very consistent with their individual sounds. The following consonants are very consistent between grapheme/phoneme—b, d, f, h, j, i, m, n, p, r, s, t v w and y. with high frequency of use, I would stress the importance of pupils learning the following consonants : b, d, m, n, p, r, s, t and w. These consonants have very few exceptions to being consistent between symbol and sound. The following are some exceptions :

1. the letter "b" is silent in the word "debt".
2. the letter "p" is silent in the word "pneumonia".
3. the letter "s" sounds like a "z" in the word "resides".
4. the letter "w" has a "wh" sound in words such as "why",

"what", and "when". When I was an undergraduate student in a teaching of reading class, the instructor mentioned strongly that the "wh" sound is made with pronouncing the "w" and then at the same time blowing the light out an a candle. We think in most cases we cannot distinguish between the two initial consonant of "w" with the words "where" and "when".

In context, then, single consistent consonants, between symbol and sound, need to be taught. These are very helpful for learners to use in addition to context clues to unlock unknown words. Functional use should be made of these consonants. They are not to be learned for their own sake, but rather for application and use.

Short vowel sounds are next in importance for pupils to study. The consonant/vowel/consonant pattern are relatively easy for many pupils. These sounds are common in such words as the following : run, sun and bun. These words pattern with a short "u" sound. Ran, ban and man pattern with the short "a" sound. Hen, men and pen pattern with the short "e" sound. Sit, pit and hit pattern for the short "i" sound. Cot, lot and tot pattern with the short "o" sound.

Long vowel sounds can have a pattern when taught to pupils. For example, there are numerous words that follow the consonant/vowel/consonant/silent "e" (CVC silent e) pattern, such as bake, cake, make, fake, sake and lake. Vowel digraphs include s*ai*l, p*ai*l, m*ai*l and r*ai*l. Here, there are two vowel letters that come together with the first being long and the second silent in sound.

Initial consonant digraphs taught by the teacher may assist many pupils to become proficient in word recognition. Generally, two consonant letters make for one sound. These individual letters cannot be taken apart and make sense, such as the following : "th" as in *th*ought; "sh" as in *sh*ine; "ch" as in *ch*air;; and "ph" as in *ph*one. The words listed here for the consonant digraphs are commonly used words. The consonant digraphs listed are used very frequently. Within context, there are pupils who need assistance here since the separate letters do not make for consistency between symbol and sound.

Ending consonant digraphs are more difficult for pupils to master as compared to those coming in the beginning. Many pupils have been guided to improve reading through identification of ending consonant digraphs such as : ch as in ben*ch*, sh as in pu*sh* and th as in wid*th*. Games may always be played with pupils to see if they can provide additional words that have a beginning or ending consonant digraph. One of us observed a student teacher and her cooperating teacher have pupils brainstorm consonant blends and pupils wanted the lesson to continue beyond closing time. There was excitement and interest in continually naming more consonant blends.

Consonant blends or clusters are made up of two or three letters, each making its separate sound. The sounds come rather close together. There are pupils who have difficulty making these blends of two consecutive letters with their individual sounds. Her are some common blends : bl as in *bl*ow and *bl*ue; cr as in *cr*y, *cr*ystal and *cr*ow; fr such as in *fr*uit, *fr*ail and *fr*y; sn such as in *sn*ow, *sn*ail and *sn*ake and str such as in *str*eet, *str*ay and *str*ike.

Phonograms are interesting for many pupils to experiment with. Phonograms are short words found within a larger word. Examples of pupils discovering phonograms are the following : *at* as in hat, *eat* as in seat and *ate* as in skate. Sometimes a new "unknown" word is not impossible to identify. Thus, the word may appear unknown, but the learner knows enough about phonograms that he/she can identify the word correctly.

There are pupils who face an "unknown" word until they notice familiarities therein, such as a prefix. There are very common prefixes that hold true quite consistently. These include *un* meaning *not* such as *un*popular and *im* meaning not such as in *im*polite. The unfamiliar becomes familiar when pupils notice suffixes such as *less* as in child*less* and *ful* such as in cup*ful*. By noticing the familiar such as the root word and adding either the prefix and/or suffix, many pupils can determine what the new word is.

Diphthongs may cause selected pupils problems in word recognition. Why ? Here are two vowel letters that are together and yet their sound is different then any short or long vowel sound as well as being different in pronunciation. The following are examples : *oil* (the oi letters make a unique sound) and *oy* as in oyster (the oy make a unique sound also). These sounds are not like the individual letters or like a short or long vowel sound would make.

Another problem in sound/symbol relationships are words governed by a final "r". Notice the following words : *fir, fur, fer*, a syllable as in trans*fer*. The first word "fir" refers to a fir tree. The second "fur" refers to the hair on an animal, such as "The dog had shaggy fur". The third 'fer' is common as a suffix to many words. Sometimes, there are no governing principles in analyzing an unknown word. With the sight method in oral cooperative reading by pupils and the teacher, an unknown word becomes a known word. The following words, for example, follow a spelling pattern, but their individual pronunciations certainly do not : though, through, tough, bough, cough and dough. These words are spelled in an irregular manner and must be learned as sight words, even though a spelling pattern is there.

We generally oppose in teaching phonics prior to the time it is needed. To be functional, phonics should be taught when the need arises. Thus, when a pupil is reading silently or orally, he/she may need assistance on word identification. There is that teachable moment in time when a pupil might well benefit from selected phonics learnings. Thus, if a pupil is reading, "The Henry family liked to take—during holidays", the pupil may not know the word in the blank space. When using context clues, there are many words that would fit in according to meaning theory. The words that do not begin with the correct initial consonant can then be eliminated. If the pupil does not know the sound that goes along with the initial consonant letter, he/she may now be taught the grapheme/phoneme correspondence.

There is another suitable time to teach phonics and that is when learners may see patterns pertaining to the word not identified in oral or silent reading. Not always, of course, are there patterns in evidence. But, when a pupil does not identify the word "soil" in reading, he/she may be assisted to notice words which pattern such as boil, toil and spoil. The patterns approach has helped many pupils to identify unknown words when reading. Then too, a pupil who does not identify the word "soil" when reading may be asked to give other words that begin like "s" or end like "l". Why is this important ? The teacher may then appraise if the pupil can see and hear these phonemes/graphemes.

The question always arises as to the teaching of phonics to pupils who truly cannot hear sounds. A colleague of one of us as a sophomore in college in teacher education could not hear sounds. He was an avid reader and comprehended well. At the time he was doing student teaching during his sophomore year for a sixty hour certificate, he was called down during a lesson taught. The calling down occurred in front of pupils being taught. The student teacher had stated in the elementary school class that a vowel sound in reading was long when actually it was a short vowel sound. A colleague felt very badly for this happening and was ready to quit student teaching. At the last moment he decided to continue and be certified with a sixty hour certificate for teaching. This colleague had taught for forty-two years at the time he was dying of cancer. His teaching was done on the fifth and sixth grade levels where phonics instruction in reading was minimal. He seemed to have done well as a classroom teacher. This teacher should no doubt rely very heavily upon whole language approaches when teaching pupils. This might not always be possible when the pendulum swings to a heavy dose of phonics for all pupils. One thing my colleague did during his teaching years was to mark vowel sounds carefully before each day of teaching. He checked with a dictionary as to the accuracy of the making.

Basic Principles in Teaching Phonics

There are basic principles that teachers should adhere to when teaching phonics to primary and intermediate grade pupils.

1. Pupils should be ready for the new lessons to be taught. This would include learners having an attention span adequate in duration. They should be able to hear likenesses and differences in sound.

2. Pupils should experience lessons in phonics that are taught in an interesting manner. This would mean that drill would be greatly minimized and stimulating games would receive primary emphasis in the teaching of phonics.
3. Pupils need to experience sequence in ongoing lessons and units of study. One of the most important factors in teaching is that pupils perceive learning activities as being sequentially more difficult and yet readiness is there for attaining goals in phonics instruction.
4. Pupils need to be attentive during the time phonics is taught. If pupils are not attentive, they will not benefit from ongoing instruction. A teaching strategy needs to be in evidence whereby pupils develop and maintain their attentiveness.
5. Pupils should experience success in learning. If pupils experience failure, the chances are they will not benefit much from phonics instruction.
6. Pupils should receive feedback on how well they are achieving in phonics instruction. In this way, pupils know what they need to concentrate on in phonics lessons.
7. The teacher needs to monitor pupil progress in phonics. Thus, there are indications that pupils are achieving and learning if careful monitoring is done.
8. Pupils need to use what has been learned in phonics; otherwise phonics may be learned for its own sake. The only reason for teaching phonics is for pupils to become capable readers and spellers. Knowledge needs to be used and application made to new situations encountered.
9. Pupils need to assist each other in learning about and using phonics in reading instruction.
10. Pupils should appraise themselves personally to notice progress in phonics knowledge acquired and application made.
11. Teachers need to evaluate themselves to notice what pupils have achieved and work for improved instruction.

12. Objectives chosen for phonics instruction need to be relevant and achievable by learners.
13. Learning opportunities in phonics should provide for individual differences regardless of ability levels and socio-economic status.
14. Evaluation techniques should be aligned with the stated objectives so that the objectives provide direction for instruction.
15. The phonics program needs to be assessed frequently and modified to provide the best instruction possible for each pupil.

We need to emphasize again that phonics should be taught as a means to an end, not an end in and of itself. The end being to produce readers who enjoy reading and like to solve problems through the act of reading.

Philosophies of Phonics Instruction

There are diverse philosophies of education stating how phonics should be taught. One philosophy stresses the basics idea whereby there is essential information that needs to be taught to all pupils. Phonics is conceived to be the basics by selected authors in education as well as teachers. These individuals believe that phonics is rather consistent between symbol and sound. Thus, the grapheme/phoneme correspondence makes it so that teachers can be certain that consistencies do exist between symbol and sound as pupils learn to read.

Advocates of the basics believe that there is a core of phonics principles and generalizations that pupils should learn and use. More people then would learn to read than ever before, according to advocates. A strong scope in phonics needs to be identified. The scope or breadth of phonics content to be taught needs to be identified. Specialists in phonics instruction should be on committees to choose *what* is silent to teach pertaining to phonics. These phonics learnings might be graded so that pupils and parents would know what the minimal level of achievement should be for pupils to achieve on a grade level or at the end of a semester. The determining of *when* phonics objectives should be emphasized in teaching stresses the concept of sequence. Thus, there are phonics objectives that would be taught on the kindergarten, first and /or second grade level. There are teachers who emphasize a very strong program of phonics instruction with a well developed scope and sequence.

Reasons given for a strong program in scope and sequence in phonics are the following :

1. the English alphabet is rather consistent in stressing each grapheme (symbol) equals a phoneme (sound).
2. the key to success in reading is becoming an independent reader and that is through the study and use of phonics.
3. once the graphemes/phonemes have been mastered, pupils can do more and more independent reading.
4. pupils can enjoy ideas in reading when studying and using phonics. It is not an either/or situation such as either studying and using phonics versus obtaining ideas and enjoying reading.
5. phonics instruction can be made enjoyable with games and stimulating exercises. The teacher may use a phonics text or workbook in teaching and still promote pupils interest in learning to read.

There seems to be general agreement that good auditory and visual discrimination are pre-requisites for learning sound-symbol relationships. We know that children must be able to distinguish one letter from another and one sound from another before they can associate a given letter with a specific sound. Visual discrimination refers to the ability to distinguish likenesses from differences among letters and auditory discrimination refers to the ability to distinguish likenesses and differences among sounds. To achieve these skills, children must first understand the concepts of like and different among forms. Also to achieve auditory discrimination, children must first have phonemic awareness or the awareness that speech is composed of separate sounds (phonemes). They must be able to hear sounds within words or they will be unable to form mental connections between sounds and letters (as quoted in Burns, Ross and Roe, 1996).

Somewhat toward the opposite end of the continuum, there are teachers who believe in holism, only, in the teaching of reading. They stress pupils reading the entire story or reading selection without having lessons on phonics. These teachers believe that phonics instruction destroys interest in reading. Thus, pupils with teacher assistance should read the selection together. In this way, all pupils can orally read the content and identify all words. Re-reading is also stressed so that pupils and the teacher read over again the same selection. Generally stories chosen are quite predictable in that pupils have some idea of what will occur in sequence. Predictability of content assists pupils to ascertain what the unknown words are in pronunciation and in meaning.

Individualized reading is a holistic approach in reading instruction. The teacher here needs to have a rather large supply of library books from which each pupil will select sequential content to read. Learners generally select sequential books to read that are interesting and on their own unique reading level. Positive attitudes should be an important and on their individual reading level. After the completion of reading a library book, a conference is held with the teacher to determine comprehension and reading skills of the pupil. Attention is paid to phonics individually or in a committee when pupils reveal a need for help. It is important to notice that pupils reveal help needed as they read orally to the teacher a chosen selection. Assistance is provided pupils then as the need arises in reading and not before any selection is to be read.

Reasons given for using whole language approaches in teaching phonics within a quality reading program are the following :

1. Pupils learn phonetic elements within context as library books are read and holistic procedures in reading are emphasized.
2. Ideas acquired are the major ingredients of a good reading program for pupils. With interest and purpose in reading, the pupil hurdles many difficulties in reading, including associating sounds with symbols.

3. Pupils need to read to become better readers, not study phonics for its own sake.
4. The whole is greater (content in reading) than the sum of the parts (phonics).
5. Phonics is a tool to be used to obtain ideas from reading, not an end in and of itself.

In a psychological reading curriculum which is child cantered, the pupil is strongly involved in a selecting objectives, learning opportunities, and evaluation procedures. This is the heart of a pupils centered curriculum in reading. Humanism as a psychology of learning is then being emphasized. A humane reading curriculum, according to its advocates, stresses the individual learner being involved in decision making in the reading curriculum. The pupil is at the center of developing the reading curriculum (Ediger, 1997).

Behaviourism and the Reading Curriculum

Behaviourism a psychology has had much influence in education. With behaviourism, objectives for pupil achievement are stated prior to instruction and in measurable terms. Teachers can even announce prior to teaching what pupils are to learn from the lesson. It is very precisely written in the objective as to what each pupil is to learn. The learning activities are aligned with the objectives. The teacher then ultimately measures, after instruction, what pupils have achieved that was stated in the objectives. A pupil either achieves or does not achieve an objective since each is stated very precisely. Reasons given for using behaviourally stated objectives in teaching are the following :

1. Learning standards are written with precision so there is certainty in knowing what pupils are to learn or have learned.
2. Careful selection is given to objectives when each is very important and carefully defined in measurable terms.
3. Clarity is involved when communicating pupil results to parents. The results can be given in numerical terms.

4. Much attention can be paid to sequencing of objectives so that pupils experience as much success in learning as possible.
5. Pupils may receive continuous feedback on how well they are achieving.

Phonics objectives for pupil attainment may be stated precisely or behaviourally. Careful selection of phonetic elements to be taught needs to be inherent in the stated objectives. A good teaching strategy needs to be in the offing so that pupils may achieve the sequential objectives. The teacher ultimately appraises pupil achievement to notice if objectives have been achieved.

Conclusion

There are numerous decisions to make in the teaching of reading. First, which objectives should pupils achieve? There are implications here for stressing holistic approaches in teaching of reading versus analytical procedures. The objectives chosen will reflect one's beliefs pertaining to the teaching of reading. Under which conditions do pupils learn to read best? Second, which learning opportunities should be selected so that pupils will achieve the stated objectives. This includes the role of the basal textbook in the teaching of reading. In addition to basals, there are many other materials in reading instruction as learning opportunities such as the use of CD ROMS, computer packages (drill and practice, tutorial, games, simulations and diagnostic approaches), Big Books, picture books, library books, encyclopedias, filmstrips and slides with accompanying print materials, among others.

Third, how should the reading curriculum be organized ? There are numerous procedures available such as a separate subjects approach involving reading and literature only; correlation such as reading/language arts and social studies taught as being related; fused curriculum such as reading/language arts, social studies, science and mathematics, taught as being related. The inter-disciplinary reading curriculum integrates subject matter from all disciplines of knowledge. Problem solving procedures are best to use in inter-disciplinary approaches in instruction. Regardless of the academic discipline, that subject matter is used which assists in solving a problem.

The role of the reading teacher is to stimulate pupils to identify problems within the framework of a stimulating environment. After a problem has been clearly identified, related information is gathered to solve the identified problem.... Based on the data, a hypothesis is developed in answer to the problem. The hypothesis needs to be specific so that it can be tested. The hypothesis is tentative, not an absolute. With further reading experiences, as well as use of audio-visual activities, the pupil with teacher guidance tests the hypothesis. The hypothesis, as a result of testing, may be accepted as is, refuted, or modified.... Problem solving skills are usable in all curriculum areas, as well as in the societal arena...

Curiosity of the learner is salient when he/she selects a library book to read. With curiosity, interest accrues. Interest in a particular topic may well spur pupils on to a greater desire to read (Ediger, 1997).

Fourth, how should pupil achievement be evaluated? There are many techniques to use in evaluating pupil progress in reading. These include standardized and norm referenced tests, teacher written tests, teacher observation, anecdotal records, checklists and rating scales, pupil self-evaluation, as well as peer appraisal. The purpose of evaluation is to determine how well the pupil achieving in reading. A philosophy of constructivism in evaluation may also be emphasized in that pupils reveal in context what has been achieved in word recognition techniques and in comprehension. This can provide feedback to the teacher and the pupil in deciding upon what he/she needs to emphasize as objectives.

A quality reading program then stresses the following:

1. Each pupil begins at a point where he/she is ready to achieve as optimally as possible.
2. The learner experiences continual progress successfully in reading.
3. The four vocabularies—listening, speaking, reading and

writing—are integrated in a quality reading program.

4. Word recognition skills, such as phonics, syllabication, context clues and structural analysis, are taught within a framework of interesting content to be read.
5. Major emphasis is placed upon reading literature, not analyzing words into component parts.
6. Multimedia approaches are used to motivate pupils so that an inward desire in learning to read is inherent.
7. Problem solving, critical and creative thinking, as well as application are salient concepts stressed in teaching reading.
8. The best sequence is used to guide each pupil toward optimum achievement in reading.
9. Learning to read as a life time endeavour is stressed.
10. The use of relevant research results is important in the teaching of reading (Ediger, 1997).

References

Burns, Paul C., Betty D. Roe and Elinor Ross (1996), *Teaching Reading in Today's Elementary Schools.* Boston : Houghton Mifflin Company, 114.

Ediger, Marlow (1997), *Teaching Reading and the Language Arts in the Elementary School.* Kirksville, Missouri : Simpson Publishing Company, 32.

Ediger, Marlow (1997), *Teaching Reading and the Language Arts.* Kirksville, Missouri : Simpson Publishing Company, 37.

Ediger, Marlow (1997), "Perspectives in Teaching Reading", *Reading Improvement.* 34(2), 52–53.

Van Den Broek, Paul (1996), "On Becoming Literate : The Many Sources of Success and Failure in Reading", *the first R. every child's right to read*, Graves, Van Den Broek and Taylor, (Editors), 193.

10
Reading Poetry in the Language Arts

An important type of reading for elementary age pupils is to read poetry. There are pupils who love to read poetry and unfortunately others either are neutral or react negatively to its reading. My hope in this writing is that all pupils will read and react more positively to diverse forms of verse and their contents. Pupils in classrooms where I have supervised student teachers and cooperating teachers are somewhat eager to express their opinions about the study and writing of poetry. Some of the recorded comments we have written down of these opinions include :

1. I do not understand what is written.
2. I would rather read stories from library books.
3. The language used is confusing.
4. I like to read poems that rhyme.
5. I would rather do something else than read.
6. I like poetry that has animal content.
7. I like to read poetry and other literature.
8. I do not like to memorize poetry.
9. I feel that the words used in poems are difficult to understand.
10. I wish more time would be given to the study and reading of poetry

From the above comments, it is quite obvious that there are mixed feelings toward the reading of poetry. Certainly, the teacher will need to establish objectives in which each pupil learns to love the studying and reading of poetry. This can be a difficult task and yet the teacher needs to try to get pupils actively engaged in units of study pertaining to poetry in the elementary school. We would suggest that a major goal of instruction should be to assist pupils to love and appreciate poetry. Additional objectives include obtaining meaning and understanding of poems read, desiring to write different forms and types of poems, working harmoniously with others in reading and writing of poems, increasing vocabulary development through poetry writing, improving reading skills in word recognition and comprehension (Ediger, 1997), relating poems read to different curriculum areas in the elementary school, building and developing background information to use in diverse subject matter areas in the curriculum, as well as increasing in the desire to learn, grow and achieve. To write quality poetry, the pupil needs background information. The teacher needs to have a rich learning environment in the classroom. We believe in having many learning centers in the classroom só that learners may look at what is at each center. Objects, items, audio-visual aids, realia and library books with other print materials need to be located at each of these centers. The teacher needs to introduce each center briefly as well as motivate and assist pupils to move forward with achievement in poetry writing. Pupils need to browse through books containing poetry. First, lets take a look at how the poetry curriculum may be organised.

Organizing the Poetry Curriculum

Teachers need to think of how to organize the poetry curriculum so that more optimal pupil achievement is in evidence. We have observed teachers teach entire units on poetry as a separate subject. The unit involved here may be entitled "Reading and Writing Poetry". Why do selected teachers teach separate units on poetry? Depth teaching might then be involved in that the focus is upon poetry only in its many forms. Here, the teacher may have pupils concentrate on rhymed, unrhymed but with a certain number of syllables per line and no rhyme and no specific number of syllables per line. When readiness is in evidence, pupils may compare and contrast diverse forms of poetry studied and written. Ingredients in poetry writing may also be emphasized here with imagery, alliteration and onomatopoeia. In the separate subjects approach of units on poetry in the elementary school, pupils may focus in depth upon what goes into the different forms of verse to emphasize poetry in its diverse manifestations.

For example, in studying imagery, pupils may learn in depth what is involved here with metaphors and similes. Thus, pupils need to understand that metaphors do not require words including *like* and *as*. Creative comparisons may then be made: The moon, a yellow flame of gold, moves rapidly in space. Here, the moon is compared creatively with, "a yellow flame of gold". This is a metaphorical comparison.

A second form of imagery is to use similes whereby the words "like" and "as" are used to make creative comparisons: The clouds in the sky look like sheep walking on blue grass. The simile her is "like sheep walking on blue grass". Thus, a creative comparison is made between "The clouds in the sky", and "sheep walking on blue grass".

In addition to the separate subjects poetry curriculum, the teacher may also wish to correlate reading and writing poems with different curriculum areas. Here, the teacher attempts the best possible to have pupils directly relate each poem studied to social studies, science, mathematics and the language art areas. Thus, if a social studies unit on the Civil War is being taught, the teacher may assist pupils to read and study literature written during this war. Social Studies and literature are being correlated. Perceiving relationship of knowledge by pupils is a major goal of the correlated curriculum. There are fewer separate subjects to be taught in a given day. The elementary school curriculum tends to be crowded as it is and teachers do welcome certain curriculum areas to be correlated.

In correlating social studies and poetry, one pupil in the fifth grade wrote the following quatrain containing patterns of rhyme :

The Holy Land
Moslems, Christians and Jews
Each have their own unique views
Mosque, Church or Temple
Religion is taught as an example.

When pupils perceive that knowledge is related, it becomes easier to remember what had been learned. Why? One idea obtained triggers off others that are related. In a separate subjects poetry curriculum, the pupil may perceive content in isolation and thereby not sense that facts, concepts and generalizations can be learned as a unity or as ideas related to each other. There are fewer separate subjects to teach if correlation of content is in evidence.

A third way of organizing the poetry curriculum is to stress an integrated curriculum. Here, the teacher leans upon social studies, science, mathematics and literature, among other academic disciplines, to provide content for poems written by pupils. Each academic discipline tends to become blurred with the integrated curriculum. Pupils then have even greater chances of understanding how knowledge can be related. Many educators would argue that pupils here should retain subject matter in memory longer due to using it and in this case not being a separate subject.

How the teacher wishes to organize the poetry curriculum depends upon many factors. These include the number of curriculum areas taught which can be emphasized satisfactorily as related by the teacher. Sometimes the integrated curriculum is also called the interdisciplinary approach for organizing instruction.

One pupil wrote the following triplet with all ending words rhyming and indicating an inter-disciplinary curriculum :

The Dome of the Rock in the Holy Land
The Dome of the Rock has an octagonal design
(mathematics)
It is used for worship by the Moslems as a sign
(social studies)
With all of its beauty viewed by yours and mine
(art).

The poetry curriculum needs to be carefully developed with quality objectives, learning opportunities and evaluation procedures. In making these three decisions, the teacher also needs to think of organizations such as the separate subjects, the correlated and the integrated approach in teaching and learning.

Alliteration and Onomatopoeia in Poetry Writing

Pupils with teacher guidance should learn to use alliteration in poetry writing. Poets use this device frequently in writing. Alliteration tends to stress two or more sequential words that begin with the same sound. Learners find it fascinating to create verse whereby the two or more initial sounds are the same in an ordered way. A committee of three children collaborated on writing the following containing alliteration :

The Dead Sea in the Holy Land

With *s*alty *s*ea water at sight
And *l*ow *l*evel elevation of land
I find the *d*ear *D*ead Sea to lack life.

We feel that writing poetry with alliteration assists pupils in recognizing the role of phonics in reading. Creatively determining words that start with the same sound stresses sounds, not spelling. For example, the words *cent* and *sent* have identical sounds but these words are spelled differently with the initial consonant sound.

Another device that poets use in writing poetry is onomatopoeia. Here, words used must make the sounds that one hears in the natural environment. If one throws a rock into the water, the sound made is similar to splash ! Thus, the word splash makes that sound, in degrees, when a rock is thrown into the water. A pupil I observed while supervising student teachers in the public schools wrote the following containing onomatopoeia in a science unit of study :

The Sound of Wind

Why does the wind sound like *swish*, *swoosh*, *slosh*, *slash* and *spash* ? The unequal heating of the earth's atmosphere makes for movement of air.

The movement of molecules through the air say travel, move and go!

The underlined words in the above poem seem to indicate in degrees the sound of wind. The pupil has included onomatopoeia in the first line only of this poem.

Poems That Rhyme

One important kind poetry does rhyme. Others do not. The following are examples of rhymed verse which pupils may write when readiness is in evidence (Ediger, 1988). Couplets contain two lines with ending words rhyming, such as in the following poem:

The Forty Niners

The Forty niners went to the West
To look for gold with great zest.

One teacher mentioned to one of us while supervising student teachers that the whole word method only or largely was used when she attended public schools. Major learnings came from studying rhymed verse. In her school, the teacher would have pupils brain storm ideas on how many words would rhyme with a particular word printed on the chalkboard. These listed words were then to be used in poetry writing.

Triplets have three lines with all ending words rhyming. From a brain storming session on ideas about the zoo, a committee of three wrote the following triplet :

The Zoo

I like to visit the zoo to see large lions
We have studied these animals in science
They live in a few nations with different biomes.

The quatrain was discussed above and needs a little review. Quatrains have four lines with lines one and two rhyming as well as lines three and four rhyming. Sometimes, all ending words rhyme of the four line poem. A dyad of two pupils wrote the following within a unit of study :

An Inventor

Thomas Edison invented the light bulb with much work
His efforts helped all to see better at night with little quirk
The light bulb was here to stay
And make life better with more pay.

Selected pupils like to work together with others in the classroom in writing a poem. The number here needs to be kept small so all may participate such as a dyad of two members of a maximum of four pupils writing collaboratively.

Limericks are a very popular kind of poem for pupils to write. Generally, this poem starts with the words "There once was a—The limerick has five lines comprised of a couplet and a triplet. Lines 1, 2 and 5 form a triplet whereas lines 3 and 4 form a couplet.

Kindness

There once was a man in a large city
Who felt sorry for poor people in a pity
He raised much money for the poor
And felt he needed much more
That wonderful man worked on a committee.

It is excellent if pupils volunteer to write poetry; however, there are learners who do not participate with intrinsic motivation and may need to be assigned to a committee which is highly accepting and provides for all pupils to succeed.

Unrhymed Verse

Many pupils are surprised that there can be unrhymed poetry which provides for interest and purpose on the part of the learner. They find free verse to be challenging and relatively easy to write. After all, pupils should enjoy reading and writing poems. Intrinsic motivation is important in all learning as an ideal. Many pupils are motivated from within and do not need inexpensive prizes as rewards for learning. For those lacking intrinsic motivation, the teacher may need to use an award system and, hopefully, pupils will wean themselves from extrinsic motivation as time goes on. We do not count verbal praise as extrinsic motivation. Honest praise is good for pupils and should be used judiciously. We believe that quality learning takes place best with intrinsic motivation, but a few pupils will need rewards and prizes as motivators. Two pupils wrote the following haiku containing five-seven-five syllables for each of three lines:

The Goat

The goal is a joy (five syllables)
In the grass among the trees (seven syllables)
A lovely sight seen!

A tanka has two more lines, each having seven syllables:

The Tall Camel

I like to see far	(five syllables)
Where camels roam in deserts	(seven syllables)
And chew scarce rare feed	(five syllables)
Up, away go the camels	(seven syllables)
Where grass and water abound.	(seven syllables)

Writing Free Verse

Free verse is a very open-ended kind of poetry. There does not have to be any rhyme nor syllabication. Many pupils enjoy brain storming lines for free verse. The following free verse was composed by four pupils collaboratively :

The Shepherd

Alone with the sheep in the field
plays on the flute to maintain entertainment
watches and cares for each and every sheep
is careful with the little lambs
herds the animals to good grass
throws stones at cement fences
does not mind being alone
relishes time with the sheep
ever faithful and kind

Conclusion

Pupils need to experience reading and writing different kinds and forms of poetry. There are rich meanings and messages in poetry. The novel use of words adds to the learning repertoire of pupils. There should be poems for pupils to read that deal with diverse topics and genres. The poems should be on appropriate reading levels of individual pupils for maximum achievement to take place. The teacher needs to read poetry frequently to pupils in an enthusiastic way. Each pupil may wish to collect his/her favourite poems for enjoyment and future reference. Pupils need to become motivated through the use of different stimuli in order to read and write more poetry. For selected pupils, reading much poetry has been a way of increasing skills in learning to read more proficiently.

References

Ediger, Marlow (1997), *The Modern Elementary School*, Kirksville, Missouri : Simpson Publishing Company, 206.

Ediger, Marlow (1988), *Language Arts Curriculum in the Elementary School*. Kirksville, Missouri : Simpson Publishing Company, 29–36.

Rao, Digumarti Bhaskara and Pushpa Latha, Digumarti (1993). *Achievement in English*. New Delhi : Discovery Publishing House.

11
Spelling and the Language Arts

Pupils need to become good spellers to communicate effectively with others. Spelling is a tool to use to make known personal needs as well as to communicate feelings and appreciations. Correct spelling of words will always be necessary, even with the mass amount of technology available to many in society. Why? a person does not always have a computer at a specific place to process words. If the word processor is available, individuals still need to spell words reasonable close in accuracy for the spell checkers program to work and be effective. Thus, if a word is misspelled greatly, spell checkers will not list the needed correct spelling of the word on the monitor. Then too, sometimes it is more convenient to use long hand in writing rather than starting a computer up and using the attached printer. A personal message written in long hand may convey information to the reader better as compared to a printed document. How then might pupils be assisted to become proficient spellers?

Guidelines for Teaching Spelling

We would like to state selected guidelines which good teachers have used successfully in the teaching of spelling. First, pupils should understand the meaning of words to be mastered before studying their spelling. Meaning theory suggest that if pupils understand context, they will learn more effectively and depth learning may then be in evidence. Teachers need to take time for pupils to give definitions and/or be able to use a word contextually within a sentence. Some words are difficult to define and should then be used by the learner in a meaningful sentence. If a word can be defined and a pupil is ready to explain the meaning, he/she should do so. We believe that being able to use a word in a sentence and with a clear meaning, the learner is then ready to study the correct spelling of that word. We hope that words mastered in spelling will also be retained in memory for reading content as well as for writing in different academic areas. It is good if a pupil makes use of spelling words in many ways such as in reading those same words in literature, social studies, science and mathematics content. If pupils do not identify words correctly or a halting procedure is used in reading, the chances are comprehension will suffer in the process.

Second, the teacher needs to provide a variety of learning opportunities to assist pupils in learning to spell words correctly. Do I approve of the use of spelling textbooks in guiding pupils in learning to spell? It is not the textbook that is good or bad, but it depends upon how they are used by pupils and the teacher. There can be selected fascinating activities for learners within the confines of a spelling textbook that has been carefully chosen. Thus, here are activities that truly benefit and make spelling enjoyable. For example, in one lesson in a spelling textbook, there are the usual list of words for pupils to master. How are they to achieve this task? One approach in the text is to have pupils fill in blank spaces in sentences given, whereby the words for the fill in, come from that list. Pupils can be very attentive in doing this when application is made of the new words to be mastered in spelling. Seemingly, many pupils are interested in this activity even though it does occur generally in each weekly lesson. We think that the activity has variation each week due to changing words that are used to fill in the blank spaces within sentences. The teacher should always observe pupils to notice if boredom sets in and, if it does, to switch to a different experience. The teacher cannot do a prefect job of varying activities when boredom sets in, but he/she can do the best possible to keep pupils on task. With twenty to thirty pupils in a classroom, it is difficult to provide for individual needs of all pupils. Additional tasks in a textbook to be used to help pupils learn to spell words correctly are cross word puzzles that use words from the weekly list in the spelling text. Friendly and business letters are to be written using selected words from the spelling list. The teacher needs to be creative in text use in teaching spelling by thinking of and implementing other learning opportunities than those indicated in the weekly lesson.

Third, we believe that pupils should develop a definite methodology in learning to spell words. A good speller, no doubt, has a workable method of learning to spell words correctly. Those who do not spell words correctly, in many cases, may need a new methodology in mastering the correct spelling of words. We like the method that many pupils have used correctly in learning to spell. Thus, the pupil needs to look at the new word carefully. It is doubtful that a teaching strategy will work if the pupil here does not look at the word carefully if pupils are truly focusing upon a word to acquire in correct spelling. Next, the pupil should pronounce the word correctly. Spelling errors are made due to inaccurate pronunciation of words. Hopefully, the pupil will listen to all the sounds with that word being studied for mastery in spelling. Involved sounds need to be associated with the correct graphemes or symbols. The learner then should practice writing the word once. The written word may then be checked with the correct spelling. Too frequently, pupils are asked to write a word five or ten times immediately; the word written might be misspelled then ten times. Better it is, to write the word once and check accuracy of spelling. Once the word is spelled correctly, the pupil may wish to write it several times in a contextual situation.

Fourth, pupils need to perceive reasons for learning to spell a given set of words, be if from the textbook or from other sources. Purpose is vital for success in learning to spell words correctly. The teacher may say why it is important to learn to spell words correctly in a specific lesson. A deductive approach is then in evidence. Inductive procedures may also be used such as a teacher asking questions of learners so that the latter understands the merit of learning to spell a given number of words correctly. Extrinsic rewards are used by some teachers to motivate pupils to study and master the new set of words in spelling. Thus, a teacher may say how many words need to be spelled correctly by Friday to receive a prize. These prizes are generally visible to pupils. Learners then know what to do to receive the award. We recommend that if extrinsic awards are given for learning, pupils should, as soon as possible, feel a desire from within to learn to spell words correctly as an intrinsic motivational device. The extrinsic rewards should be removed as soon as possible and not become a crutch or lever used to spell words correctly.

Fifth, pupils should learn to spell words correctly in a contextual situation. The new words are then used in functional situations. Words and their correct spelling are meaningful within a practical endeavour. We recommend that pupils determine useful ways to spell words correctly within contextual situations. The learner may then use the new words when writing an invitation for his/her birthday party. Further uses include writing business and friendly letters, content in greeting cards, prose and poetry, poetry, narrative and expository accounts, short stories, announcements and thank you notices, among other functional writing activities.

How many words should a pupil learn to spell correctly per week? This depends upon the present achievement level of the involved learner. To be sure, too many words may be required for a pupil to master in spelling. The opposite extreme would be too few words are learned to spell words correctly in a given time interval. The teacher needs to observe each pupil and notice what a reasonable number of words might be. There is nothing sacred about mastering twenty spelling words per week in the third grade, for example. It is important always to challenge pupils to do their very best in all curriculum areas.

Sixth, the spelling curriculum should be as individualized as possible. To some educators this means that each pupil should have a unique set of words to master in spelling. These words may come from those the learner misspelled from diverse writing activities the preceding week. The number of words in this list must be adjusted to fit the abilities of the individual learner so that too many or too few words are not required for mastery within a designated time. This seems to work fairly well in the spelling curriculum provided that learners do not refuse to use words in writing unless they are spelled correctly. The reason for doing this pertains to keeping the number reasonable of those words misspelled and needing to be studied for mastery. Another approach that might be used pertains to adjusting the number of words from the spelling textbook that need to be spelled correctly per week. Pupil A then may find it easy to learn to spell all words correctly plus a bonus list of words per week. Pupil B might be able to spell ten of the twenty words correctly per week. Once Pupil B has experienced success, he/she might become motivated to increase the number of words spelled correctly per week. We have noticed that pupils who are successful do volunteer to do more work then formerly and go beyond minimal levels. It takes time and effort for the teacher to make these adjustments for individual pupils. But with good teaching, teachers attempt to provide for individual differences among learners in the classroom. Even though the spelling curriculum is individualized, there may be pupils who wish to work collaboratively. Learning styles differ from one pupil to another such as wanting to work intrapersonally or by the self as contrasted with interpersonal or committee work. Here, pupils should have a voice in how they wish to study and learn, individually or in a group, to achieve more optimally in spelling.

Seventh, we recommend that creatively be stressed in pupils learning to spell words. So often, spelling is taught as role learning and memorization. Rather, the pupil should have ample opportunities to spell words correctly within creative poetry and prose written or within plays and stories written. Here, we recommend that pupils evaluate correct spelling of words after the creative product has been completed, not during the writing endeavour. Pupils may wish to assist each other when correct spelling of words is emphasized at the end of the creative writing experience.

Eighth, we recommend strongly to provide incentives for pupils to volunteer to learn to spell more words correctly, than those assigned or even going beyond the bonus words. It is surprising what pupils will do to put forth effort when the sky becomes the limit. Intrinsic motivation certainly can come into being when pupils feel rewarded and successful in learning. The teaching of spelling is not known to be the most stimulating curriculum area, but the teacher can work in the direction of it becoming motivating and challenging.

Which Words Should Pupils Master in Spelling ?

This question has been debated for a long time. There are teachers who assume that the spelling text alone contains salient words for pupils to master in spelling. The text has had a long history of use in teaching and learning situations. We have looked at spelling texts that came out in the early 1930s. These books had lists of words only for pupils to memorize in spelling per week. There were no suggested learning activities. The teacher each week needed to work out all learning activities that would assist pupils in learning to spell each word correctly. Presently, there are teachers who believe that no spelling texts be used and believe better teaching is an end result. A well chosen textbook should definitely not hinder good teaching. Ingenious teachers can stimulate pupils to learn with interesting activities that capture pupil attention. No textbook needs to be followed religiously in terms of the recommendations in the manual. The good teacher chooses from among the different activities stressed in the manual section. Additional learning opportunities are brought into the teaching and learning situation that provide for individual differences among pupils. No writer of quality materials would suggest following the manual 100 percent. Writer realize that the teacher is the one to implement the teaching suggestions and must vary the kinds of learning opportunities provided for pupils so that securing the attention of pupils is there and pupils are actively engaged in learning. No using a basal textbook, in and of itself, does not make for good teaching. The teacher is there to study and implement teaching strategies that assist pupils to attain relevant objectives in the spelling curriculum.

If the teacher uses words for each pupil that the latter missed in everyday functional writing, the teacher still needs to have quality approaches in teaching so that individual pupils learn and achieve. Pupils need to be motivated when attempting to master the spelling words missed in daily writing. The number per week to be mastered needs to be adjusted to what a child can achieve in a reasonable manner. Certainly, a pupil may experience failure if too many words need mastering or become bored if too little is expected in a given time interval.

There have been successful teachers whom we have observed that emphasize spelling words that have been chosen for pupils to master which are based on research study of pupils' writings were selected by the teacher within a list for mastery learning by local pupils. The Dolch List (1954) has been used in teaching spelling by many teachers, even though it is not a recently developed list. This list has 220 words that Dolch's research found should be learned by pupils as sight words. This might then cut down on the number of errors that pupils make in spelling as well as in word identification in reading. These are the most frequently occurring words in spelling errors in pupils' writing, according to Dolch. We feel the Dolch List still has much merit because these words are commonly used by pupils in everyday writing and reading today. The word list is not divided by grade levels but is contained in one listing. We recommend that teachers study pupils' writings to notice which words are used most frequently. Teachers should be involved in doing research and may come up with a revision of the Dolch List. With personal computers in the school and in the home, the statistical procedures, we believe, have been greatly simplified and become user friendly. With personal computers and assistance from educational researchers, teachers now have more opportunities to engage in research and attempt to solve classroom problems than ever before.

There are numerous statements of objectives in spelling that educators have developed over the years. We believe the following are worthy for teachers to emphasize in the curriculum:

1. Assist pupils to master those words which are needed in order to express oneself clearly and accurately in writing.
2. Guide pupils to achieve good study habits which assist the learner to pursue diverse kinds and types of writing experiences. Preservance is a key concept here. Pupils need to establish plans in writing, work toward their achievement and personally monitor progress. We have noticed pupils who attempt to give up too soon on assigned or voluntary written work. Encouragement by peers and the teacher will go a long way in motivating learner achievement. Pupil pride in achievement aids in setting higher goals in spelling within the writing activity.
3. Develop within pupils a set of standards in learning that will help pupils to spell words correctly. These standards

involve using phonics to make associations between symbol and sound where this consistency is in evidence. Pupils also need to learn to spell selected words by sight when the consistency between symbol and sound and sound just is not there. Correct pronunciation of words is important so that spelling errors are not made due to that factor.

4. Help pupils to realize that correct spelling is a social courtesy and incorrect spelling may reflect negatively upon the pupil.

5. Direct quality teaching to have pupils, when ready, learn keyboard skills to use the personal computer to engage in writing. This is necessary for all pupils. Spell checkers can do much to minimize spelling errors when word processing is used. Computers are increasingly becoming user friendly.

6. Provide friendly assistance to pupils who need help in spelling so that success can be stressed as much as possible in the writing curriculum. A good speller in the classroom may also provide this help. If the latter approach is used, change or rotate who gives the assistance. Each pupil also needs to pursue his/her own interests in purposeful learning.

7. Emphasize the interest factor by letting pupils choose the topic to write on, regardless of the purpose involved. Thus, if pupils are to write limericks, the learner may select within that framework the contents of the limerick. Interest goes a long way in providing effort for learning.

8. Let pupils work together in the writing activity involving spelling. Observe theat each is participating actively in the spelling/writing experience.

9. Involve pupils in self-evaluation as well as the teacher participating actively in appraising learner progress. Collaboratively, a learning community may be developed that stresses quality writing in the curriculum.

10. Establish quality sequence in pupil learning to spell words correctly. If pupils are involved in determining which words

need to be learned in spelling, a psychological spelling curriculum is in evidence. Sequence then resides within the learner, not in other sources. Should the teacher determine sequence in pupil learning to spell words, a logical approach is in evidence since the teacher determines the order of learning activities for pupils (Ediger, 1988).

Pupils should definitely realize that spelling and reading are related, not isolated entities. Being able to spell more words correctly as time goes on should reflect learners' increasing abilities to become better readers. The goals of spelling and reading instruction should develop confidence in the learner to achieve at a higher level commensurate with inherent abilities of the involved pupil (Ediger, 1998).

Cautions in Learning to Spell Words

There are selected cautions that teachers need to be aware of when teaching spelling. Pupils and the teacher should not go overboard on phonics when correct spelling of words is being emphasized. Thus, there are numerous words that lack consistency between symbol and sound such as my, pie, buy, sigh, kite, white and bye. Each of these words contains the long *i* sound and yet that sound is spelled differently from word to word.

Second, pupils need to learn to spell vital words that are truly useful. Too frequently, words listed in a spelling textbook may not be important enough for pupils to learn to spell. We believe the teacher needs to study word lists in spelling texts, if used and ascertain the worth of learning to spell each word. There is so much to learn that it behooves the teacher to choose carefully what pupils are to learn.

Third, if pupils are to learn to spell a given set of words, they should make application of what has been learned. Much forgetting occurs of mastered words in spelling if there are no related practical endeavours, meaning that applying what has been learned is important. We believe much time is wasted in learning if pupils are tested only, on the number of words spelled correctly on Friday and yet the involved pupil perceives no practical application of these kinds of learning activities.

Fourth, too frequently, memorization of correct spelling of words is emphasized and yet meaningful experiences are lacking. Generally memorization is done for the sake of passing a test and in this case to receive a good grade from the teacher. We would like to see the evaluation process change to where more emphasis is placed upon pupils' making application of words being studied for correct spelling in ongoing lessons and units of study.

Fifth, pupils in many cases lack readiness factors for learning to spell words correctly. What are these readiness factors? Certainly, a pupil should also be able to use the new words being studied contextually in a sentence that makes sense. Pupils individually need to use the proper tools at hand to analyze parts within a word such as grapheme/phoneme relationships. For those irregularly spelled words, a basic sight vocabulary needs to be developed by learners.

Sixth, too often, pupils in a class are taught as if all possess readiness for the same number of words to be mastered in spelling. Pupils are individuals, not a mass of objects. Learners come with feelings, dreams and hopes. They need to be treated as human beings with much worth. Thus, the teacher needs to help each pupil to learn as much as possible. The opportunity for pupil learning is now and we need to take advantage of these opportunities.

Seventh, there is a lack of emphasis upon diagnosis and remediation when teaching spelling. We need to determine why pupils individually are making errors in the incorrect spelling of words. Do pupils go by phonics too much when learning to spell words and yet one or more of these words are not that phonetic in sound/symbol relationships? Is legible handwriting a cause for improper; spelling of words? Pupils need to experience as much success as possible so that motivation is there to learn, grow and achieve.

Technology and Spelling

There definitely is room for technology use in the spelling curriculum. Its use is one way to strengthen teaching and learning in ongoing lessons and units of study. Computer use should be made available to teachers and learners. The software content of the computer should not duplicate with other materials of instruction, but should provide learning activities which also assist pupils to improve in the area of spelling. There are drill and practice exercises which truly help pupils to achieve more optimally. Words here need to be highly useful with strategies of learning that provide for each pupil's ability level. The drill and practice experiences give learners an opportunity to rehearse the correct spelling of words. There are needs for drill and practice so that pupils may practice and retain the correct spelling of words at a more optimal level of achievement. Much of what we remember has been presented to us in different ways using a variety of learning activities. Here software and computer use can provide this variety with innovating ways and procedures displayed on the monitor. Also, there are numerous games that pupils may engage in individually or collaboratively that stress the correct spelling of words, as shown on the monitor. These games may provide wholesome competitive activities between two or three sides. Thus, in rotation, one side may score points for the correct spelling of one or more words whereas the two other sides or single side, in sequence, may come back with spelling other words correctly to score points. The winner has the most words spelled correctly. Games in spelling are good for pupils to play competitively, if appropriate attitudes are in evidence.

Tutorial software programs provide new words for pupil mastery, as shown sequentially on the monitor. Diverse learning opportunities are provided so that pupils may master these new words in spelling. Also, there are simulations that attempt to represent life-like situations whereby pupils are to engage in problem solving in virtual reality. The encounters here are quite realistic and provide for situations involving higher levels of cognition such as critical and creative thinking as well as problem solving. At the same time, pupils are engaged in attempting to spell words correctly. Since a more utilitarian situation is involved in simulations, pupils tend to find these activities to be challenging and real.

We find that pupils engaging in using the word processor to write creatively or functionally is one of the better ways to stress correct spelling of words. Here, pupils need to be proficient in spelling during the actual composing situation when using the words processor. It is true that spell checkers does provide much assistance in helping pupils make corrections in spelling. However, the commands provided by the learner in writing content into the computer need to be very close in correct spelling or spell checkers cannot provide the correct spelling on the monitor of the word processor. All pupils, when ready, should master use of the word processor to write prose, poetry, or utilitarian content. Mehlinger (1997) asks the following provocative questions when using computers in the curriculum :

1. How would teachers teach if textbooks were replaced by small multi-media devices that serve as both computer and communications tool ?
2. What would school libraries be like when students have access to the libraries of the word ?
3. How would teaching change when students can contact experts who know more about a single topic than the teacher ?

These are three excellent questions that need pondering for all educators. We recommend both technology and textbooks, carefully chosen, be used to provide for individual differences among learners. Diverse kinds of materials need to be used in teaching and learning. Individuals possess diverse learning styles and the professional teacher attempts to harmonize instruction with pupil learning styles. Bermman and Tinker (1997) discuss a seminar method of instruction with the use of technology :

Many teachers who experiment with on-line courses report being overwhelmed with enrolments of 10 or 12 students because they set up e-mail conversations with each student. The better model is more than a seminar, in which the teacher determines the topic and activities, encourages substantive interactions among students, monitors and shapes the conversation and promotes an atmosphere in which students respond to one another's work. This model results in more conversation, is far more likely to be constructivist and builds on the rich learning that takes place in groups.

Collaborative endeavours that stress the learning of correct spelling of words within purposeful writing activities certainly do emphasize positive ways in the use of technology. Interactions among learners do tend to make for higher levels of cognitive endeavours within the framework of critical and creative thought as well as problem solving.

Handwriting, Spelling and Print Discourse

Illegible handwriting may be major cause for incorrect spelling of words. Handwriting as a separate subject is receiving much less emphasis than formerly. When attending the elementary school years from 1934 to 1942, handwriting received considerable time for instruction; approximately, fifteen minutes per day was spent in handwriting instruction. We learned to write in the air to form individual letters correctly. The making of ovals so that no line was crossed with another received much emphasis as did push and pull exercises, again with no strokes crossing each other. May be these activities had something to do with a transfer value in becoming better handwriters. We truly doubt if this was the case, however. Probably, more time should have been given to the actual writing of prose and poetry, as well as other forms of print discourse. Thus, use needs to be made of what has been learned in handwriting experiences.

What might the teacher do to assist pupils to improve in handwriting? Here, the teacher needs to give much attention to child growth and development characteristics. A lengthy period of time given to handwriting instruction may not harmonize with psychomotor skills and readiness of the learner. Much tension may be built up by the leaner if he/she is required to write extensively. Activities may be changed so this does not occur, such as changing to a reading experience. It is always good procedure in teaching to observe the attention span of pupils to notice when sequential activities need to be changed. We strongly recommend handwriting be taught within an ongoing activity involving purposeful writing. Application might then be made of what is being emphasized in terms of objectives of instruction. Handwriting and content written become one, not separate entities.

The objectives of handwriting need to be chosen carefully so that relevance is in evidence. The making of ovals and push/pull exercises were eliminated from the elementary school curriculum some time ago due to a lack of significance involved. To spend hours and hours on drill pertaining to a set of letters certainly is misusing teaching time. We believe legibility is a key concept to emphasize in the handwriting arena. A pupil does not need to conform specifically to models of upper and lower case letters of the alphabet presented in a handwriting text. The model letters, however, may be used as a guide for pupils to develop legibility in handwriting. If we can read a pupil's written products readily, then we are satisfied with the quality of his/her handwriting. If illegible handwriting is in evidence, then objectives of instruction need to be developed and implemented so that the child becomes a writer of legible content.

Pupils should feel successful in ongoing experiences. Thus, a pupil is making progress over his previous work in handwriting. Learners should not be compared with each other in legible handwriting. Why? Pupils individually are at different achievement levels in using neuromuscular skills. Teachers need to develop interest within pupils in achieving at a higher level in handwriting. Three kinds of objectives need to be stressed in handwriting. These are knowledge objectives whereby pupils have the needed content about legible letters, words, phrases, sentences and paragraphs to write in a illegible way; skills objectives whereby learners use what has been learned; and attitudinal objectives in which learners develop positive feelings in wanting to improve over previous levels in handwriting.

More specifically, objectives of instruction in handwriting should achieve the following :

1. how to form letters legibly.
2. how to align letters appropriately.
3. how to space letters and words properly.
4. how to stress proper proportion of letters within words.
5. how to achieve overall legibility in written discourse.
6. how to appraise the self in the quality of handwriting

exhibited.

7. how to emphasize neatness in all written products as final copies.

Skills objectives should emphasize the following :

1. form letters and' words illegibly.
2. align letters and words properly.
3. appropriate proportion of letters and words.
4. proper spacing of letters and words.
5. self-evaluation in achievement in general as well as specific skills in handwriting.
6. neatness in the handwriting arenas.

Attitudinal objectives for pupils to achieve should place importance on the following :

1. desiring to improve in the area of handwriting.
2. wanting to improve in the area of letter formation.
3. developing positive attitudes toward having proper proportion.
4. feeling a need to space words and letters properly.
5. voluntarily assessing personal achievement in handwriting.
6. emphasizing neatness in activities involving handwriting.
7. respecting the progress of others in handwriting.

There needs to be proper balance among understandings, skills and attitudinal objective in handwriting. Pupils do need knowledge pertaining to what makes for quality handwriting, but the knowledge needs to be implemented as skills. Hopefully, positive feelings as attitudes within learners will develop as a result.

Quality Handwriting Across the Curriculum

Good handwriting that is legible needs to be stressed throughout the different curriculum areas in the school setting.

Thus in mathematics, written work of pupils becomes difficult to evaluate unless good handwriting is there. Good handwriting needs to infiltrate numerals written as well as story or words problems composed by learners. Reports written such as biographies of famous mathematicians provide more opportunities to have pupils practice proper handwriting skills.

In science, pupils individually or in committees may write up the results of a science experiment, a method of procedure in doing an experiment, a report written on a self selected topic in science, bar or line graphs developed on temperature readings on a daily basis, notes written on content read in science from a well known encyclopedia, an outline written from a variety of reference sources in science, criteria written on being an effective member of a discussion group in science, as well as summaries on main ideas obtained from a video tape.

In social studies, pupils may write business letters to order free and inexpensive materials pertaining to an ongoing unit of study, friendly letters to pen pals, generalizations involving content read from diverse reference sources, relevant facts in reaction to a question raised by pupils in the classroom, as well as announcements to other classes to come to visit the pupil's classroom to observe completed projects related to an ongoing unit of study in social studies. Additional learning opportunities involving handwriting in the social studies include the following:

1. Speaking parts for pupils involving early days of Puritans in the New World.
2. Directions written for making a relief of the continent being studied in the social studies.
3. Standards may be written for evaluating an oral report.
4. An outline might be written to cover content pertaining to conclusions reached on an important selection read from social studies materials.
5. Hypothesis written involving one or more hypotheses written in a problem solving activity.
6. Notes taken on a selection in reading in the social studies.

In the literature curriculum, there are many opportunities for pupils to practice handwriting, including the following :

1. Labeling objects in the classroom in a reading readiness program.
2. Using handwriting texts as the need arises, such as for a model in the writing curriculum.
3. Developing experience charts written by pupils with teacher guidance in a reading readiness class.
4. Writing ideas involving reading for a variety of purposes, such as from critical reading, reading to follow directions, factual reading, reading for a sequence of ideas, creative reading, reading for main ideas and reading to develop generalizations.
5. Pupils need ample time to do practice forming letters correctly, writing letters and words with proper alignment, slanting letters correctly, spacing words and letters properly and using proper proportion of letters.
6. Pupils with teacher guidance need adequate time to write news articles. The resulting newsletter could be sent home weekly, bi-weekly, or monthly on important happenings in class.

In the health curriculum, the following writing experiences involve handwriting :

1. Learners may take notes on a talk given by a physician pertaining to improved health practices in everyday living.
2. Main ideas might be written on a set of slides or illustrations presented by a registered nurse on improving healthful living in the community.
3. Each pupil might write a personal experience chart pertaining to content from a filmstrip related to a facet of healthful living.
4. Letters may be written to the city council making recommendations on improving a polluted area.
5. Menus may be written for a week on implementing

balanced diets in the school lunch program.

6. Business letters may be written to order free and inexpensive materials relating to an ongoing health unit of instruction.

Conclusion

Handwriting errors certainly may cause spelling errors. The teacher needs to do much diagnosing to ascertain why pupils misspell words in writing. Writing needs to be emphasized in all curriculum areas. Improved communication results when quality spelling and handwriting are involved. Courtesy is also inherent when the learner exhibits the best spelling and handwriting in ongoing contextual writing activities. Purposeful writing experiences propel pupils to put forth effort to attain worthwhile objectives. Quality knowledge, skills and attitudes as three categories of objectives should be achieved by pupils. Pupils need to practice much writing so that increased proficiency is in evidence. The writer has treated spelling and handwriting within the broader perspective of writing. Spelling and handwriting skills can best be developed in context within the writing activity. Successful learners in writing will increase their abilities in spelling and handwriting. Careful selection of objectives, learning opportunities and evaluation procedures need to be in the offing.

References

Ediger, Marlow (1998), "Goals of Reading Instruction", *Experiments in Education*, published by the SITU Council of Educational Research (in India), 11–19.

Ediger, Marlow (1988), *Language Arts Curriculum in the Elementary School*, Kirksville, Missouri : Simpson Publishing Company, 73–81.

Dolch, Edward W. (1955), *Methods in Reading*. Champaign, Illinois: Garrard Publishing Company.

Mehlinger, Howard D., "The Next Step", *Electronic School*, A22–A24.

12
Reading and Literature for Children

There are many reasons for emphasizing a quality literature curriculum for children. Reading instruction too frequently has centered upon word recognition skills such as using phonics, syllabication, structural analysis, context clues, picture clues and configurational clues. It is important for pupils to possess these word recognition skills to identify unknown words. But quality literature has more to offer than word recognition skills. Also, thinking skills are stressed such as critical and creative thinking, problems solving, as well as reading to obtain facts, concepts and generalizations. However, important these thinking skills are and they are indeed important, literature for children incorporates, but goes beyond these skills (Ediger, 1997).

Why Children's Literature ?

There are many excellent reasons as to why there should be a good children's literature curriculum in the school setting. First, pupils may experience life vicariously. No one would wish to experience whatever life had to offer directly in all of its manifestations. There are too many negative occurrences which one definitely would prefer not to experience. These items include being robbed, fired from a job, death of a loved one, harsh climates for a long period of time, poverty and other negative happenings. However, pupils may experience these occurrences in a vicarious way. We learn from the experience of others. One's life consists of experiences which makes possible for new ways to respond and live. There are many choices to be made and the arena of decision making increases in options as more possibilities are in the offing. Reading then provides opportunities for vicarious experiences. These vicarious experiences might limit the negative that can occur to an individual. They do provide more indirect experiences which might be used in the decision-making arenas. Thus, there are things that one does not want to experience directly, but in a wholesome manner the experiences can be read about.

Second, choices are made in life involving standards to be used in relating to others. Values are involved in decision making. These values can be dictated to children. Many times dictated values do not work. If pupils live without a set of guiding principles they may falter and fail in possessing that which gives a person criteria or standard to live by (Leming,1996). Children's literature can deal with the values dimension in its many manifestations. Values are secured by learners from diverse sources and children's literature may make its numerous contributions here. Children's literature may make its numerous contributions here. Children's literature needs to meet needs of pupils from different backgrounds and cultures in the values dimension. Obtaining the interests of learners is important; otherwise pupils will not be engaged in reading about and considering various values. Pupils should reveal that core values are being achieved as they interact with pupils of different beliefs and religions. Pupils need to receive insight into the structure of values and how these may provide needed guidance in relating to others in school and in society. Learners may experience unique endeavours in learning about values such as in creative and formal dramatics, pantomime and socio-drama. Positive values studied and acquired through children's literature need to be used. Application needs to be made of knowledge, skills and attitudes achieved. The practical situation provides ample opportunities for pupils to use and make application of a values system.

Third, children's literature provides avenues for relaxation and recreation. We prize very highly the ability to read well. With reading, we are able to entertain ourselves and grow in appreciation for quality literature that has enduring values. These values will provide direction for us and they will be acquired through reading for recreation and relaxation. There certainly is a refreshing component when thinking of reading during one's leisure time. To spend even a few minutes of time in reading does help one to feel renewed with energy and purpose.

Each person needs to find ways of dealing with stress. Life can indeed be very stressful. Blessed is that person who finds ways that are effective in dealing with stress. Certainly, reading can be an approach in minimizing the stressful components of life. Children's literature may well provide that avenue. Teachers, supervisors and parents should make an all out effort to assist each pupil to read well so that recreational reading may become a relevant purpose.

Fourth, reading of children's literature can be a guidance resource. Difficulties are involved when facing problems. These problems need to be identified and relevant solutions sought. Literature for children might well be a vital resource to provide assistance in counselling and guidance. Pupils face diverse kinds of problems, such as extreme shyness, aggressive behaviour, hostility, negativeness, ill-health, obesity and loneliness among others. There are books written for children which can provide assistance in dealing with these kinds of problems. Bibliotherapy as a concept stresses using library books to deal with problems faced by pupils which seem overwhelming. Teachers and guidance counsellors need to be very familiar with the wealth of library books that might well assist pupils to cope with endearing problems. We have observed in classrooms whereby teachers have suggested library books to pupils which were very helpful in dealing with and even overcoming what seemed as a major problem. For example, a girl felt she was much too tall compared to others in the classroom. She did fit into the category of being tall. After reading several library books on how individuals coped with their feelings, this girl was better able to accept herself by using personal strengths possessed to achieve, grow and develop.

Fifth, pupils can become knowledgeable about different careers that are in the offing. Career selection can indeed be a problem for many young people. Career exploration is vital for any elementary school child. The learner needs to acquire information about different careers and what is involved here when moving on to the work place as an adult.

There are numerous quality library books on careers. One of us well remember supervising a student teacher and cooperating teachers in a classroom in which two pupils did extensive reading from library books to develop a career manual. The career manual written and illustrated for fourth grade pupils contained explanations of what training is involved for the careers being studied. Drawings were made of individuals involved in each career write-up. These two pupils interviewed individuals in diverse careers. Here, pupils revealed much purpose and interest in their study. Reading of library books was central to this project. These two learners were greatly interested in careers. Later on in the high school years and beyond, these same two boys found the world of work to be enjoyable and interesting. We recommend having plenty of library books out to assist pupils with reading in the vocational and work arenas.

To learn to read well, the pupil needs to read, study and think. We have noticed effective teachers do a good job of introducing carefully selected library books to children by telling some interesting aspects of these books. Also, numerous teachers have developed excellent bulletin board displays on library books in the classroom and centralized library which capture and fascinate learner interests and provide readiness of reading. The teacher also needs to be a good story teller so that pupils perceive sequence, plot, characterization, theme, point of view and setting. Both student teachers and cooperating teachers whom one of us have supervised have told about numerous good story tellers who have come to class and engaged in the telling of stories. Story telling seemingly motivates pupils to do more reading. Sometimes, the stories told have come from a library book in school. Many pupils then wish to read this library book.

Sixth, children's literature provides a springboard for creative thinking activities on the part of pupils. After pupils have completed reading a library book, learners volunteer to do a creative dramatics activity pertaining to the subject matter. Roles are selected and learners use speaking parts spontaneously without looking at print discourse. At other times pupils individually wrote parts from a library book read. Each pupil then might have a role to play in presenting content written as play parts. Creative dramatics has no written script but may be based on contents contained in a library book whereas formal dramatics had parts written down for each role. The parts may be memorized and presented to the class and other classrooms of children. Quality presentations have been developed whereby pupils orally read or speak their part in sequence with others in formal dramatization. Creativity knows few bounds when children's literature provides the basis for this learning opportunity.

Seventh, children's literature may be related directly to social studies, science, mathematics, the language arts, art, music and physical education (Templeton, 1995). There is literature written for pupils which pertains to each of these subject matter areas. In the social studies then, there are library books written on many nations on the face of the earth as well as on minority groups and diverse cultures. In science, library books on astronomy, geology, chemistry, physics and other areas other numerous in their offerings. In mathematics, library books are valuable on history of mathematics, uses of mathematics and biographies of famous mathematicians. In the language arts, there are fairy tales, myths, legends, tall tales, poetry and different novels written to meet needs of pupils. In art, music and physical education there are also interesting library books written. We always enjoy reading biographies of well known artists, musicians and basketball/football/baseball stars. There are library books written to meet interest and purpose needs of pupils as well as being on the diverse reading levels of individual pupils.

Each school needs to have ample library books in the offing which encourage reading and reflection on content read. Reading across the curriculum is an excellent concept to stress in the curriculum. One of the finest science units we observed as supervisors of student teachers and cooperating teachers stressed the title, "Our Changing Environment". Here, pupils read library books on that unit title instead of the basal science textbook. It was amazing how pupils contributed in the discussion pertaining to content read on volcanoes, hurricanes, tornadoes, wind and water erosion, as well as other natural disasters in the world of science. Pupils individually in their reading of library book content were able to relate ideas to the ongoing interaction and discussions. We wholeheartedly recommend teachers giving this procedure a try in unit teaching. Using a variety of approaches in teaching is challenging and brings in the new to pupils.

Pupils with teacher assistance need to understand and attach meaning to concepts such as setting of the story, characterization, plot, point of view, theme, irony of the situation, as well as satire. These literary concepts are used by novelists and writers in the world of literature (Ediger, 1988).

Teacher Self Evaluation in the Literature Curriculum

The teacher needs to be a good evaluator of the self in determining pupil achievement. We would suggest the following as guidelines for the teacher to assess his/her achievement in guiding optimal pupil achievement in children's literature :

1. The teacher should be an avid reader of literature, be it for children or for adults. Pupils need to realize that the teacher does much reading and does not operate on the principle that children alone are to do the reading of divers topics in literature.

2. There needs to be a literature program that is planned with an appropriate scope and sequence. A planned literature curriculum stresses that pupils read many library books on diverse topics and on unique individual levels of reading. The plan should include literature being emphasized across the different subject matter areas. Each unit of study taught should be integrated with library book content coming from different academic disciplines as well as from the vocational arenas. The literature curriculum should have its own objectives, carefully chosen, for pupil attainment.

3. The teacher needs to be fascinated with literature and indicate these interests to pupils. Here, the teacher may tell pupils about what he/she has read as it relates to what is being taught. In sharing time, the teacher might also indicate enthusiasm for reading in general. We believe enthusiasm to be very contagious. Pupil enthusiasm for

reading is motivating and stimulating to do further reading. A literate society is needed. Literacy can be stressed in any curriculum area (Ediger, 1997).

4. Pupils need to find pleasure in reading. Using leisure time wisely has been a goal of education for a long time. Wise use of leisure time is important. We would suggest that teachers work in the direction whereby reading literature becomes recreational as well as utility in emphasis. Pupils need to love reading in its diverse manifestations.

5. There needs to be rational balance between scheduled literature sessions as well as pupils reading during free time. We believe pupils need to be given ample time to read during spare time in school. Sustained Silent Reading (SSR) may also be emphasized. Here, everyone in school reads at a given time. Pupils then see models in reading to emulate. They may also notice how people of all ages become interested in reading library books and other kinds of reading materials. We have observed SSR being stressed with student teacher and cooperating teacher guidance. We believe it is one answer to problems in encouraging learner interest in reading. In SSR, individually select a library book to read. The learner, not the teacher, does the choosing of which books to read sequentially.

6. Ample time needs to be given for free reading in the classroom. Pupils do tend to enjoy reading when there is time for this activity. The free reading time may emphasize pupils choosing a library book relating to an ongoing unit of study. Thus, the free reading time relates directly to what is being studied in different curriculum areas. The learner may also choose a library book to read which is recreation in nature. With free time, pupils realize the values placed upon reading by the teacher and by the school. In most cases we have observed in supervising teachers in the schools, pupils do read and not waste time in and during free reading. The teacher may need to work with pupils who have difficulties in settling down to read sequential library books.

7. Pupils should read for both enjoyment and for information

(Templeton, 1997). Both can stress assisting pupils to do well in the affective dimension. Pupils then should develop wholesome attitudes toward reading. If pupils learn to dislike reading, the chances are they will not develop the necessary literacy qualities so necessary so necessary for the twenty-first century. We believe that most individuals read well if they understand what was read from an eighth grade reader. Eighth grade readers contain content such as Charles Dicken's *A Christmas Carol*, Robert Louis Stevenson's *Treasure Island* and Edigar Allen Poe's *The Gold Bug* among others. More critics of education should pick up an eighth grade reader to notice how complex some of the reading selections are. Many would discover that an individual reading on the eight grade level can read and comprehend many kinds of recreational and vocational writings. Of course, teachers need to work in the direction of having pupils achieve as much as possible in reading and in all curriculum areas. Reading across the curriculum is important !

8. There is considerable debate, among educators in the teaching of reading, between reading narrative versus expository materials. Previously, much stress has been placed upon pupils reading narrative materials such as fictional and story content which has a definite sequence or order of events. Presently many reading specialists are recommending pupils reading more of expository content. Expository content emphasizes informational books that pupils should read. The information is more reality based as compared to narrative accounts. Expository reading materials cut across diverse curriculum areas. For example, pupils may read library books on volcanoes, earthquakes, as well as wind/water erosion when studying a unit on "The Changing Surface of the Earth". Information read may relate directly to the unit in science being taught presently. These same topics may provide content for reading in SSR or an individualized reading program. Perhaps, a rational balance should be in the offing between narrative and expository reading materials.

9. The teacher should read orally to pupils each day of the

school week and year. Books chosen for reading aloud to pupils should develop interest, enjoyment and motivation in that the latter develop an inward desire to read. The teacher needs to face pupils and have good audience contact while reading aloud. Voice inflection with proper stress, pitch and juncture need to be in the offing when the teacher reads orally to pupils. Pupils might then desire to do more reading on their own. Both narrative and expository books should be read to elementary age pupils. Recently, there have been educators who recommend that secondary school teachers read aloud salient facets from textbook content to pupils so that comprehension is possible. Not all secondary school pupils are able to comprehend subject matter read from their basal textbooks.

10. Library books should be ample in number to provide for individual differences in the classroom. Pupils are at different levels of achievement in reading and therefore the teacher needs to be certain that gifted/talented, average achievers and slow readers have access to reading materials that are understandable and comprehendible. Accessibility is a key concept to emphasize when having pupils check out reading materials. Pupils should not feel frustrated in reading by having rigid requirements for checking out different library books.

It is very important for library books to reflect the different interests, tastes and abilities of pupils in the classroom. Each pupil should be able to locate sequential library books to read which are of appeal, feeling and provide for the different reading achievement levels of pupils in class. Library books should be shown to an briefly discussed with pupils so that there is a desire to read. The teacher needs to make certain that pupils realize that there is a library book to read for each and every pupil. No pupil is left out from being able to choose and read a library book. There are large illustrations with a small amount of print in numerous library books for those who face problems in reading well. For others, there is more print discourse in library books to provide for those who read at a higher level. There should also be library books to read for the talented and gifted.

Provision for individual differences is a must.

It is important for the teacher to reveal to pupils his/her love for reading. The attitudes and feelings possessed by teachers toward reading are generally indicated non-verbally to pupils. The teacher needs to be certain that the message sent to children is that quality attitudes and values pertaining to reading in its diverse manifestations is in evidence. Teacher enthusiasm for children's literature is a must !

If pupils are to read library books for follow-up conferences, the teacher needs to be well informed about the contents of each book, if at all possible. I have observed student teachers and cooperating teachers whom I supervised in the public schools have an excellent knowledge of literature for children. One teacher, in particular, used individualized reading in the curriculum. She felt that if follow up conferences with pupils were to be successful after the learner has completed reading a library book, the teacher needs to be well versed on the contents of each book read by children in the classroom. This teacher had a good file of four by six inch cards in which key ideas were printed about each library book in the classroom. Her thinking was if pupils were to have quality conferences, the teacher needs to be well versed in organizing content of the book, completed by the pupil and discussed in a literary setting. I agree wholeheartedly. Teachers who have good knowledge of individual library books tend to enjoy reading and they do read much children's literature. Some of these teachers should teach a class in children's literature on a university campus. So often, I hear negative comments from university students on the quality of the children's literature course. An elementary teacher may be able to do a better job of preparing future teachers for the literature curriculum. One of my cooperating teachers mentioned one time that our student teachers did not read well orally to pupils during the student teaching program. In my Teaching of Language Arts class, immediately added a requirement for the course in that student were to read a section from a children's library books using appropriate criteria. These criteria included having eye contact with pupils when reading aloud, showing the illustrations inside the library book to pupils as the related oral reading activity proceeds, observing pupils to notice engagement with the subject matter as it is being read and pronouncing words clearly and accurately when reading orally. I like feedback from cooperating teachers in public schools who have suggestions to give to improve the curriculum. (Ediger).

Evaluating Pupil Progress in Children's Literature

One of the first things that a teacher needs to do in the classroom is to observe individual pupils reading library books. Pupils must read continuously if they are to become proficient in reading. Reading content in the basal reader and other materials of print discourse requires skill, knowledge and quality attitudes. With practice in reading diversity of materials, the pupil certainly will increase abilities to read. The pupil needs to develop a positive attitude toward reading. There are numerous ways of doing this. One way is to have pupils listen to the teacher read orally with appropriate stress, pitch and juncture as well as using good audience contact. By observing learners, the teacher may notice how well pupils like what is being read. Feedback from pupils here is important. Another way is for the teacher to show pupils newly arrived library books and have pupils hypothesize as to what the contents might be. The teacher then should observe which of these books pupils chose to read on their very own. We recommend that pupils in a small group take turns reading a library books among themselves. One pupil may start to read aloud, followed by others. A creative teacher finds ways of getting pupils interested in reading alongwith developing positive attitudes toward reading. Developing an appreciation for reading children's literature is an important goal for pupil's to attain.

Reading widely on diverse subject matter areas is salient for learners. Pupils individually need to experience ideas and content on diverse topics. It might be all right for pupils to read on a single topic initially to develop a desire in learning to read, but the content read needs to be broadened so that learners will find themselves more fully in a job or in life outside the work place. Thus, each pupil should find his niche in life to the best possible. A quality resource may be exploration through literature written for children. There are books written on different vocations for pupils, as well as those that assist pupils to achieve selected values and the ability to solve problems. This is continuous and ongoing throughout life. Reading on a variety of topics then is important for pupils. Hopefully, the enjoyment ingredient will be there in processes involving reading.

When supervising student—teachers and cooperating teachers, we pupils very informally why they chose a certain book to read. Pupils answer with giving purposes such as the following:

1. I like to read about dinosaurs.
2. I enjoy reading about famous people in history, but I do like to read also about people of other lands.
3. I choose books about farming first, maybe its because my grand-parent still live on the farm.
4. My favourite library books are those that emphasize fishing and fish. My father and I go fishing very frequently in summer.
5. I read on almost any topic since I enjoy reading.

There are many purposes involved in reading. Pupil purpose is important when he/she chooses library books to read. Pupils who have narrow interests in reading as reading skills permit should be encouraged to select a wider variety of topics when choosing library books to read. A broadly educated child should be in the offing so that he/she has more options available for decision making. However, the teacher should never minimize pupils individually reading for sheer enjoyment. Pupils may need assistance to make sense out of what is being read.

From skills developed in more formal reading programs, the child should be able to identify unknown words, especially in the use of context clues and initial consonant sounds. Then too, there are times when words need to be pronounced directly to the reader. Hopefully, there will be a short time elapse for the child to determine what the unknown word is. Independent readers is an important goal for the teacher to stress. This includes word recognition skills that are developed as well as meanings attached to content read. An ultimate goal should be for pupils to reflect upon what has been read. Analyzing content in terms of reality versus fantasy, accurate from inaccurate ideas and cognitive versus the feeling dimension needs emphasis in the literature curriculum. Hopefully, pupils will become more creative in interpretation of content read. There are numerous interpretations that can be made of content read. Then too, learners should be able to bring to bear relevant solutions to personal and social problems faced. Attaching meaning to subject matter is so very important. What is written by an author may have an agenda or personal bias and the reader needs to interpret to perceive understanding of the ideas presented in print discourse. Certainly, the pupil should be able to make use of and apply what has been learned. Use and applications can be made in ongoing social studies, science, mathematics and English units taught.

Metacognition is important for pupils to engage in. With metacognition, the pupil monitors his/her achievement in comprehension as the reading activity progresses. The child then does not read words only, but the words read mean something and it is up to the learner to bring forth meanings as abilities and progress indicate. Organization of content read is important such as sequence, main ideas, subordinate ideas and details. Thus, in metacognition, the pupil monitors or evaluates on a personal basis if comprehension is occurring and main ideas are clarified from subordinate ideas. It is important for all people who read to be able to clarify with self check the progress that is being made in reading comprehension. There are pupils and undergraduate students in universities who believe that if they have "read" the content that is all there is to reading. In other words, merely pronouncing the words and then *ipso facto* they have understood content read is a grave misinterpretation of what reading is all about. Reading is a process that involves understanding and applying what has been read. There are many criteria then that teachers should use to appraise the quality of pupils' reading children's literature.

Conclusion

We, as teachers, can assist learners to achieve in an optimal manner in reading achievement, be it in a formal or informal approaches in teaching and learning. When pupils are taught in formal reading, such as in the use of basal textbooks, they should be assisted individually and in groups to provide for continual progress and achievement. When choosing library books, pupils individually select and sequence their very own progress and achievement.

References

Ediger, Marlow (1995), *Philosophy in Curriculum Development.* Kirksville, Missouri : Simpson Publishing Company, 13–15.

Ediger, Marlow (1997), *Teaching Reading and the Language Arts in the Elementary School.* Kirksville, Missouri : Simpson Publishing Company, 141–42.

Ediger, Marlow (1988), *Language Arts Curriculum in the Elementary School.* Kirksville, Missouri : Simpson Publishing Company, 103.

Leming, James (1996), "Teaching Values in Social Studies Education: Past Practices and Future Possibilities", in *Critical Issues in Teaching Social Studies*, Massialas and Allen, Editors. Belmont, California : Wadsworth Publishing Company, 145–50.

Templeton, Shane (1995), *Children's Literacy.* Boston : Houghton Mifflin Company, 27.

Templeton, Shane (1997), *Teaching the Integrated Language Arts.* Boston : Houghton Mifflin Company, 209.

13
Reading and Vocabulary Development

Developing a rich listening, speaking, reading and writing vocabulary is important in all curriculum areas. In the reading curriculum, in particular, a quality vocabulary needs to be achieved by each pupil. One reason that pupils do not read well is that they do not possess a functional vocabulary for reading. Enriching and developing pupil vocabularies should be a major goal in each academic discipline. The following are reasons for teachers guiding leaners to possess a rich vocabulary :

1. Subject matter and ideas are expressed with more clarity and accuracy.
2. Proficiency in the work place might well depend upon individuals having a quality vocabulary.
3. Individuals seemingly have more prestige if their listening, speaking, reading and writing vocabularies are adequately developed.
4. Greater enjoyment of reading is in the offing if a person has a rich functional vocabularies.
5. Vocabulary development is salient in problem solving. A person with a rich vocabulary should have a better opportunity to develop his/her vocabularies.
6. Conversations carried on with other persons require a rich vocabulary. There needs to be an appropriate number of words used that carry intended meanings.
7. Variety in selecting words to convey accurate meanings is necessary in speaking and writing, the outgoes of the language arts.

8. Use of diverse terms and concepts in speaking and writing adds variety to quality communication. Vocabulary development becomes a tool to take in, such as listening and reading, as well as provide communication to others within the framework of speaking and writing.

Very closely related to the background knowledge required for reading a text is vocabulary knowledge.....By about the third grade and certainly by the fourth grade, most of the selections of the newer reading programs are drawn from independently published materials, as compared to selections created by a publisher for inclusion in their series. The newer basals are virtually anthologies. Authors of the selections are professional writers using the best words available from the general vocabulary to communicate their ideas. Thus, the kind of vocabulary control found in the older basals is not in evidence in current programs. The sophisticated vocabulary in the selections from the newer basals has both positive and negative potential for students. The negative potential is obvious—too many unfamiliar words will cause comprehension problems. The positive potential is also obvious—children can add words to their store of vocabulary.

Vocabulary development strategies created for each story lesson begin with the identification of a subset of words that developers believe may cause meaning or decoding difficulty. These words are listed in the teacher's manuals. By the third or fourth grade the programs assume competent decoding : most of the words noted in the teacher's manuals are of the meaning variety difficulty. These words become "target words" for vocabulary development activities. Traditionally, the development of word meaning is attended to by instructional events that occur prior to reading, during reading and after reading.... (Beck, 1984).

Developing the Vocabulary of Learners

The reading teacher needs to select quality objectives for pupils to achieve in the areas of vocabulary development. These objectives need to emphasize that is relevant and functional in vocabulary development. Certainly, pupils should be able to use what has been learned. Learning should not be for its own sake but rather be for personal use and application in society. Important vocabulary terms should be acquired by pupils. Adequate time must be given in choosing what pupils need to learn in vocabulary development. This cannot be hurried, because vocabulary development emphasizes that which must be learned in depth, not survey approaches.

Objectives pertaining to vocabulary development need to stress securing the interests of pupils in ongoing lessons and units of study. Ways of developing and maintaining pupil interest in learning must be emphasized in vocabulary studies. If pupils do not reveal interest in learning, they will not achieve as optimally as possible.

There needs to be objectives reflecting pupils working collaboratively. Within the cooperative endeavour, pupils listen to others and use oral communication with opportunities to achieve in vocabulary development. There are definite social goals here in that pupils need to learn to work harmoniously with others. And yet pupils also should be able to work by the self and achieve on an individual basis.

Vocabulary development emphasizes that pupils seek purpose in learning. Purposeful learning in vocabulary development means that pupils perceive reasons for learning. I think that one cannot stress too strongly that vocabulary development for pupils should have as a goal that purpose is involved in learning. Purposeful learnings have as a goal that pupils perceive the values inherent in vocabulary activities. If these values are lacking, the teacher should stress other vocabulary development lessons for learners.

Objectives in vocabulary development need to emphasize the importance of meaningful learnings. If meaning is lacking, the chances are pupils will memorize terms and concepts for testing purposes only or largely. Meaning stresses the importance of pupils understanding that which has been learned. Use cannot be made of a new vocabulary term unless understanding of prerequisites in vocabulary terms is prevalent. With prerequisites, background information is needed to attach meaning to vocabulary terms being studied.

Objectives in vocabulary development for pupils should emphasize pupils experiencing the concept of providing for individual differences. There are pupils who learn more rapidly that others while some pupils take more time to learn the same content/skills as written in the statement of objectives. Each pupil regardless of socio-economic level must be accepted as a human being and taught in a manner which provides for all pupils.

Learning Opportunities to Achieve Objectives

To achieve vital objectives in vocabulary development, the teacher needs to select worthwhile activities for pupils. These activities need to be selected carefully so that each pupil's achievement is as optimal as possible. Pupils should not be labeled as being fast, average, or slow learners. Rather all should be accepted and develop feelings of belonging to the group.

To achieve objectives in vocabulary development, We recommend selected learning opportunities that student teachers and cooperating teachers whom we supervise have used successfully.

Each day the teacher should read aloud to pupils during story time. The book chosen should interest pupils and keep their attention. Voice inflection using proper stress, pitch and juncture should be in the offing when the teacher reads during story time. Words should be pronounced clearly and accurately. The teacher should have good audience contact with listeners. For young children, it is especially good to show the book's illustrations to pupils as the library book is being read. Throughout the story time activity, pupils should understand an increased number of facts, concepts and generalizations. Knowledge received provides background information for more complex ideas that should be forthcoming. Knowledge is sequential and cumulative for learners. A love for learning by pupils might be a further end result when the teacher reads orally to pupils during story time.

A second activity stressed pupils discussing ideas obtained from listening to the library book read or from personal reading pursued. Through discussion participation, pupils should learn effective ways of working within a small or large group setting. Pupils should learn to be polite, accepting and cooperative in the discussion learning activity. Being a good listener, valuing the thinking of others and actively participating in a polite manner should help a discussion to move forward in quality. Thus, the processes of being a member of a discussion group need to be emphasized continuously.

Then too, during the discussion, pupils should achieve quality ideas, facts, concepts and generalizations. Learners need to stay on the topic to achieve subject matter learnings during a discussion. Straying from the topic at hand merely wastes time. Ideas need to circulate within the group so that all have opportunities to participate. Active participation by each pupils should be an objective. Use of language during a discussion helps pupils to achieve more optimally in speaking. This translates content acquired to be used to comprehend subject matter in reading. The content and vocabulary gained by the learner might then provide background information for reading. Generally, what pupils are able to discuss represents meaningful subject matter. The subject matter might then provide the necessary knowledge, prior to reading, which helps pupils to understand increasingly complex vocabulary read.

Third, it is good to have once or more listening centers in the classroom. There are excellent cassette tapes related to an ongoing lesson on unit of study. Information gleaned from listening to a tape may guide pupils to answer related questions contained at the center. The information might well assist pupils to use this as background content to understand better what will be read from a basal or library book.

At the listening center, pupils may choose sequential tapes to listen to, for a variety of purposes. These purposes might well be the following in listening for :

1. facts, concepts and generalizations.
2. information to use in problem solving.
3. critical thinking purposes such as separating facts from opinions, accurate from inaccurate information and fantasy from reality.

4. opportunities to do creative thinking in the reading curriculum such as coming up with novel, unique ideas and originality in thought.
5. obtaining directions in reaching a certain place.
6. securing a main idea when relating facts, concepts and generalizations.
7. obtaining the setting of a story.
8. securing ideas pertaining to characterization within a writing.
9. determining the plot of a selection in reading.
10. understanding the theme of the speaker.

Fifth, the reading teacher needs to have one or more speaking centers in the classroom. Listening (discussed above) and speaking are interrelated. We will mention some activities here that emphasize speaking more than listening.

1. Giving oral reports on library books read, related directly to the ongoing lesson and unit of study being taught. The oral report should follow good sequence in content presented. The ideas need to be presented clearly and at an appropriate rate of speed so that listening comprehension is optimal. The pupil presenting the oral book report needs to have the content well in mind. An outline, in proper form, should be used to convey the contents therein. The presenter of the book report should have good eye contact with the audience. Reading for enjoyment and for solving problems are two purposes in having pupils become proficient in reading.
2. Having pupils video-tape their individual oral book reports given to the class. Here, pupils individually or with a peer may appraise the quality of the oral report given. Standards used to appraise may be the same as under number two above. The contents of the videotape may also evaluate distracting mannerisms of the speaker such as rubbing the nose excessively. It is good to have the presenter appraise the quality of his/her own oral report in terms of quality

standards. Vocabulary terms are developed from the reading of library books as well as from the oral presentations given of library book content.

3. Interacting with audio-visual materials to locate information for problem solving. The AV materials may include video-tapes, CD ROMS, films, filmstrips, large illustrations, snapshots enlarged for class viewing with an opaque projector, internet and worldwide web, as well as computer packages. Among others. With pupil interaction with AV materials of instruction, there are many opportunities to gather information for a committee project such as developing a mural. The mural must be planned cooperatively with all participating and no one dominating collaborative endeavours. After the planning, the implementation of the plan comes in sequence. With implementation, each pupil on the committee does his/her fair share of the work. The project represents the best work each pupil can do. Thus, neatness, accuracy and attractiveness become key ingredients when appraising the mural. Art work correlates well with reading. Through art, pupils may reveal what has been learned. Vocabulary development is definitely inherent in planning, implementing and appraising the project.

Sixth, ample emphasis should be placed upon pupils doing much writing. With writing, pupils read their own written products as well as read those of other learners whose works are posted on the bulletin board. Reading and writing cannot be separated from each other but are complimentary. There are numerous forms of written work that pupils may engage in. Journal entries should be written freely to indicate what had been learned in a given lesson. Diary entries may be written each day and should be dated. These diary entries portray what pupils learned for a day. As pupils write these diary entries, they read written content. In this way pupils also review that which was learned previously from reading and re-reading diary entries covering subject matter learned. Additional written work may included the following :

1. **Logs**—logs summarize what was contained in diary entries for one week. Clarity of ideas and proper sequence is important in writing logs.

2. **Book reports**—these relate to an ongoing lesson or unit of study. Meaningful content in an appropriate order must be inherent in the written work.

3. **Outlines**—here proper style needs to be used such as Roman numerals to indicate main ideas, capital letters in sequence to indicate subordinate ideas and Hindu-Arabic numerals to reveal details. The subordinate ideas relate directly to the main ideas whereas the details tell more about the subordinate content. Outlines are very helpful to use in giving a report on a certain topic to classmates. Thus, the oral report will have improved sequence to ideas presented as well as if the pupil forgets certain ideas, the outline is there to aid memory in oral communication.

3. **Poems**—poetry written in any lesson should relate to an ongoing lesson or unit of study. There are opportunities for pupils to write poetry in each curriculum area. There can be unrhymed verse written such as free verse. Or poetry written may contain rhyme such as couplets, triplets, quatrains and limericks. Poetry written may also include a selected number of syllables per line such as Haiku (5-7-5 syllables for each of three sequential lines). Tanka contains 5-7-5-7-7 syllables per line for each of five lines.

It is quite obvious that there are many writing opportunities for pupil pertaining to each curriculum area and within each lesson taught. Pupils engage in much reading, re-reading and proofreading when engaging in writing experiences. Vocbaulary development opportunities are numerous.

Seventh, pupils may engage in developing a dictionary Even though there are pictured dictionaries, grade level dictionaries, unabridged dictionaries, as well as glossaries in basal textbooks, it can be highly profitable for pupils individually or in committees to develop their very own dictionaries. Why? Perhaps, there are many new words brought into the lesson or unit of study by the teacher. It is good to alphabetize these new words and write meaningful definitions for each. Dictionary entries need to be functional so that they may be used as needed to obtain contextual information. It is good for pupils to be able to alphabetize and re-read the necessary entries.

Eighth, pupils and the teacher should engage in story telling activities. Content for the story needs to follow a certain order to be meaningful to the listener. Thus, sequence of ideas in story telling is important ! A clear speaking voice with proper enunciation helps the oral presentation to be more effective. Having a pleasant speaking voice with quality eye contact with listeners assists in the communicaiton of the story. When pupils hear stories told, especially pertaining to a specific library book at an interest center, interest in reading that book tends to be generated. Background experiences are also developed within pupils for reading additional books in ongoing lessons and units of study.

When engaging in story telling, pupils should be developing poise and gracefulness in the process. Pupils need ample opportunities to appear before others in informal and formal experiences. No doubt, skills and attitudes are being developed here that will have life-long values and worth. Shy pupils, in particular, need to appear before others in a variety of roles so that feelings of poise and worth are inherent. The confidence that can come from these experiences might well have carry over values to other endeavours.

Tenth, reading co-operatively in small groups can provide much enjoyment and interest in literature. Being with others is a favourite leaning style of selected individuals. They prefer to work together rather than working on an individual basis. Pupils too receive practice in reading. Cumulative practice should make for increased knowledge, skills and attitudes toward reading. With co-operative reading, three or four pupils may take turns reading a library book. If one copy only of a library book is available, sequential pupils may read aloud as the others in the group listen carefully to the contents. The contents may also be tape recorded so that individual pupils may re-read the library book. Then, if a word is not known in identification, the recorded voice provides the needed information.

If multiple copies of a library book are available, the small group of three or four pupils may follow along in their own library book as the sequential oral reading takes place. Thus, one person reads aloud as the others in the committee follow along in their own library book. Shared reading experiences has many intrinsic rewards for pupils. There should also be ample opportunities for those who like individual endeavours to read a book by themselves.

Eleventh, there should be many objects and items at an interest center whereby pupils may discuss each. I have observed many aquariums and terrariums in classrooms which provide stimulating situations for pupils to provide content for an experience chart. Sometimes a teacher has numerous potten plants in the classroom which may provide pupils an oppportunity for informal conversation and also ideas for an experience chart. A rich learning environment helps pupils to think about the contents. The resulting ideas assist pupils to use oral language, engage in written work, read about similar situations or subject matter and/or listen to the thinking of others. A stimulating environment needs to be in the offing so that pupils have purposes for engaging in reading and language arts activities. For example, on the early primary grade level, pupils may observe and experience objects on an interest center. They may then provide content to the teacher who in return prints in neat manuscript letters what pupils have said and discussed. After the write-up of the contents, the pupils with the teacher pointing to words and phrases being read may comprehend the ideas presented int his experience chart. This approach is sound in that :

1. pupils have the background information to begin with by looking at and discussing objects at the center.
2. pupils present ideas for the experience chart. Learners then have chances to speak and to listen to others. What is said should be meaningful since it is based upon personal experiences of pupils. When the techer points to words and phrases, he/she together with pupils read orally content from the experience chart. Here, young learners should be developing an enriched vocabulary with a larger basic sight vocabulary. These sight words become the building blocks for future reading activities. The contents of the experience chart may be re-read as pupils desire. Many pupils like to read over again what has been read

previously. Practice here assists pupils to retain basic sight words better than would otherwise be the case.

Twelfth, a quality spelling program should help pupils to become better readers. There are numerous places where spelling words in vocabulary developemnt may come from for pupils to master. Individualized spelling stresses learners mastering a reasonable number of words that come from what was missed in spelling words correctly from every day writing occurrences. The teacher needs to decide here how many of these misspelled words can be spelled correctly within a week or whatever the designated time would be. Words may also come from a quality basal spelling text, new words in a lesson for pupils to master as listed in the basal reader, words that research states are important for pupils to master in spelling such as the Dolch list (1955). As pupils practice the correct spelling of words, they are becoming involved in vocabulary development and reading. learners need to see print as often as feasible in order to become good readers. Spelling need not be dull and dry with memorization of words. Rather pupils should experience interesting activities by;

1. using these words in writing letters to parents and friends, devleloping a related cross word puzzle and playing games with peers.
2. working with peers in learning to spell words correctly. Co-operative learning may be a preferred style of learning for selected pupils.
3. pantomiming the meaning of selected words. This could involve the playing of charades whereby a pupil chooses a word for spelling at random from a box, pantomimes it and then asks others in the classroom to identify which word is involved.
4. dramatizing the spelling word. A pupils may select a spelling word at random and use puppets or marionettes to dramatize its meaning. Classmates may guess what the spelling word is. Creative dramatics may also be used. Here, the pupil chooses a word at random from a box and uses words and actions to indicate which word is being

focused upon. The word wanted is not mentioned orally in the creative dramatics presentation. Several pupils could also be involved in this activity.

How much of the spelling curriculum should stress inductive and how much deductive thinking? We would suggest a balance between the two appraoches. Thus, when using a spelling textbook in teaching, the teacher assigns words for pupils to master. This is a deductive approach. Furthermore, the teacher has pupils learn a strategy for learning to spell these words such as:

1. looking at the spelling word carefully.
2. saying the word accurately.
3. saying clearly the parts of the word, such as pronouncing each syllable carefully and accurately.
4. writing the new word without looking at it.
5. comparing the written word with that contained in the basal spelling textbook.

The teacher here is empahsizing a deductive method of spelling words correctly. Why is this a deductive approach? The teacher has determined what and how pupils are to learn.

An inductive approach stresses pupils being involved in curriculum devleopment such as, pupils seeing how many homonyms or synonyms to find in a homonym/synonym hunt. Pupils might have suggested this activity when studying a unit containing a few of these words. Also, the teacher may have suggested the activity and pupils individually or on teams volunteered to see how many could be found. The sky is the limit in the number to be located. Perhaps, the teacher needs to have a balance between deductive versus inductive approaches in having pupils learn in the area of spelling. If a basal spelling text is used and there are a few rhyming words in a weekly list, pupils could locate additional ones to go along with those given in an inductive approach in learning. With a deductive procedure, the teacher may challenge gifted learners with additional words to master in spelling in addition to those listed in the text. By studying the correct spelling of words, pupils should increase their skills in vocabulary development and reading.

Thirteenth, we recommend pupils learn to spell relevant words contained in computer packages. There are drill and practice activities, tutorial, gaming and games, simulation and diagnostic/remedial packages. Reading teachers need to evaluate each package carefully to determine which relevant words in spelling pupils should master. Use should be made of spelling words for retention to take place. Spelling words may be used to write;

1. friendly and business letters.
2. notices, announcements, plays, reports, poems and stories.
3. names and addresses.
4. birthday greetings and holiday messages.
5. notes of sympathy and condolence.

As pupils participate in these writing activities, they need to proof-read content. The skills of reading are very much in evidence then. The spelling curriculum should be based upon words that pupils need to learn to spell. The needs of pupils are very important when developing any curriculum area. Beyond the goals of learning to spell words correctly are skills in reading for a vareity of purposes that should be upper most in the minds of learners. Narrative, expository and creative writing should all be emphasized in ongoing lessons and units of study. Vocabulary development is an essential part in any listening, speaking, achieve as optimally as possible in vocabulary development and its related component—reading.

What then should be guidelines to use in assisting pupils in vocabulary development?

1. Word study should be integrated with prior knowledge and with learning in the content areas.
2. Word study should involve intensive "deep" study of some words, involving many exposures to the words in meaningful contexts, both in and out of texts.

3. Teachers should engage in direct teaching or modelling, talking explicitly about word meaning and structure.
4. Students should be actively involved in instruction; an important side effect of this involvement is the development of favourable attitudes toward words and word learning.
5. Students shoiuld be taught strategies for learning new words independently.
6. Teachers should introduce words in meaning "families" so that semantic and structural relationships among the words are made explicit.

These principles are more applicable at the intermediate grade levels and beyond, when student's cognitive development has advanced to the point where they can explicitly deal with increasing conceptual abstraction. Nonetheless, you will see aspects of these principles at work; in work study at the primary grade level as well....(Templeton, 1997).

Conclusion

There are numerous opportunities for pupils to engage in vocabulary development. Each curriculum area provides these learning activities to increase proficiency in the use of vocabulary terms. The teacher needs to establish objectives, learning opportunities and evaluation procedures within individual academic areas to guide pupils in acquiring a rich listening, speaking, reading and writing vocabulary. The objectives of instruction need to stress relevant, functional words for pupils to master. Learning opportunities in vocabulary development should assist pupils to achieve the stated objectives. These activities need to be interesting, purposeful and meaningful. Evaluation procedures to appraise learner performance in achieving objectives need to be valid, reliable, varied and encourage further learning.

In evaluation Ph.D. theses for Sri Ramakrishan Mission Vidayala College of Education in India, the author of the study listed the following sequence in vocabulary development (Ayyappan, 1997) :

The confrontation phase empahsizes the teacher presenting relevant data pertaining to the concepts as well as important related definitions. Students then generate questions pertaining to the concept or vocabulary term. Phase two is the concept information phase. Here, students compare the attributes given and relate them to form the concept of vocabulary terms taught. Learners discuss with other pupils the distinguishing features to identify the concept.

In phase three, the teacher obtains responses from pupils in a stimulating discussion. Pupils then identify similarities and differences from the information presented. Pupil hypotheses are then appraised involving the tentative concept. In phase four stressing the concept development phase, the teacher presents related tasks for pupils to complete pertaining to the concept stressed. Probing of pupil knowledge pertaining to a concept is important. References are also made to the textbook while discussing the concept. The major classroom interactions are :

1. Teacher interaction/introduction/informatin
2. Activities for pupils include media interaction, consulting text, and peer interaction whereas feedback includes evaluation and teacher interaction (Ayyappan 1997).

One of the finest procedures in vocabulary development, one of us have observed in supervising student teachers and cooperating teachers, was the Hilda Taba inductive method used with a class of sixth graders. Here, the two teachers had pupils view a filmstrip on *Life on a Manor*. The teachers, after having pupils view the contents in the filmstrip, asked:

1. Tell us in a single word or phrase what you learned from watching the filmstrip. The following responses were given by pupils; castles, moats, draw bridge, the mill for grinding grain, oxen pilling a plow, peasants cutting wheat by hand, peasant cottages, the three field approach in farming, fallow, boblemen, tournaments, page, knight, guilds, apprentice, master and wars.
2. How would you combine or join together the concepts you mentioned for number one above? Here, a vareity of

answers were given in and for an open-ended question. One grouping of vocabulary terms given by pupils was the following :

oxen pulling a plow, peasants curring wheat by hand, the three field appraoch in farming and fallow were joined together.

3. What name would you give to the joined together vocabulary terms? The answer provided was "cultivating the soil".

Refernces

Ayyappan, R. (1997), *Concept Development in Electronics at Higher Secondary Level.* Coimbatore, India : Bharathiar University, Ph.D. thesis.

Templeton, Shane 91997), *Teaching the Integrated Language Arts,* Second Edition, Boston : Houghton Mifflin Company, 287–88.

14
The Psychology of Teaching Reading

Teachers need to be aware of a psychology of teaching in reading and the language Arts. There are numerous psychologies available which provide guidance to the teacher in helping pupils learn. Behaviourism has its strong advocates in teaching and learning. So many educators and stated departments of education desire objectives to be stated precisely. Some advocate they be stated so precise that there is no leeway in determining what is to be taught. For example, the teacher could write as a behaviourally stated objective that pupils are to spell words correctly with 90% accuracy from unit ten in the basal spelling textbook.

After instruction, it can be measured by testing pupils if the behaviourally stated objective has been achieved.

Behaviourally stated objectives work better in some areas of the curriculum as compared to others. Note in the previous objective, it can be measured if a pupil has or has not ached the stated objective. If pupils are to write haiku poetry, the teacher can measure of consecutive lines have a 5-7-5 progression of syllables per line. But what about creativity ? Creativity should be at the heart of writing poetry. Behaviourism as a psychology of learning has a difficult time measuring pupil creativity in writing poetry.

Behaviourists like specificity in talking about knowledge. If we would say the room temperature is pleasant, the behaviourist would not be satisfied with that statement since a numerals is wanted to state precisely what the room temperature is, such as eighty degrees. Or the behaviourist would not be satisfied with a person saying he/she has a fever and having a high temperature reading. The behaviourist would want to know what the exact temperature reading was, such as 102 degrees.

Thus in teaching, the teacher writes behaviourally stated objectives, in measurable terms, prior to instruction. The teacher may state to pupils what they are to learn before instruction takes place. This provides security to pupils in that they know what is be learned without guessing. A teaching strategy needs to be developed to provide for individual differences so that all are attentive and can attain what is written inside the measurably stated objective. By stating ahead of time prior to instruction what is to be learned, pupils perceive purpose or reasons for achieving. There are behaviourists who advocate which inexpensive prizes pupils may obtain if they achieve what the behaviourally stated objective describes. After instruction, the teacher tests pupils to see if the objective describes. After instruction, the teacher tests pupils to see if the objective was achieved. Those achieving the objective may go on to the next sequential lesson. Those not being successful achievers may need a different teaching strategy so that objectives may be achieved.

The following are provided as examples of objectives for pupil achievement pertaining to vocabulary development in reading :

1. The pupil will orally present five definitions of the concept "animation", as it relates to stories in reading. Here, the teacher may measure if a pupils has/has not achieved this objective as a result of instruction.

2. The pupil will write a setting of a story containing at lest fifty words.

Behaviourally stated objectives should be written at different levels of complexity for pupils to achieve. The following are examples, starting with the lowest level of cognition or mental operations :

1. The pupil will give the names of eight parts of speech in the English language. This objective is on the *recall* or

memorization level.

2. The pupil will explain in his/her own words consisting of atleast fifty words the meaning of what is meant by the concept *plot* in a story. This objective is written on the meaning or understanding level.

3. The pupil will write a poem using the elements that make up a tanka poem. Here, the pupil applies or uses what has been learned previously.

4. The pupil will analyze an Editorial from a newspaper in terms of statements being factual versus opinions. Here, the pupil needs considerable background information to know if accounts in an editorial are factual or opinions.

5. The pupil will rewrite the Editorial, number four above, to indicate an explanatory account of a happening or an incident.

6. The pupil will indicate the value or worth of what was written in an explanatory approach, number five above. Here, the pupil is making a value judgement as to the affect of the writing upon the human population. This objective might even contain the number of words to be written by the learner.

Student teachers and cooperating teachers whom we supervised in the public schools have stated that lower cognitive levels of behaviourally stated objectives are easier to give pupils a pass or fail mark for achieving or not achieving. Certainly in objective number one above, all teachers would agree if a pupil can list in writing the eight parts of speech as a result of instruction. This is the lowest level of cognition ;and is a memory task. Objective number two is more difficult to assess in that answers will differ from pupil to pupil as to what a plot is in a story. To be sure, there will be some consensus or the objective is meaningless. Objective number three stresses pupils writing a tanka with a 5-7-5-7-7 progression per line, each indicating how many syllables are expected. The measuring of syllables per line, such as 5-7-5-7-7, is relatively easy for a teacher to do. However, to ascertain how much creativity there will be or is for the tanka makes for subjectivity in appraising progress. Objective number four is a complex objective to achieve. How complex it is for pupils to achieve this objective depends upon the difficulty of the reading materials. If there are many new words in the section or if the style of writing is unfamiliar to the child, the learners may experience problems in attempting to achieve objective number four. In addition to comprehending what has been read, the pupil also needs to possess background information in terms of subject matter in order to separate facts from opinions. There can be much subjectivity involved when one or more teachers evaluates pupil responses to objective number four. We will just briefly comment on numbers five and six.

Objective number five brings in much subjectivity for the teacher in knowing what is strictly an explanatory account of pupil writing when synthesizing information from objective number four. Objective number six certainly stress subjectivity in that the pupil is to explain the worth or value of explanatory writing product. We would suggest here to draw up a set of standards to appraise the explanatory writing. These standards to be used for evaluation could include the following:

1. The content is based upon current societal thought as to what is relevant. This standard does indicate it takes knowledge to understand concerns of society. It will be difficult to emphasize here what is relevant in society.

2. The content is comprehensive in covering diverse facets of what the public considers to be relevant. Subjectivity is involved in that the breadth of content written about can be broader or more limited. A minimum number of words could be written into objective number six in terms of pupil responses.

3. another evaluator may be asked to appraise the pupils' written responses and work out an agreement with the original evaluator as to what is relevant and has adequate breadth of content.

The use of behaviourally stated objectives is quite popular on the state level of instruction. About three out of four states in the union require the use of behaviourally stated objectives for instructional purposes in elementary, middle and senior high schools. Thus, there are many school systems in the United States that do use behaviourally stated objectives in the instructional arenas.

What have been the advantages in having used behaviourally stated objectives in teaching?

1. It has made educators more cognizant about having more precise objectives in teaching. Objectives can certainly be too broadly stated whereby they have little or not meaning, such as "To develop the democratic citizen". Perhaps, no one knows what pupils are to learn when viewing a vague objective such as this. Vague objectives provide no guidance to the teacher as to what is to be taught.

2. It has assisted educators in looking at objectives more thoroughly in terms of what is relevant. Why? High quality behaviourally stated objectives are time consuming to write and therefore, I believe, makes the writers conscious of the importance of what pupils are learning. If too many objectives need to be written, the chances are pupils are to learn isolated trivial facts. Good behaviourally stated objectives are clearly written and state vital subject matter that pupils are to learn.

3. The evaluation process is simplified in that either a person has/has not achieved, after instruction, what is written in the behaviourally stated objective. The teacher can be relatively certain that objectives have been achieved if written in a precise manner.

There seemingly is an opposite and equal reaction to any trend in education. Our personal objections are the following to behaviourally stated objectives :

1. They can make teaching to factual in subject matter stressed in that rote learning is emphasized. It is easiest to write behaviourally stated objectives that stress factual learnings for pupils.

2. We have noticed how difficult it is to write these kinds of objectives that stress higher levels of cognition. Living

in society require individuals be able to think critically and creatively as well as engage in problem solving. It takes knowledgeable and superb writers to encourage inclusion of these higher cognitive domain objectives.

3. It is very difficult to write attitudinal objectives in measurable terms. How would one write even a few behaviourally stated objectives in the affective, attitudinal domain ? Here is one example : The pupil will show interest in vocabulary development by volunteering each school day to look up the meaning of one/two concepts. The concepts will be written up in a special notebook.

Behaviourists recommend a logical curriculum in that the teacher sequences the order of objectives for pupils to achieve. These objectives are arranged in ascending order to difficulty from the easier to those gradually more complex, harmonizing with a pupil's individual stage of development. Learners too may achieve the individual objectives in an optimal manner based on differences in achievement among learners.

The Psychology of Learning Using Task Analysis

Related to behaviourism, there are strong advocates of a task analysis approach in teaching. Robert Gagne (1984) has been a strong advocate of the task analysis approach in planning for instruction. The eight sequential steps stress the following:

1. ***Signal learning.*** Classical conditioning is involved here in that pupils learn to respond to a stimulus that is neutral initially to a response. The Russian physiologist in the early 1900s conditioned a dog to salivate with the sound of a bell only. Prior to this occurrence, Pavlov noticed that dogs salivate with the sight and smell of meat. The meat (unconditioned stimulus) is the stimulus and the response by the dog is to salivate (unconditioned response). Next in sequence, Pavlov sounded a bell (conditioned stimulus) before and with the meat and, of course, the dog salivated. Later, the bell was sounded only (the conditioned stimulus) and the dog still salivated. However, after a period of time, the dog no longer salivated with the bell's sound only. We have observed teachers using classical conditioning in the

classroom, even without knowing about this theory of learning. For example, a teacher conditioned pupils to stop visiting and talking by turning off the lights in the classroom with no words used. The turning off the lights (conditioned stimulus) was followed by pupils indicating readiness for being attentive in the classroom and hopefully for learning.

2. ***Stimulus-Response learning.*** This concept emphasizes operant conditioning. Thus, a teacher has an objective for pupils to achieve. A reward has been announced prior to instruction as to what a pupil can obtain if successful in goal attainment. If a pupil learns, what was stated prior to instruction as a reward, he/she receives the reward. The reward may be an inexpensive prize such as a few readouts. With a correct response from the pupil, Stimulus-response theory of learning emphasizes rewarding good and correct responses. The emphasis is upon the correct response with its accompanying reward, according to operant conditioning.
3. ***Chaining.*** A series of correct responses is necessary from the pupil in an ongoing lesson or unit of study. Thus, in a dramatic activity, the pupil correctly pantomimes sequential content in the drama. This involves a series or ordered set of psychomotor responses that are viewed as being appropriate.
4. ***Verbal association learning.*** The pupil in a creative dramatics presentation uses words appropriately in a sequence or order to convey what is in the story being dramatized.
5. ***Multiple discrimination.*** The pupil is able, during and/or after lesson presentation to analyze and separate into component parts. For example, the pupil on his/her optimal developmental level is able to separate contextual from non-contextual words when reading content or subject matter.
6. ***Concept learning.*** The pupil is able to learn concepts such as nouns, verbs, adjectives and adverbs.
7. ***Rule learning.*** Rules are generalizations. If pupils are to

learn the following generalization : Verbs are words that indicate present or past tense as well as indicate an action taking place or a state of being is in evidence.

8. ***Problem solving.*** This is the highest level of Gagne's hierarchy of objectives in task analysis. Problem solving is important in school and in society. Individuals and groups face problem which need identification and solutions. Much information is necessary in most cases to be able to solve problems. There are problems that are easier to solve as well as those which take a long time or may never be solved.

There are numerous advantages in using a task analysis psychology in preparing an instructional sequence. For example, a pupil that cannot solve a problem such a writing a "thank you" note for favours received may lack pre-requisites in the task analysis. The teacher than needs to evaluate if the pupil lacks rules (step seven), meaning he/she does not possess the content needed for writing the "thank you" note. There are definite parts that should go into the writing of the note. Should the pupil lack knowledge of the rules, he/she may need to learn vital concepts (step six) in Gagne's task analysis plan of teaching. This may mean the pupil needs to be taught these important concepts for a "thank you" note. A quality plan of task analysis for teaching may truly assist the teacher to teach pupils sequentially and successfully vital subject matter. As the reader can see, there is much time and planning going into a lesson plan or unit of study which includes task analysis. The plan of task analysis stresses lower cognitive objectives such as signal learning (Classical conditioning) and stimulus-response psychology in operant conditioning (rewards provided for pupils who respond correctly in achieving precise objectives).

Dr. Gagne' has worked out a plan here in educational psychology in having pupils work from lower to higher cognitive level objectives. The plan helps teachers think of sequence when preparing what pupils are to learn.

The Structure of Knowledge in the Curriculum

During the 1960s and 1970s, the structure of knowledge psychology of learning was stressed much. Here, specialists in their academic areas of specialty worked in the direction of attempting to identify key concepts and generalizations in subject matter knowledge. We believe attempting to identify key concepts and generalizations in diverse academic disciplines is as important as ever. Pupils should learn what is salient, not the trivia. Academicians certainly do have a very important role in choosing what is vital for pupils to learn. Thus, in reading and the language arts, the structure of knowledge, consisting of main ideas needs to be determined. For example, linguists have identified the following sentence patterns with examples provided :

1. subejct—predicate

   Cats run.

2. subject—predicate—direct object

   Ralph saw people.

3. Subject—predicate—indirect object—direct object

   Mary gave Irma gifts.

4. subject—linking verb—predicate adjective

   Flowers are beautiful.

5. subject—linking verb—predicate nominative

   Robert was a clown.

6. subject—linking verb—predicate adverb

   Mother is away.

7. subject—predicate—direct object—adjective

   Jim painted the barn red.

These sentence patterns are used again and again in listening, speaking, reading and writing. They provide structure or a blue print for how the English language works or operates.

Linguists have also identified ways of expanding each of the seven above named sentences. These are:

1. using modifiers such as single word adjectives and adverbs as well as adjective and adverb phrases.

2. using appositives
3. using subordinate clauses
4. using independent clauses.

These four approaches in expanding sentence patterns work again and again. Thus, they do present a structure of the English language.

In a nutshell, these have been key concepts and generalizations that have been identified by linguists. There are many other key ideas that linguists have to offer which assists pupils to achieve more optimally in reading and the language arts.

Teachers, we believe, have always tried to determine what is major and what is of lesser importance to teach. When doing this, teachers have been looking for major concepts and generalizations to teach. Key ideas or the structure of knowledge as the teacher sees it is being emphasized. The original intent of the structure of knowledge psychology was to have academicians, generally Ph.D. professors in their respective academic discipline areas from leading universities/colleges, get together and select, after much deliberation, what pupils should learn in terms of concepts and generalizations. These key ideas would then be available to teachers to emphasize with inductive teaching in the classroom. What actually happened at that time was that educational publishing companies hired selected academicians to have these professors write materials of instruction which stressed structural ideas. These commercial productions for teacher use have almost become extinct.

We would suggest that structural ideas be sought after continuously by academicians, teachers and administrators. It is very important to choose the best subject matter possible to teach pupils. The subject matter must be important, not trivia. There is no reason that pupils could not learn some of the content inductively. However, I recommend both inductive and deductive procedures. Sometimes in our teaching pupils can learn much and in a short time with explanations and direct teaching. At other times, it is good to have pupils discover and find out on their own.

For example, in using context clues with an unknown word in reading, it is good to have pupils hypothesize what the unknown word is. These might well be good educated guesses. At other times, the teacher may wish to pronounce the unknown word to pupils due to their lacking consistency between symbol and sound. The teacher should still give learners time to determine the identity of these words. Brief explanations (deductive methods) my be used by the teacher as to why there is a lack of phoneme/grapheme correspondence.

In situations in life, we learn through deductive and inductive approaches. The following are every day examples of deductive learning :

1. listening to news broadcasts and weather forecasts.
2. obtaining information on how to repair an item.
3. following directions for making something such as baking a cake.
4. looking at a new car manual to ascertain when services needed to be provided such as tire rotation or the changing and filtering of a oil.

Inductive thinking in life occurs when situations such as the following are in evidence :

1. finding out what is not functioning well with one's car.
2. discovering how to attach a doorbell to the house.
3. reading about and determining how to implement a school of thought pertaining to disciplining children in the school setting.
4. determining how to make a picnic table that is sturdy and beautiful.

We recommend that teachers and supervisors use much of what structuralists have to emphasize and that is to re-examine subject matter to determine its relevancy and importance. Structural approaches in curriculum development have always stressed evaluating current subject matter thoroughly to see if it is vital for pupils to achieve. Trivial skills and content need to be culled.

Jean Piaget and Readiness for Learning

Piaget studied middle class children for over forty years in Geneva, Switzerland. He came up with valuable conclusions from his research findings. Biological maturation was a key concept in findings pertaining to child growth and development. The stages that a child goes through from birth to eleven years and beyond covered the following approximate stages :

1. Psychomotor Intelligence. This stage incorporate birth to two years of age whereby the child learned through the use of the muscles and the readiness phase. Thus, a youngster may learn to hold a ball, touch objects, taste, smell and hear sounds in the environment. Object permanence is a very important learning to the psychomotor development pupil.

2. Preoperational Intelligence. This stage of development occurs from ages two to seven. Here, the child perceives one variable only or largely, such as seeing the height of a container or its width. There are many implications for teachers in the child of preoperational intelligence and that is not to present too many variables at one time. With Piaget's research, we have doubts pertaining to how this harmonizes with the many abstract symbols that are in evidence when pupils work in a strong program of scope and sequence phonics instruction. There are many variables emphasized with abstract symbols in the phonics curriculum. Thus, the teacher needs to be concerned about the number of variables stressed in a phonics lesson or unit of study for early primary grade pupils.

3. Stage of Concrete Operations. Here, the pupil, as previously, needs adequate concrete materials when the abstract is emphasized in teaching and learning. It is important then to stress the abstract subject matter directly related to concrete situations. Perhaps, this should be emphasized throughout the kindergarden through grade five or six age levels. Meaning accrues when pupils can experience the concrete (objects and items) along with the symbolic or abstract words. If pupils are listening to subject

matter, speaking about experiences, reading about reality and writing about what has been encountered in the real world, the concrete situation is inherent. The teacher as well as pupils may bring into the classroom numerous items and objects pertaining to what has been studied.

When using the above example pertaining to the stage of concrete operation, we have to think of the experience chart. Here, the pupils experience the concrete world, such as objects on an interest center. In sequence these pupils present ideas for an experience chart. This encourages speaking activities that refer directly to the items and objects on the interest center. Writing is in the offing for pupils. The experience chart, in and of itself, may consist of the teacher writing the ideas presented by pupils. Learners may then see talk written down. Finally, pupils together with the teacher read the abstract words on the chart.

The experience chart then follows the thinking of pupils seeing and experiencing objects and having their related comments recorded. In sequence, oral reading follows:

4. Formal or abstract thought lasts from eleven years and up pertaining to the age of the child. Here, pupils may now read the abstract without referring to the concrete materials.

According to many observations, Piaget and his research have made the following contributions;

1. The teacher must study the maturation levels of pupils in order to know what and how to teach these learners.
2. There can be much wasting of time in teaching what the maturational level of the child is not ready for...
3. Hastening the readiness of a pupil for learning.....does not work. The maturational level of the child will indicate what can or cannot be taught.
4. There needs to be an adequate amount of concrete material available for teaching through the age of eleven, approximately.

5. Securing attention for learning is salient since learners do not achieve unless they mentally operate upon the content being presented (Ediger, 1997).

According to Piaget and Imhelder (1969), there are definite factors that impinge upon pupils as they progress in intellectual development. These are biological maturation; interaction with experiences in the environment; social activities and homeostasis, a balance between the self and experiences in the physical environment.

Biological maturation stresses pupils going through the stages of sensorimotor, preoperational, concrete operations and formal thought. However, there are factors that influence these stages of biological maturation. One factor is pupils interacting with the natural environment. The richness of experiences here has much to do has much to do with learners developing biologically.

Learning Styles of Pupils

There are educators who are strongly emphasizing evaluating the learning styles of pupils to notice factors dealing with the psychology of learning. The Psychology of learning emphasizes stressing that which assists pupils to achieve more optimally. Bernice Mc Carthy (1996) stresses the 4 MAT approach in providing for learners in the classroom. She identifies four types of learning styles among pupils.

1. The highly creative pupil with a feeling and reflective style of learning. These pupils ask many questions in ongoing lessons and like brainstorming methods of instruction.
2. The analytic pupil who is well organized in classifying and analysing details.
3. Problem solvers in thinking who are doers and like concrete situations, not reading activities, basically.
4. Learners who like to work cooperatively as well as independently on open-ended tasks in which inductive learning is stressed using kinesthetic/audio/visual materials. First hand experiences are important to these pupils in teaching

and learning. Learners in this category do not like formal, rigid schedules.

In the above named four types of learning for pupils, a natural cycle sequentially of feeling, reflecting, thinking and acting or doing occurs.

In commenting about each of the above names styles of learning, the following are examples also harmonizing with the numerals indicated :

1. Pupils might brainstorm characteristics pertaining to the major character of the story. Here, pupils are generating as many ideas as possible, without repeating previous responses. To generate new ideas in brainstorming requires the unique and the original.
2. Analytical pupils might contrast characterization of the major character of the previous story with that of the present one being studied.
3. Pupils who are problem solvers like to identify stimulating questions or problem areas. The Why and How kinds of questions are very important. They require securing information in answer to the question/problem. An hypothesis needs to be developed. The hypothesis is a tentative answer to the problem. Deliberation and thought are needed here in decision making when trying out the hypothesis. Generally, the tentative hypothesis is tried out in a life-like situation. Revisions may need to be forthcoming if the evidence is warranted after the trying out of the hypothesis. Reading and the language arts together with academic/practical knowledge may assist in providing acceptable solutions.
4. There are selected pupils who like to work in groups or committees, not by the self. Others prefer to work by the self in an ongoing learning activity. Both sets of pupils like life-like experiences which are open-ended, not assigned activities. These pupils may find interesting tasks within the assigned. Hands on approaches in learning should be in the offing for these pupils. The tasks may not stress problem solving, but emphasize the useful and

the utilitarian through learning by discovery. Finding out on their own is desired by these learners.

Conclusion

The psychology of learning provides the reading/language arts teacher with a basis for making sound decisions in lesson and unit construction. The psychology of learning attempts to guide teachers on how to aid pupils to attain more optimally. Thus, behaviourists advocate the writing of precise objectives prior to instruction. The teacher may announce to learners who is to be achieved when teaching occurs in sequence. Pupils then may tend to the presentation with certainty as to what is to be learned. After instruction, pupils are measured in achievement to ascertain if the objectives have been attained. There is a certain structure involved in developing lessons and units of study. The emphasis is upon selecting with much care the objectives of instruction. Adequate time needs to be spent on choosing objectives for pupils to attain.

Advocates of task analysis stress a carefully developed sequence of learning opportunities going from lower to higher levels of cognition. If a pupil does not achieve an objective, he/she can always be guided to be taught at a preceding level of achievement. The preceding level provides readiness for the new objective to be achieved by pupils.

The structure of knowledge approach will always be important in that teachers and supervisors need to analyze and study presently what is taught with hopes of obtaining something better. The something better should emphasize an improved structure of reading and the language arts.

The 4 MAT approach stresses learning styles of pupils. The psychology of learning herein emphasizes different styles of pupils in learning from the creative pupil to those stressing being analytic, problems solvers and/or desiring hands on approach in learning.

We believe we can use the best of all four strategies in teaching such as having;

1. clearly stated objectives as advocated by behaviourists.

2. quality in sequence in pupil learning as advocated by tasks analysis psychology.
3. good problem solvers in school and in society among pupils, as emphasized by problem solving advocates.
4. styles of learning which harmonize with a pupil's intrinsic make-up in terms of how the individual learns.

References

Bhaskara Rao, Digumarti (1997), Educational Psychology. Guntur: Creative Press (in Telugu language).

Beck, Isabel (1984) "Developing Comprehension : The Impact of the Directed Reading Lesson", Learning to Read in American Schools (Edited by Anderson, Osborn and Tierney). Hillsdale, New Jersey : Lawrence Erlbaum Associates, Publishers, 9 and 10.

Dolch, Edward (1955), Methods in Reading. Champaign, Illinois: Garrard Publishing Company.

Ediger, Marlow (1997), Teaching Mathematics in the Elementary School Kirksville, Missouri : Simpson Publishing Company, 31.

McCarthy, Bernice (1997), About Learning. Barrington, Illionois : Excel, Inc..

Piaget, Jean and Barbara Imhelder (1967), Science of Education and the Psychology of the Child. New York : Viking Press, 26.

15
The Teacher, Reading and Parents

Many writers and speakers on educational topics, as well as educators, believe that parental involvement in their child's education is of utmost importance. Too frequently, parents have not been actively involved in assisting their children to do well in school. Perhaps parents have been left out of planning for the education of their offspring or there has been parental indifference toward the welfare of the child in the school setting.

There are many factors that need to be taken into consideration by reading teachers in planning the curriculum. Among others, the following are important :

1. Interests possessed by individual pupils in subject matter read.
2. The complexity level of the reading material.
3. Purpose for reading that a teacher can develop within pupils.
4. Meaning attached by pupils to story content in materials read.
5. Amount of assistance that a pupil needs to achieve more optimally in reading (Ediger, 1997).

Teacher Education

Teacher education at colleges/universities lack experiences for future teachers in working with parents. We believe there should be at least a three semester hour course for all pre-service teachers in working cooperatively with parents. The three semester hour course should involve students working directly with parents such as in parent/teacher conferences, open house, parent's night and PTA meetings. The most important of the previously mentioned items for students to experience would be the parent/teacher conference. Here, the student has the opportunity to notice what a professional teacher does to get parents to work cooperatively for the good of the child in reading and other curriculum areas. The goals of the parent/teacher conference should be spelled out here. How to fulfill meeting these goals needs to be in the offing. Activities and experiences to meet objectives of parent/teacher conferences should be clear and outcomes oriented. Sequences in the strategy must be carefully considered. Certainly, after the conference, there needs to be a time for reflection to notice if the goals have been achieved. Also, it needs to be noticed which additional elements need to be covered in the future.

We will spell out a model conference situation between the teacher and parents in a conference setting for reading instruction.

1. Have evidence ready to discuss with parents where the child is achieving presently in reading. The evidence may consist of actual reading by the pupil on video-tape or cassette.

2. Display pupil written work related directly to reading such as outlines, summaries, journal writing, book reports and precis' writing.

3. Discuss reading problems faced by the pupil with parents.

4. Detail what parents can do to assist the pupil to read better. It is important to agree upon a plan of action. If another parent/teacher conference is held in spring, comparisons can be made of evaluation results in fall.

5. Conduct the conference in an atmosphere of trust and respect. Nothing is gained with hostile remarks by either teachers or the parents.

6. Be well prepared for the conference and adhere to time limits in a schedule if others also have come for a conference.

7. Get to know the aspirations parents hold for their offspring. Notice how parents feel toward their child. What benefits are the parents able to give the child, such as after school lessons of diverse kinds, such as playing piano. There are also parents who expect too much of their child with all the after school formal activities that are transpiring.

Students need to have ample opportunities to practice being involved in parent/teacher conferences in mock situations as well as in reality. The techniques and practices use, including the above seven flexible steps may be modified as the need arises. Parent/teacher conferences need modification if evidence suggests that changes should be made. Models are flexible devices that provide guidance and direction, but are not absolutes. Students like to hear of diverse techniques that might be used in conducting these conferences. We have noticed a few conferences where the adding of the involved pupil assists in improving the setting with parental involvement. Thus, the pupil may also comment about his/her school work and state improvements that need to be made in personal school achievement. Active involvement by the learner is important in ongoing lessons and units of study and might be equally important in parent/teacher conferences. The school principal may occasionally visit the conference setting to add to improving the personal child's curriculum. There are principals of schools that are highly interested in each pupil and make definite efforts to assist in the child's welfare and achievement. Each participant in the parent/teacher conference should help to develop the best objectives, learning opportunities and evaluative procedures for the individual pupil. It is good to have follow-up activities to determine how beneficial the conference has been to the individual pupil.

The concept of parent involvement is interrelated with parent and teacher efficacy/involvement. Parental efficacy of self-image, locus of control, developmental status and interpersonal support are linked in more effective parent involvement. Specific teacher strategies in the areas of communication, shared learning and guidance are specified as ways to nurture parental efficacy and strengthen parent-teacher relations (Swick and Boradway, 1997).

There are parents who have become involved as volunteers in school due to having participated in parent/teacher conferences. This is a point of contact between the home and school that is vital. Teacher education students then need to realize the importance of parent teacher conferences that are scheduled as well as unscheduled. By phone, teachers can call parents at home to commend a child's achievement at a given point or to call attention to where the child needs more help. Trust and cooperation needs to be built up in a positive way. There is so much parents can do in the home setting to assist their child in reading. These include the following ways :

1. Reading orally to the young child. What is read should be interesting and capture learner attention. Ideally, when ready, the pupil should follow along with the words being pronounced by parents as the story is being read. However, as a major goal, the pupil should obtain ideas read and view the related illustrations in the library book. The child should be encouraged to bring library books home from the school library.

2. Parents should be encouraged to take their offspring to the public library and checkout books, generally with no charge, to read at home. If the child is secure enough in reading silently or orally to parents, he/she should do so. Otherwise, the parent should help with word identification that the child is not able to identify.

3. Library books should be given as gifts for birthdays and holiday seasons. Learners should realize the importance of obtaining and reading library books.

4. Specific assistance may be provided pupils in the home setting in reading with consistent symbols and sounds when pupils reveal problems in reading.

5. Parents need to read to themselves in order for pupils to see a model to emulate in reading.

6. Rewards may be given to pupils for reading a certain amount or number of library books. Best it is if pupils read because intrinsically they enjoy the contents of reading. Hopefully, all pupils will read because of fascinations for

subject matter contained in library books. There is much that is missed in life by these individuals.

7. Parents and the pupil need to realize that the latter needs to do the learning in becoming a reader. The teacher does not have a magic wand in having a child become a good reader. The teacher must do the best job teaching possible, but it is the learner that must do the learning. Learning to read can be enjoyable. We remember certain things and no others and yet both were vital in one's life.

8. Quality sequence in reading materials pursued is vital to ensure success in becoming a good reader (Ediger, 1996).

There are pupils who will need to work very hard to become good readers while others will hardly remember how they learned the complex act of reading. Pupils need to realize that beginning with the formal years of schooling, no class time must be wasted in learning to read. Pupils and parents who feel it is funny to disrupt the class are hurting themselves. Later on, they will realize how foolish it was to do these kinds of negative things. Recently, a first grader said to the teacher at the beginning of the school year. "I will see to it that you are removed from your teaching position unless you quit making us read so much". Children at a young age learn the sophisticated methods of :

1. I will see to it that the school gets rid of you.
2. my mother said I did not have to do the work you assigned to me.

There are articles in top educational journals that state if the pupil did not learn it, it was not taught. We think we all have to realize that there are teachers who truly do an excellent job of teaching and yet pupils are there to disrupt and not learn. May be, much more accountability should be the role of the pupil and the parents. When a pupil cannot read after graduating from twelve years of schooling beyond the kindergarden level, then there must be problems whereby it is nearly impossible for the pupil to learn to read. Educators, medical doctors and psychiatrists may not be able to diagnose and remedy the problems involved. If a pupil graduates from high school and cannot read whatever definition is used to describe, "being able to read", the following questions need to be raised:

1. Was it due to poor teaching for twelve grades? We cannot imagine having poor teachers in all classes where reading was emphasized during these twelve years.
2. What did parents do to help the pupil to read? Did the child attend school regularly unless there was a need to be absent, such as being in poor health? If poor health was the case, how many days of school were missed?
3. What kind of home life did the pupil have?
4. What kind of encouragement was given to the pupil to learn to read?
5. why did the pupil not have a desire to learn to read on his/her very own?

From this discussion, we recommend that teachers try to impress within all pupils the necessity of studying hard each school day and make the most of the time available in learning to read well. Time moves by rapidly and time wasted cannot be made up unless one considers the time that should be given to accomplish new goals in reading. Opportunities go by rapidly unless they are taken advantage of. These opportunities may come only once and then they are gone. Thus, in learning to read, the individual throughout his/her lifetime must avail the self of opportunities in learning and developing. The student teacher needs course work and field experiences in possessing knowledge pertaining to involving parents in guiding pupil growth in reading achievement. The regular classroom teacher and student teachers have identically the same responsibilities in the classroom.

Conferences at Other School Events

Too frequently, the annual parent/teacher scheduled conference is looked upon as the only time to discuss pupil progress in detail in reading. The time usually is too short for conference time when meeting with many parents and discussing their questions. Thus, there needs to be numerous additional occasions when the teacher may talk to parents about pupil progress in reading.

Using the telephone can be an appropriate media to use in talking with parents. We would suggest here that the messages be very positive. The pupil's progress in reading is then discussed first. This can lead into discussing problems faced by the learner in achieving needed reading skills. Thus, if a pupil is facing problems in using context clues in reading, this needs to be discussed. The child is too valuable as a human being to lose out on needed abilities and attitudes in order to do well in society. The teacher needs to provide ways then of parents helping the pupil to use context clues to unlock unknown words. If parents are not home at the time of the call being made, most homes have an answering machine to return calls. If the news is all positive about a pupil's progress in reading, the recorded voice might well be adequate for communication purposes. However, if suggestions need to be made, such as how to assist a pupil in using context clues, then a more extended two way street of communication is necessary.

Open house can be a time to meet with parents and, perhaps, discuss achievements and problems a pupil has in reading. Generally, the time is very limited in open house in speaking with parents. The teacher, however, needs to make the best use of time possible. The teacher here, as always, needs to be caring person who desires to guide pupils to do well in school. Teachers are in a helping position; they do not sell items nor are they in the business world. Teaching is a helping profession and has its intrinsic rewards in assisting pupils and parents in educating the former, in particular.

To strengthen the teaching profession, the pre-service teacher should attend parent parent/teacher conferences, open house and PTA meetings, as well as other relevant school functions. Attending PTA meetings provides opportunities to meet parents and talk briefly to parents about their child's progress in reading. Course work and field experiences are vital here ! Reading content cuts across all curriculum areas including mathematics, science, social studies, literature, art, music and physical education. The relevance of reading in each curriculum area and to the future world of work for the pupil needs to be discussed with the involved parents.

Palardy (1997) indicates three characteristics of a successful literature based curriculum. These are.... instruction is designed around and under-graded with one of the basic tenets of language learning. Reading, lots of reading, must be and is a basic activity....A second characteristic of literature-based instruction is that it provides youngsters the opportunity to self-select their own reading materials within a print-rich environment....Third, there is a notable amount of social interaction as youngsters share, debate and compare the materials they read.... Palardy (1997) goes on to say there are four critical needs that teachers must meet to implement successfully literature-based instruction. First, and perhaps most important, teachers must become familiar with the diverse and ever expanding world of children's literature, in itself a difficult and time-consuming task.....Second, literature-based instruction requires teachers to have good planning and organizational skills, not only from an instructor's point of view, but also from a curriculum perspective....Third, an adequate supply of materials is essential. With today's funding crunch extant in most states and localities, this is not an insignificant element.....Lastly, the need for accountability has to be addressed up front through cogent and close communication with parents, administrators, other teachers and the youngsters themselves.

PTA Meetings and the Teacher

PTA meetings provide further opportunities for parent/ teacher involvement in discussing educational trends and pupil progress.

During a school year, there is much assessing of pupil progress. Much of the assessment information gathered during the school year serves as a basis for ongoing dialogue between teacher and students. Parents need to know how their children are doing. If teacher-based assessment is to inform public accountability, the evidence must take a form appropriate to this need. How can the classroom teacher effectively transform the data to suit these different audiences ? And beyond these client groups, how can the evidence be effectively employed as teachers reflect on their instruction individually and as members of a professional community ? Reporting in the new approach occurs at least three levels. Student and teacher engage in an ongoing discussion of growth and quality, based on actual performance and a common understanding of the rubrics. Quality parent-teacher conferences for parent-student-teacher conferences in which students reports and reflect....are the occasion for a summarative report. Tied to reporting is grading, often a problem for alternative assessment advocates. If one believes that each student can excel (or not excel) in a variety of ways, then what is the meaning of a grade ? On the other hand, in a competitive society such as ours, parents want to know, "How well is my kid doing ?". Finally a number of districts and states are turning to alternative assessment methods as a basis for public accountability. The "public" is the audience for these reports; practically speaking, the public wants numbers, averages, "hard data", and "bottom lines". The challenge is to transform soft data collected under non-standardized conditions into trustworthy and interpretable indicators (Graves, Van Der Brock and Taylor, editors, 1996).

We would like to discuss at this point issues in the teaching of reading. There appears to be a continuous debate between advocates of testing to determine pupil achievement as compared to the use of portfolios as an alternative assessment method. We believe portfolios have a tremendous advantage over test scores solely, in reporting pupil achievement. With a variety of pupil products in a portfolio, the scope of what is being evaluated for the pupil is much broader and more inclusive.

Whole language versus phonics approaches in the teaching of reading emphasize another continuous debate. We believe both whole language and phonics should be emphasized in the teaching of reading. If whole language is used only, pupils might well be at a loss in having an approach in identifying unknown words. If phonics is stressed excessively, then ideas to be obtained in reading may suffer. Therefore, we strongly encourage teachers to emphasize reading for meaning and also phonics instruction as it is needed, not for the sake of teaching phonics.

Phonic principles and generalizations taught should be relevant in learning to read better. Phonics instruction should be vital for the task at hand and that is to identify unknown words in reading. We have observed phonics lesson after phonics lesson taught with no attempt made for pupils to apply what has been learned.

Stop the sound and fury of the phonics vs. whole language war. We need both....Beware of the "one true method" imposed from on high ! Different children learn to read differently (Chase, 1997)..

Another issue in reading that may be discussed with parents is the use of workbooks. Workbooks should assist pupils to comprehend better what has been read and also to become more skillful in analyzing words so that identification of unknown words in reading is possible. Workbooks should stimulate interest in reading, not minimize or destroy it. Content in workbooks need to guide learners to achieve vital goals in reading instruction. They may be one activity, among others, in teaching pupils how to read. Activities chosen for pupils in workbooks should be reasonable in length. They should be relevant in emphasizing a certain objective such as having young pupils learn to use picture clues to identify unknown words. The exercises pupils work in from the workbook should relate to a larger whole or be related to ongoing lessons and units of study in reading. Isolated activities should not be stressed, nor should the workbook be used as busy work merely to occupy pupil's time.

PTA meetings may lend themselves to discussing issues such as the above involving testing versus portfolio use to appraise pupil achievement, whole language versus phonics in reading instruction, as well as the issue involved in using workbooks in the teaching of reading. Perhaps, teachers and the principal could arrange a panel presentation to present at a PTA meeting on issues in teaching reading. Questions from the audience should help clarify ideas in reading instruction.

Teachers sometimes feel as if there is not enough time to interact adequately with any one parent at a PTA meeting. We would say make the best use of time possible to communicate with parents. Bring in as much information as possible pertaining to understanding and improving the reading curriculum. The trained and educated teacher must have much knowledge pertaining to the teaching of reading and needs to share this information with patrons in the school district.

There are numerous civic and social organizations in the community in which reading teachers may speak and tell about what is done in the curriculum to assist pupils to learn as much as possible in becoming a good reader. There should also be adequate time to answer questions from the audience pertaining to reading instruction.

Human Relations in the Reading Curriculum

There are many times in which the teacher needs to be strong in human relations when working with children and adults. These times include parent/teacher conferences, open house and in teaching and learning situations. The teacher is in a critical situation here. Parents may become angry at the teacher and school for various reasons, logical or illogical.

First, the teacher must never show anger toward parents. If an angry parent comes to school, take time to work in a positive manner with the problems involved. Pupils do go home and say things that did not really occur in school and sometimes there is a misunderstanding by the parent of what the child said. When our three children were growing up, we asked them what they learned in school and so often the answer was, "nothing". Our children were so busy wanting to play that they had no time to discuss what was learned in school. At the super table, it was quite obvious that much had been learned in school that day when our children started to tell about what they had read and the humorous things that happened that day in school. Sometimes, our children would say more about what was learned than on other days. In general, we were happy, as parents, as to what was taught and learned in school.

After the angry parent has become more rational, then discuss what he/she has in mind as a problem. We like to look at problems in reading as something to identify and then solve. The solution must then be tried out to see if it truly works.

There are parents what come in to talk to the teacher in a friendly, concerned manner. These parents too may wish to discuss what to do with a child that is not doing well in reading. The teacher must take time to discuss the problem thoroughly. It is a professional responsibility to do so. The parent needs to take adequate time to discuss the problem with the reading teacher. If the child reads in a somewhat halting manner, the learner may need help in reading in thought units or phrases. Additional ways to solve the problems might involve.

1. Securing more reading materials on the reading level, not frustrational level, of the pupil.
2. Reading together more selections with others in a whole language approach so that the learner can hear and see the words pronounced accurately. Then the pupil has a better chance to read less haltingly and comprehend the contents better when re-reading occurs. In this way, the involved pupil receives more practice in identifying words in a fluent manner.

It is important to accept parents and pupils in a respectful way. No one should be minimized nor treated abruptly or rudely. The teacher, as a professional, must always be respectful regardless of the feelings parents bring in as complaints. If parents reveal extreme negative feelings, the principal should be contacted and cooperatively with the teacher work with the dissatisfied parents. Problem solving is the best procedure to use in situations involving parental complaints. With the solving of problems, better human relations should be an end result. Sometimes, teachers, like other professional, do not have answers to some of the problems brought in by parents pertaining to reading instruction. The remedial teacher, the guidance counselor and the supervisor need to be resourceful in suggesting specific specialists who might be able to guide the pupil to overcome difficulties. Severe behavioural difficulties that are beyond the capability of help that a teacher can provide may make it so that the involved pupil does not achieve at all in reading. The extreme cases of dyslexic behaviour in reading might tax a true specialist that specializes in helping these kinds of learners. With milder cases of dyslexia, the teacher may receive assistance from the remedial readıng teacher. Methods such as the following may be used for these pupils :

1. Tracing plastic raised letters moving from left of right only.
2. Writing one or more supervised sentences from left to right solely.
3. Varying the materials used from using raised plastic letters to the use of sandpaper letters in writing strictly from left to right.
4. Looking at a sequence or illustrations from a left to right perspectively. Each illustration needs explaining moving from left to right therein.
5. Reading numbers on a yardstick in a left/right progression.

.....there is now overwhelming evidence that a primary cause of variability among children in growth in early word reading skills involves individual differences in the ability to process the phonological features of a language. At present, the most important of these phonological skills appears to be phonological awareness and the rapid automatic naming ability....(Torgesen and Hecht, 1996).

In summarizing implications for teaching pupils with disabilities in reading, the following emerge :

1. If preventative remedial approaches to reading instruction with reading disabled children are to be successful, they must lead to the development of accurate and fluent text-based word reading skills.

   These children also may need special instruction in comprehension skills, but the first goal of instruction should be to ensure that they can read words fluently and accurately.

2. As the basis for early independence in word recognition and gradual development of effective visual codes for words, the early growth of alphabetic reading skills must be fostered.

   These are precisely the reading skills that most reading disabled children have difficulty with.

3. As a basis for the acquisition of the alphabetic principle, instructional interactions must stimulate the growth of phonological awareness.

   Phonological awareness provides the basis for understanding and utilizing the alphabetic principle in reading.

4. In order to receive the maximum number of opportunities to acquire accurate orthographic representations for words, children must be taught explicitly to integrate the use of phonological cues and context in order to arrive at accurate pronunciations of words in text.... It also seems important to involve reading disabled children in manageable and meaningful reading experiences from as early in the instructional process as possible (Torgesen and Hecht, 1966).

Pupils with dyslexia need much practice and guidance in moving from left to right in printed and other kinds of materials. The reading teacher needs to study and use information pertaining to dyslexia and how to assist a pupil with this problem. Knowledge needs to be present of what to say to parents in advising them on how to work with their children in the home setting when dyslexia is in evidence. Quality human relations stresses the importance of being knowledgeable and helpful when called upon to guide pupil progress in reading.

Observing Where There is High Parental Involvement

Reading teachers need to observe in schools where there is high parent involvement. Time off from teaching and paying needed expenses for these observational visits is time and money well spent. There are many questions that teachers should have before making these arranged observational visits. Journal articles read and teacher education textbooks used in studying how to involve parents before visiting schools where there is much success in involving parents are prerequisites ! We have observed the following in schools where a considerable number of parents are involved in working with their children in the home setting and in the school arena.

1. Parents feel that the public schools and their child's education is important.

2. Parents believe they can help to achieve in the home setting which will assist in achieving more optimally in school.
3. Parents liking teaching and learning believe that helping in the school setting is enjoyable and personally satisfying.
4. Parents believe that all children are important and need to learn as much as possible.
5. Parents believe that the center of life should be the home and the school.

Those schools and individual teachers who appreciate the role parents can play in school send out notices for parental assistance in the educational arena. A personal welcome is also given at parent/teacher conferences, open house and PTA meetings for more parental involvement in the school setting. For those who assist in the classroom, guidelines are printed and distributed so that the parent feels welcome and has considerable knowledge as to what is desired as parental help. The classroom teacher further welcomes and provides necessary communication as to how the parent is to help in teaching and learning situations. Schools need to develop brochures and school publications whereby parents have an inward desire to work in school and feel rewarded intrinsically for doing so. Pre-service teachers should find that working with parents has many rewards. They feel more inclined then to use parental assistance in their own positions later as public school teachers.

Parents should have a voice in determining what they wish to contribute in the school and classroom setting. The following were offered by parents at one school :

1. Serve as a resource person on environmental problems. This person was a biologist by profession.
2. Serve as a room mother for planning and serving holiday treats to pupils.
3. Listen to pupils read and read stories orally to pupils.
4. Help check pupils' papers in arithmetic and go over the errors with individual pupils. This person had been a former elementary and secondary mathematics teacher.

5. Assist in taking pupils on excursions such as to the local museum or one from school house.

It appears quite obviously that parents do have a desire to help out in a positive manner in the classroom. They do participate actively when asked to do so and they can assist pupils to achieve, develop and grow. One school one of us visited in supervising student teachers and co-operating teachers used a brain-storming approach in determining how parents can assist in the school setting and classroom. Here, a former art teacher who became a housewife wanted so badly to be involved in children's art work. Later, she came to school to show several classrooms, art work she had completed including the making of five beautiful puppets which she had used in a program at a local club meeting. There is much talent in any community and these talents should be used to improve objectives, learning opportunities and evaluation procedures for pupils in the classroom setting !

A Reading Party

As a first grader in a five teacher rural school, I (Ediger) participated in a reading party during the 1934–1935 school year. I was a first grader in a combination room with second graders. Invitations were sent home with pupils for the date of the reading party. Each pupil, with teacher assistance, selected a story to read to the parents who were present. There were thirteen first graders who participated. Parents could then hear and listen to their child read orally to the group. Pupils individually had chances to practice reading their selections over and over again so that the oral reading activity for each was a success. I must say the event was enjoyed by pupils and parents. Refreshments were served, such as coffee and doughnuts, after the reading party. This event was held during the height of the depression years with great success ! The event sticks out clearly in my mind. Since the reading party was for first graders in the combination room, these pupils with teacher assistance displayed the following as it related to ongoing lessons and units of study in reading :

1. Art work to indicate compression of content read from a library book.

2. A small mural made by two pupils to show the setting where a story took place.
3. Several dioramas to reveal the character of a story read by learners.
4. Dictated work to show an experience chart developed cooperatively by pupils. Yes, we had experience charts in our school during the early to middle 1930s.

The reading party was used as a way to communicate with parents in the teaching of reading. Parents cold see and listen to their offspring read orally. They could look at the products of pupils from the reading of children's literature. Of major importance was the asking of questions by parents of the teacher as to what could be done to assist the pupil to improve in reading. I felt that the conversation was rich indeed in parents learning more about reading instruction and about how to assist their offspring to achieve more optimally in reading. Parental involvement was certainly in evidence here in developing and in understanding better the reading curriculum.

Conclusion

Early in the primary grade reading program, adequate emphasis should be placed upon writing as being directly related to reading instruction. We have noticed in the experience chart that the teacher records the ideas of children for content to be read aloud cooperatively, by the teacher and the children. Here, children have had adequate opportunities to see talk written down. Their own ideas then have been encoded or written on the chalboard, chart, or computer.

Pupils individually may also dictate content for the teacher, an aide, or other child to record. As pupils become increasingly more mature with print materials, they should do their very own writing. After the act of writing has been concluded with very short or more lengthy papers, learners need to re-read the contents. Other pupils will also wish to share their written ideas.

Print is one way of sharing ideas and must be used widely to increase pupil proficiency in reading and writing. Multiple intelligences theory (Gardner, 1993) emphasizes that pupils possess nine areas of intelligence. These are verbal/linguistic such as in reading and writing, logical/mathematical, visual/ spatial such as in art work, musical, bodily/kinesthetic such as in physical activities, interpersonal such as in cooperative learning, intrapersonal such as in personal endeavours, scientific and the human experience such as in history. Thus, there are numerous ways of showing achievements in any curriculum area, according to multiple theory intelligence. Multiple intelligences theory stresses pupils reading and in different curriculum areas. Here, reading of print materials may also be correlated, for example, with visual/spatial intelligence such as a pupil doing art work related to what has written or printed. Involving parents in all educational endeavours is the challenge so that the home and school work together for the good of the child.

References

Chase, Bob (1997), "Teaching the first R : Is There a Best Way ? *NEA Today*, 16(5), 2.

Ediger, Marlow (1997), *Teaching Reading and the Language Arts in the Elementary School*. Kirksville, Missouri : Simpson Publishing Company, 187.

Ediger, Marlow (1997), "Perspectives in Teaching Reading", *Reading Improvement*, 34(2), 62–63.

Ediger, Marlow (1996), *Elementary Education*. Kirksville, Missouri: Simpson Publishing Company, 38–39.

Gardner, Howard (9193), *Multiple Intelligences, the Theory in Practice*. New York : The Basic Books.

Graves, et al, Editors (1996). *The First R. Every Child's Right To Read*. New York : Teachers College, Columbia University, 231.

Palardy, J. Michael (1997), "Another Look At Literature-based Instruction, *Education*, 118 (1), 68–69.

Swick, Karen J. and Francis Broadway (1997), "Parental Efficacy and Successful Parental Involvement, *Journal of Instructional Psychology*, 24(1), 69.

Torgesen, Joseph and Steven A. Hecht (1996). "Preventing and Remediating Reading Disabilities : Instructional Variables that make A Difference for Special Students", in *The First R. Every Child's Right to Read*. New York : Teachers College, Columbia University, 133–141.

16
The Reading Curriculum

Language arts and reading across the curriculum is certainly in vogue. Professional writers and speakers in education strongly recommend that all teachers, regardless of academic area taught, emphasize the language arts areas of listening, speaking, reading, writing, spelling, handwriting and word processing skills, as well as non-verbal communication such as facial expressions, gestures and body movements. Reading is an inherent part of the language arts and yet, due to its vital importance, is treated as an entity by the writer.

Reading in the Curriculum

Reading as a skill permeates all curriculum areas be it literature, social studies, science, mathematics, health, music, art and physical education to some extent. What should be emphasized in a quality program of reading instruction starting with young primary age pupils?

The teacher should do much oral reading to young learners in particular. Stories chosen by the teacher or recommended by pupils should be on the letters understanding level. Thus, pupils need to comprehend the contents of oral reading. Otherwise the teacher's and the pupil's time is not being used wisely. Learners need to enjoy the contents of trade books read oral to them. This is one way for the pupil to build background information so that more difficult content sequentially can be understood. Then too, with the enjoyment to read on their own. Later on when reading to themselves, pupils will understand subject matter better due to having the necessary background ideas that might well have come from being read to orally by the teacher. Subject matter acquired by pupils from oral reading activities provides needed content to understand new facts, concepts and generalizations.

When reading orally to pupils, the teacher should maintain good eye contact with as many learners as possible. This indicates to the learner that quality communication is taking place. For young learners, it is salient that the teacher show illustrations in the story or book being read. These illustrations should be shown in context. Thus, when the abstract words are read orally, the teacher shows to pupils the related illustrations. Voice inflection when reading orally is necessary so that pupils find the content presented in an interesting way. The teacher then should use proper stress, pitch and juncture in the oral reading experience. Pupils also need to learn that content read orally has a certain sequence of ideas. The writer cannot over emphasize the importance of teachers of young children being read to orally with carefully chosen literature that is interesting, meaningful and has perceived purpose.

Second, pupils need to experience a wide variety of trade books at a reading center. These books can be checked out readily for school and home reading. Teachers need to encourage pupils selecting books for silent reading. The trade books should be on different topics such as animal life, people of diverse nations, travel, historical fiction, biblio-therapy, biographies and autobiographies, among others. Topics on reading from trade books should be as broad as the interests possessed by pupils. These books must be on different reading achievement levels so that each learner can benefit from materials read. If the teacher introduces selected books to learners in terms of subject matter contained therein, pupils should tend to have an inward desire to read due to interests developed. A stimulating bulletin board should also encourage pupil interest in reading. The bulletin board may have jackets from newly purchased books with a caption such as "HAVE YOU READ THESE BOOKS ?" Further bulletin board ideas to stimulate pupil reading might include the following :

1. list the titles of new books with an appropriate caption.
2. show a world map and indicate several book titles that would have their setting in a specific area or region.

3. have pupil draw illustrations pertaining to books read and post these on the bulletin board.
4. encourage learners to make puppets involving characters from stories and show these to all pupils in class.
5. let pupils do bulletin board displays based on trade books read.

With quality bulletin board displays, pupils should feel motivation to do more reading. Learners must experience challenge in wanting to do more reading so that knowledge, skills and attitudes are being developed in becoming proficient readers.

Using Basal Readers

Most teachers use basal readers published by a reputable company to teach reading to pupils. Basal readers by themselves will not automatically do the job of providing for individual reading needs of pupils. The teacher needs to use supplementary readers as well as trade books to assist each pupil to achieve as optimally as possible in reading. Basal readers, however, can provide a quality framework for the teaching of reading. The teacher needs to emphasize readiness activities before pupils are to read a given selection from the basal reader. Thus, the teacher should introduce new words that pupils will meet, when reading silently or orally. These words should be printed in neat manuscript letters on the chalkboard or on a transparency. Each new word may be presented in isolation or within a given sentence. The writer prefers the latter since pupils then may see each new word in context. Generally, words are viewed in context as one reads for a specific purpose. Learners need practice at the time of word introduction to be able to identify these words later when reading silently or orally. Being able to recognize the new words in print when reading is salient. Learners then have benefited from being introduced to the new words form the chalkboard or overhead projector.

Pupils need to understand the meaning of each new word. Perhaps the meaning comes from the contextual situation of the word. The meaning then comes from the rest of the words in the sentence and their relationship to the new word being introduced. The Glossary of the basal reader should also be used to determine the meaning of unknown words. Generally the glossary provides definitions for these words as they will be used in paragraphs to be read in the basal reader. After pupils have observed and learned to pronounce the new words as well as understand their meanings. Pupils should also have adequate background information to attach meaning to what will be read. For example, if learners are to read a selection on *elephants* and the *rain forest*, they must have enough subject matter understandings to comprehend content on elephants and the rain forest. Illustrations in the basal reader as well as pictures form the teacher's own files can be used in discussions to guide learners to secure the necessary information to understand that which will be read. Next is sequence, the teacher must assist learners to establish purpose(s) for reading content. The teacher might state the purpose(s) and write these on the chalkboard. Pupils might also have developed questions for which they would like to receive information through reading. Perhaps, learners asked the questions when studying the new words as listed on the chalkboard or through the use of the overhead proctor. Questions from learners may have arisen when studying the meaning of these new words or when background subject was presented with the use of audio-visual aids. If pupils are not ready to read the purpose(s) from the chalkboard as printed by the teacher, the reasons for reading can be stated orally using meaningful language. Purpose(s) usually emphasize questions that learners need to answer. The answer(s) are secured through reading.

Following the reading of the content by pupils, there are recommendable follow up activities which reveal how much learners have comprehend form the reading experience. The following are recommended:

1. Discuss answers to questions stated in the purpose by the teacher. Answers to questions raised by pupils should also be discussed. Comprehension of what has been read is vital. One reads to comprehend, not for the sake of word calling.

2. Dramatize what has been read. This takes careful planning by learners with teacher guidance. Roles need to be

accepted and content to be dramatized must be understood and used in dramatic activities. Dramatic experience may consist of creative drama whereby involved pupils develop script as the need arises. Pantomime involves no spoken words but the facial expressions, gestures and body movements tell and express that which has been acquired from reading. Formal drama empathizes learners writing the spoken parts and then using these parts for presentation to an audience.

3. Critical thinking should be stressed when pupils reveal what has been learned from reading. Here, learners analyze content in terms of being fact or opinion, accurate or inaccurate and fantasy versus reality.

4. Creative thinking is also salient in that learners might brainstorm how the characters in the story could be different from what the author describes or how the setting of the story could be changed. Learners might develop a different plot from that written by the author or develop satire from selected portions of content read. Ridiculing of persons, however, needs to be avoided.

5. Problem solving procedures should become a part of the reading curriculum. Learners then identify a problem from the story, develop an hypothesis, test the hypothesis and revise it if necessary.

Pupils need to achieve skill in word recognition techniques. Perhaps, the most salient skill in word recognition for young learners is phonics. Phonics instruction should not be overdone. Phonics stresses abstract content in guiding pupils to associate graphemes (symbols) with phonemes (sounds). There are very consistent grapheme-phoneme relationships within words such as ban, can, fan, man, pan, tan and ran, among other word families. In the above listed words, each grapheme harmonizes with a phoneme. The following set of words within a family lacks rational spelling in that a grapheme does not equal a phoneme : cough, through, though, rough, trough, bough and dough. Each of these words has an "ough" ending but each has a different pronunciation. In teaching phonics, the writer recommends the following:

1. A balanced program of word recognition techniques must be emphasized in the reading curriculum. Phonics is one approach for pupils to use in unlocking unknown words.
2. Phonics due to its abstract content should not be taught for to long a period of time at one sitting for learners. Overemphasis upon phonics instruction in one lesson may make for situations involving boredom and meaningless learning (Ediger, 1996).
3. The teacher should try to start with the concrete phase of instruction when teaching phonics and then move to the semi-concrete in ongoing lessons on phonics. Thus, the teacher may show a model dog when learners are learning the initial consonant sound of "d" in the word "dog". For the semi-concrete facet of learning, the teacher may show a picture of a dog to analyze the "d" sound. Additional concrete and semi-concrete materials may then be used to show other words that begin with the "d" sound such as dog, duck, door and desk. Some words are to abstract to relate to the concrete and semi-concrete phases of teaching such as which, when, where and what. These words will have to be taught using the abstract facet of phonics such as looking at the beginning grapheme "w" to notice consistency here in pronouncing the initial sounds of words that start with the "w" letter.

Using Syllabication to Recognize Words

Most pupils can benefit from syllabication instruction to identify unknown words. If a pupil does not recognize a word in reading, he/she may identify that word by dividing it into component parts or syllables. For example, a pupil reading the word "unknown" might perceive it to be completely new. When dividing the word into syllables, the parts have been identified previously. The prefix "un" might have been read in words such as unlike and unimportant. The learner may have also read the base or root word "known" previously in a different context. Now the pupil needs to put the prefix and base word together to make the word "unknown". There are prefixes that are vital for pupils to be able to read and understand. These prefixes are consistent in pronunciation and meaning. For example, the prefix "un" means "not". The prefix is common in words read and has the same meaning each time.

Knowledge of suffixes can be valuable for pupils to unlock unknown words in terms of pronunciation and meaning. The word "runner" has the suffix "ner". The "ner" means "one who runs". Generally, there is an "er" suffix only, that means "one who" such as in the word "dancer" which means "one who dances". The "er" suffix is common in words and thus becomes useful for pupils to know and understand to recognize unknown words. If a learner reads the word "singer" in context and it appears to be a new word, the pupil may divide the word into two component "sing" and "er". Perhaps both syllables are understandable to the pupil and have been read before. The word "singer" then can result form the two syllables. The word "sing" tends to be a common word in the reading vocabulary of the learner. The "er" ending is common to numerous words and has a rather consistent pronunciation in the English language.

In teaching syllabication skills to pupils, the writer recommends the following:

1. Important syllables should be taught to pupils as the need arises, not in isolation from context.
2. Methods used in teaching syllabication should be interesting to learners. Sameness of methodology makes for boredom.
3. Inductive approaches should be used whereby pupils are guided to discover the correct pronunciation and meaning of syllables.
4. Learners should be given ample opportunities to determine the correct word before a teacher/pupil intervenes with identification of that word in reading.
5. Holistic procedures should be used in teaching reading. Words then are a part of a sentence and sentences are a part of a paragraph with sequential paragraphs following. Thus, a word is not an isolated entity but is an inherent part of a larger unit of content.

Using Context Clues

Phonics instruction and syllabication learnings should be stressed within the framework of larger units of emphasis such as context clues. If a pupil cannot identify a word, the teacher must guide the pupil to read the words that surround the unknown. Many times, the unknown word in reading can then be identified. Too frequently, pupils do not use context clues to choose a correct word for the unknown. It is not a difficult task to assist pupils to learn to use context clues. Pupils must do the learning as is true of all acquired knowledge, skills and attitudes. The teacher's role is to provide learning activities which encourage, stimulate and assist learners to be independent in reading. The writer believes strongly that the use of context clues in reading will work in many cases to guide learners to choose the correct word when the unknown appears to be in the offing. Learners need to put forth considerable effort in achieving skill to use context clues as well as phonics and syllabication generalizations.

The use of context clues in reading stresses holism in reading. The entire sentence then as a minimum becomes salient in identifying a word. To emphasize the use of context clues in identifying unknown words, the teacher needs to;

1. Encourage pupils to read the entire sentence to ascertain the correct word in reading.
2. Guide leaners to use phonics in initial sounds if there are too many words that fit in as far as the use of context clues is concerned. The initial consonant or vowel sound will then secure the answer as to which the correct word will be in reading as a result of using context clues.
3. Assist pupils to use syllabication skills if the correct word in reading cannot be selected in context due to many meaningful possibilities which are incorrect. Thus, dividing the unknown word into syllables plus the use of context clues and phonics skills should guarantee to the learner which the correct word is in the sentence. Word identification skills are complimentary, not isolated from each other.

4. Stress holism in reading such as when one reads, the entire selection provides meaning and comprehension rather than isolated parts. Gestalt psychology is inherent here in that reading for wholes supplies meaning to the reader, rather than reading small segments. Gestaltists believe that individuals always look for meaning even if the parts truly would not provide that which is understandable. Individuals still take the parts to provide a whole. The whole stresses meaning in reading, not meaningless abstractions (Ediger, 1997).

5. Pupils should attempt the use of context clues prior to using phonics and syllabication to unlock unknown words. If unknown words are unlocked through the use of context clues, the reader will become more fluent in the skills of reading. Why? Less time is taken to read a selection if the reader identifies the unknown word through the use of context clues. Analyzing a word through the use of phonics and syllabication skills is more time consuming as compared to the use of context clues.

Using Picture Clues

Early primary age pupil, in particular, find picture clues to be helpful in choosing a correct word in what was the unknown in reading. The pictures in basal readers for early primary grade learners are large and are closely related to the surrounding printed subject matter. The illustrations serve well for the teacher to use in building background information within pupils prior to oral or silent reading. With quality background content in mind before the act of reading, the pupil will understand better that which is being read. Then too, if a pupil does not recognize a word in reading, he/she may look at the illustration on that same page and, in many cases, be able to choose the correct word for that which appeared to be an unknown word. On the intermediate grade levels, the use of picture clues to identify the unknown word tends to become less useful since the illustrations are much fewer and there is much more print on each page of the basal reader. However, even here the learner should study the picture carefully to notice if a clue exists for the unknown word. This takes only a short time to do. Learners need to become independent in attempting to identify unknown words.

Determining Reading Levels

How does the teacher ascertain the level of reading achievement in relationship to the basal textbook used? Is the text too difficult or too easy for the learner when reading content ? If it is too complex, the learner will tend to become frustrated in reading. Should the basal be at a too elementary level of complexity, he/she might become bored and lose interest in reading. The basal reader used should be challenging enough and yet be understandable to the pupil. Readiness activities provided by the teacher such as pupils seeing the new words in print, knowing the meaning of these words and having a purpose for reading, prior to the actual act of reading, assists each learner to be able to comprehend and understand the contents therein. These readiness experiences guide pupils to understand that which would be too complex for reading. However, any book can become too complex for the elementary age pupil.

To evaluate the reading level of the basal used for any child, the teacher may mark off one hundred running words in the textbook at the beginning of the school year and have a pupil read the contents orally to the teacher in a private setting where no other pupil can listen in to the oral reading. If a pupil can pronounce correctly 95 to 98 of the 100 words, the basal is on the reading level of the pupil providing that another condition is met. Thus, the learner needs to also answer correctly, three out of four questions developed by the teacher which covers the subject matter read. The 95 to 98 per cent of the words read correctly and the three out of four questions answered correctly are approximate and not an absolute. One can understand as the pupil pronounces fewer and fewer of the words correctly and is able to answer fewer and fewer questions correctly how this hinders learner comprehension of content read. The approach mentioned here to ascertain reading levels of individual pupils should be conducted so that pupils have not had any practice reading the content previously nor should other pupils listen in to the informal evaluation. If these precautions are not followed, the teacher cannot not determine if the basal is on the frustrational, instructional or recreational level of reading. If a pupil can pronounce 95 to 98 per cent of the running words correctly, there still are opportunities to grow in learning new words in reading such as 2 to 5 for each 100 running words read and yet the number required here is not overwhelming.

There are standardized tests to determine reading achievement at the present level. The purpose of administering standardized tests to determining reading levels as well as using the informal 100 running word method is to match reading levels of individual pupils with materials to be read. If a teacher can locate reading materials for each pupil which harmonize with his/her present individually can be a truly enjoyable event. If a pupil cannot identify an adequate number of words read, he/she will be reading at the frustrational level. Should the reading materials be too easy, the pupil might then be reading at the recreational level whereby approximately 100 out of 100 running words are identified correctly and four out of four questions covering the content read are answered correctly, without having read the subject matter previously. Recreational level of reading is done when the learner chooses a trade book and reads the contents for sheer enjoyment. Recreational reading must be encouraged by the teacher so that learners achieve positive attitudes toward reading. The instructional level provides opportunities for pupils to learn to identify new words and yet comprehension is adequate to ensure success in the reading curriculum. The frustrational level of reading makes for pupils who feel frustrated in reading and tend not to be encouraged through subject matter read.

Problems in Reading

There are numerous problems that pupils individually may experience in reading. Problem areas need identification and solutions sought.

The following kinds of errors made by pupils in oral reading will provide the teacher with selected ideas as to what to look for when learners reveal difficulties :

1. Mispronunciation of words
2. Omitting words
3. Adding words to content read
4. No paying attention to punctuation marks.
5. Hesitation on words read.
6. Failure to associate graphemes with phonemes when consistency is in evidence.
7. Too much stress placed on phonics when there is a lack of consistency between grapheme and phoneme.
8. Insufficient emphasis on thought units when the pupil is reading.

   Thus, the pupil should read the sentence correctly in terms of thought units such as, "The dog/ran for the bone". An incorrect thought unit would be the following: "The/dog ran for/the/bone".
9. A lack of holism in reading. Thus, the pupil reads too analytical by dividing words into component segments when the learner reveals this is not needed.
10. A stress upon holism whereby the pupil must pay more attention to parts such as words so that meaning can be attached to content read.

The teacher needs to be a quality diagnoser of learner difficulties in reading and assist learners individually with problems encountered. The pupil must become a proficient reader by using different word attack skills as keys to comprehend content, not ends in and of themselves.

As pupils master word attack skills, they also need to be capable of reading for diverse purposes or comprehension skills. The following are salient purposes for learners in reading content:

1. *Reading for important facts.* Here, the pupil reads for significant specifics in a given selection regardless of the curriculum area involved. All purposes in reading must be emphasized within context, not in complete isolation.

2. *Reading to skim.* In this situation, the learner needs to read for a precise name, date, or place deemed worthy or consideration.

3. *Reading to follow directions.* There are numerous situations in which a learner needs to read directions carefully so that an exercise can be worked correctly by the pupil.

4. *Reading to develop a generalization.* To generalize, a pupil must read a selection of adequate length so that the pupil can say in one sentence what has been read. Facts provided must support a strong generalization.

5. *Reading for a main idea.* A longer selection is read as compared to reading for achieving generalizations. Thus from an entire unit of study in any curriculum area, the learner should ultimately be able to say in one sentence that which has been read.

6. *Reading to think critically.* Here, the learner separates and analyzes that which is correct form the incorrect, the salient from the trivial and ideas of propaganda from the rational.

7. *Reading to think creatively.* The learner needs to come up with unique, novel ideas when reading creatively. Thus the pupil may come up with a different ending, beginning, setting, characterization, or plot than that which is contained in the reading selection.

8. *Reading to solve problems.* A problem solver is able to identify one or more problem areas. The problems should be questions which are rather broadly stated. Information can then be gathered in answer to the problem through reading and a multi-media approach. The content read directly related to the problem area needs to be appraised in terms of being plausible. Additional reading can be done to check the plausibility of the information. A variety of reading materials should be available to meet reading needs of involved learners.

9. *Reading for enjoyment.* The pupil then selects materials to read based on personal interests, needs and purposes.

Quality trade books need to be in the offing so that each pupil may choose that which is personally beneficial. Sheer interest in reading is the ultimate goal here. Sustained silent reading (SSR) might be stressed here in which everyone in a classroom or the entire school at a given time reads a personally selected trade book for enjoyment.

10. *Reading to determine cause and effect.* Thus, the learner reads content from a basal or printed materials to notice causes for effects. When determining what made for an occurrence, learners then need to find the cause or causes.

When each of the above purposes is emphasized in reading, the pupil needs to possess reading factors to engage in each type of purpose. For example, a skilled reader on the intermediate or higher grade level can read for any of the enumerated purposes.

In Summary

A quality reading curriculum assists each pupil to attain as optimally as possible. Appropriate reading skills are needed presently by learners to do well in school as well as to attain more optimally later in the adult world of work and recreation. The pupil must put forth much effort to become a proficient reader. The pupil needs to do the learning to become a good reader. The teacher can set the stage with appropriate readiness experiences as well as challenging ongoing learning opportunities. Pupil progress in reading needs to be diagnosed and remediation procedures should follow. Word attack skills are tools in learning to read and in becoming a better reader. They are not ends in and of themselves. To be a good reader stresses the ability to comprehend and understand that which has been read. When pupils read, the approach used should stress holism as much as possible. After all, pupils read to secure ideas and holism stresses learners obtaining meaning and understanding from subject matter read (Ediger, 1995).

Word attack skills that pupils need to become proficient in are the following:

1. use of phonics and syllabication.
2. use of picture clues and configuration clues

3. use of context clues and structural analysis.

Should pupils lack proficiency in reading, the teacher needs to diagnose and determine if a pupil should experience remedial work in any of these word recognition skills.

Reading for diverse purposes is important to any reader. These purposes include the following:

1. reading for facts and main ideas.
2. reading to secure concepts and generalizations.
3. reading to skim and scan for salient information.
4. reading to obtain directions.
5. reading to think creatively and critically.
6. reading to solve problems.
7. reading to determine cause and effects.
8. reading for enjoyment.
9. reading to obtain sequence of ideas.
10. reading orally to an audience.

Each pupil needs assistance to achieve as optimally as possible in reading.

Selected References

Bhagya Lakshmi, L. and D. Bhaskara Rao (1999), *Reading and Comprehension*. New Delhi : Discovery Publishing House.

Ediger, Marlow (1995), *Philosophy in Curriculum Development*. Kirksville, Missouri : Simpson Publishing Company, 1–18.

Ediger, Marlow (1997), *Teaching Reading and the Language Arts in the Elementary School*. Kirksville, Missouri : Simpson Publishing Company, 39–48.

Ediger, Marlow (1996), *Elementary Education*. Kirksville, Missouri : Simpson Publishing Company, 37–46.

17
Speaking and the Pupil

Speaking activities should be stressed alongwith reading experiences emphasized in teaching-learning situations. A good reader has a wide range of vocabulary terms available prior to the actual reading of subject matter. A child who has a rich speaking vocabulary has an easier time of developing reading skills as compared to the learner that lacks a rich speaking vocabulary. Then too, it is much more comfortable to be able to converse well with others due to having a rich speaking vocabulary. Then too, it is much more comfortable to be able to converse well with others due to having a rich speaking vocabulary as compared to those who cannot converse adequately. Feelings of discomfort tend to arise when one is unable to join into a conversation. One needs friends for support, for entertainment, for enjoyment and for learning. Thus, it behooves the teacher to assist pupils to achieve proficiently in oral communication.

Giving Oral Reports

There are occasions when individuals are asked to give oral reports in different organizations in society. It is important then for learners to develop needed skills in reporting to others in a group setting. Any speaking activity in front of groups should satisfying so that feelings of fright are minimized. People who are afraid to get up in front of groups have experienced the unfortunate in previous settings involving speaking in front of others. The teacher and pupils in the classroom should support each other so that satisfying experiences in oral communication are an end result. Confidence in the self in appearing before groups in different speaking endeavours is salient. Learners should never be minimized for mistakes made in oral communication. Rather support must be provided for pupils to improve oral communication skills with renewed confidence.

A. H. Maslow in his theory of motivation developed a hierarchy of needs levels which indicate the necessity of fulfillment if pupils are to do well in school and later as adults. Maslow's lowest level of needs are physiological. These needs include adequate nutrition, rest, sleep, clothing and shelter. Physiological needs are the lowest level of needs that must be met if learners are to do well in school. If a pupil lacks in any of these categories, he/she cannot attain adequately in the school curriculum. The human body is like a machine and needs proper care. Perhaps, the human machine needs much more care as compared to a mechanical machine. Quality breakfasts and noon meals served in school assists learners to achieve well. Going up higher on maslow's hierarchy of needs in sequence is safety needs. To do well, all need to feel secure and safe. Weapons brought to school or fights among pupils in the school environment and in society make for a lack of security on the part of pupils. Maslow's physiological and safety needs categories are followed by love and belonging needs. Each person wishes to feel being a part of a group which is satisfying. The child who is an isolate or who is shunned does not feel as if he/she belongs to a group, be it large or small. The teacher here must attempt to guide all pupils to develop feelings of belonging and being accepted by others. Next in sequence, Maslow stressed the importance of learners having esteem needs met. Here, the teacher and learners need to recognize talents possessed by pupils. Individuals like to thought of and remembered for what can be done well. Each person has selected strengths which need to be recognized and acknowledged. Too frequently, the talents of individuals are never sought after and praised. Ridiculing or ignoring of others seems to be more the order of the day. Is it not much better to praise that which is worthy and good ? Certainly, pupils individually possess abilities that need recognition, be it in knowledge, skills or attitudes. Talents possessed by learners should be identified and used in the classroom setting. Next in Maslow's hierarchy of needs is the desire to understand. Here, facts, concepts, generalizations and main ideas of acquired subject matter become salient. Self-realization is the highest goal in Maslow's theory of motivation. To become what one wishes to become represents self-actualization. That is a complex goal to attain but must be sought as an ongoing objective. No doubt, this objectives is sequential and never attained in toto.

Feelings of self-actualization are salient in any curriculum area. Certainly, learner optimal achievement is necessary in the language arts in order to develop feelings of self-actualization. In the area of speaking and oral communication, it is vital to attain in the direction of being the self-fulfilled individual. Gestalt theory must prevail here in that the whole or entire person is involved in learning. Thus, the physiological, the safety or security facets, the belonging individual, the person with adequate esteem or recognition for that which is well done and the self-actualization concepts are vital for any person in the language arts and its sub-division, oral communication.

Carefully chosen objectives learning activities to attain the chosen ends, and appropriate evaluation procedures to ascertain if the objectives have been achieved are necessary to ensure quality in oral communication.

Objectives in Oral Communication

Objectives to emphasize in oral communication need to be carefully selected by those involved in teaching-learning situations, be it the teacher(s), principal, supervisor and other involved persons with professional training. Committees need to be at work in adequate time durations to evaluate and ultimately choose those ends which are worthwhile for learner attainment. Workshops, faculty meetings, study groups, staff development programs, research of the current literature, as well as resource personnel assistance should provide input into selecting objectives in oral communication.

The objectives need to be comprehensive and cover all relevant ends in oral communication. Objectives must be new and attainable by learners. The objectives should be arranged sequentially so that pupils might be successful in goal attainment. They need to be written precisely enough so that it is possible to appraise if each pupil has achieved the stated goals.

There are oral communication goals which would be recognized as being salient for all pupils to attain. These are the following :

1. Speaking clearly so all can hear content spoken.
2. Speaking at a rate which is comprehendible to others.
3. Speaking with voice inflection, including proper stress, pitch and juncture.
4. Speaking with the intent of involving others in an atmosphere of respect and acceptance.
5. Speaking with purpose involved be it in the making of introductions, the presenting of an oral report, taking part in discussions, participating in creative and formal dramatics, interviewing and using of puppets involving oral communication.
6. Speaking using appropriate gestures, facial expressions, body movements and eye contact.
7. Speaking with the use of agreement between subject and predicate, as well as varied sentence patterns, kinds of sentences such as interrogative, imperative, declarative and exclamatory.
8. Speaking with diverse sentences such as simple, complex, compound complex and compound sentences.
9. Speaking with the use of different reasons for oral communication such as to provide directions clearly to others.
10. Speaking to influence others in the political arena.

Learning Opportunities

A variety of learning opportunities should be provided pupils so that interest is ongoing. Then too, individual differences among learners need to be provided for in order that optimal achievement in speaking can be furthered for each pupil. There are numerous purposes involved in speaking.

1. *Discussions.* All individuals tend to be involved in discussions at one time or another. These discussions can be quite formal as well as informal. It behooves the teacher

to guide each elementary pupil to achieve proficiency in discussions. In the classroom setting, there is subject matter to discuss after pupils have completed reading a specific selection in diverse academic areas. After taking an excursion related directly to an ongoing unit of study, learners with teacher guidance discuss what has been read. The purpose for the discussion might be to determine what the individual learner has comprehended. The discussion may also zero in on having pupils extend content read in an ongoing unit of study. Discussions need to follow definite criteria so that the teacher may appraise learner attainment in the discussions using these standards. Criteria or standards to follow in discussions should include the following:

a) The discussion should be stimulating to generate interest in content presented.

b)s Each pupil should be encouraged to join the discussion.

c) No one should dominate the discussion.

d) Learners need to develop feelings of belonging when participating in a committee setting.

e) Ideas in the discussion should circulate among all group members rather than between a few members in the group setting.

f) Content must be presented clearly to others. Meaning needs to be present in learning.

g) Respect and acceptance of the thinking of others is important.

h) The teacher is a guide and not a dispenser of information.

i) Evaluation of progress in a discussion must always follow specific standards and should be stressed frequently.

j) Learners must attain and grow in becoming proficient in discussion settings.

Creativity must receive ample emphasis in any discussion. Evaluation sessions should not hinder pupil progress in revealing originality and being a quality member of a discussion group.

Making Introductions

Very frequently two or more people are introduced to each other. How is this to be done so that individuals get to know each other? Then too, introduced persons should be able to follow with conversation that is enriching to all involved. Speaking clearly and pleasantly are two key concepts here. Rudeness and being inconsiderate have no roles to play in the making of introductions. When people are introduced to each other, the names should be correctly pronounced in order that people can call each other by name. The one who does the introducing should know something about all involved in the making of introductions so that conversation may follow in sequence. If one knows something of interest about the other person, this assists in moving forward with the conversation. Each person needs to be treated with respect as a human being having much worth. Minimizing others has no role to play in the making of introductions. Eye contact in making introductions tends to show interest toward others. There are a few cultures where eye contact with those being introduced is not stressed. However, on the whole, quality eye contact with others being introduced indicates respect involving the entire introduction process. Criteria and standards to use in appraising learner progress in the making of introductions are the following:

1. Involved persons should indicate a desire to meet others. Quality introductions made should assist in this area.

2. Self-evaluation by participants is an important ingredient in wishing to make improvements.

3. Proper stress, pitch and juncture with appropriate voice inflection should be an inherent part in the making of introductions.

4. Appropriate volume and speed of oral presentations is salient in introducing one person to the others.

5. Looking at each other in face to face communication is important when making introductions.
6. Full attention must be given to each person when an introduction is being made. Being distracted by factors in the environment hinders in the making of introductions.
7. Clarity in expressions and ideas presented is a must.
8. Individuals making introductions should be interested in people. A people centered approach is recommended when introductions are made.
9. Practice is necessary in learning the art of making introductions.
10. Feedback in making introductions is necessary for improvement to take place.

Extemporaneous Speaking

Extemporaneous speaking has much merit for pupils possessing readiness for this activity. Why ? Each person is asked at diverse intervals in life to speak on a topic with little prior notice. Or, one needs to make a decision or choices in the spur of the monument. Little time is available in these situation to plan, ponder and analyze. Thus, one must think rapidly and make the best choices possible.

In extemporaneous thinking, the learner is provided with a topic or title to speak on. He/she needs to prepare a talk within the allotted time limits given, such as five minutes. The topic or title could be familiar to the pupil, or it could also be rather new or novel. The title/topic should not be excessively difficult since the time limit for preparation might be rather short such as the five minute time interval. The presentation is then given to the total class or to a committee. Extemporaneous speaking quality may be evaluated using the following criteria:

1. The speaker is able to think quickly within the prescribed time limits.
2. The speaker is able to present content meaningfully to listeners.

3. The speaker is able to obtain the attention of listeners to secure quality listening.
4. The speaker is poised when presenting content in the ongoing talk.
5. The speaker is using notes when there is a need to do so.
6. The speaker uses eye contact when presenting information.
7. The speaker faces all participants who are listeners.
8. The speaker uses facial expressions and gestures as needed to obtain the attention of listeners.
9. The speaker does not exhibit distracting mannerisms.
10. The speaker invites questions after the extemporaneous speech.

Learners need to be taken where they are presently in achievement in extemporaneous speaking and then work for continuous progress. When appraising learner progress, realistic standards must be used. A pupil cannot attain perfection in all ten standards listed above. They can make progress with diagnosis and remediation when improving performance in extemporaneous speaking.

Creative Dramatics

Pupils need to have the opportunities to participate in creative dramatics as a speaking activity. Creativity indicates novel, unique and original ideas pertaining to words and sentences used as well as in planning and implementing the dramatic activity. Being able to dramatize would indicate the need to have background information in order to role play or act out diverse scenes and situations.

Where might the content come from for the creative dramatics presentation? Basal readers, trade books, history texts and other reading materials contain content which can readily be a part of a creative dramatics presentation. Thus, the teacher should correlate content pupils have read from the basal reader, for example, with the creative dramatics activity. Speaking parts are developed as the need arises in the creative dramatics presentation. These parts are not memorized but thought and thinking is inherent as the creative dramatics activity progresses. Ideas presented relate directly to what has been read, but creativity is needed as the dramatization enfolds. Background scenery may be made by learners with teacher guidance The scenery made should enhance the creative dramatics activity. Time spent on the scenery should have value in terms of objectives to be attained by learners. Busy work is to be frowned upon. Goal centered experiences are needed in the school curriculum. Time on task is to be emphasized. The background scenery may be appraised in terms of;

1. being neatly made.
2. being directly related to the creative dramatics activity.
3. being accurate and yet novel ideas are to be encouraged.
4. being within the achievement levels of learners.
5. being worthwhile for involved pupils.
6. being purposeful for learners so that reasons are inherent for learning.
7. being able to secure the interests of pupils.
8. being a meaningful learning opportunity for pupils.
9. being of assistance to make the dramatics experience more realistic.
10. being a springboard to further interest in reading.

Formal Dramatizations

Formal dramatizations emphasize that learners write play parts pertaining to what has been read. For example in history, pupils read about events and involved people in these happenings. Thus, a committee of pupils may take what has been read and write play parts should be written. It should not be overwhelming whereby pupils lose interest in the ongoing activity. Play parts should be;

1. Accurately written pertaining to content contained in the history textbook.
2. Correctly written containing agreement of subject and predicate, accurate placement of punctuation marks and content arranged sequentially. Exceptions would be if the language needed in writing must stress non-standard English to portray the speaking part accurately of the involved culture.
3. Written on the basis of what can reasonably be expected of leaners in terms of developmental levels. Excessively high or low levels involving teacher expectations should be avoided when pupils write play parts for formal dramatics activities.
5. Challenging and motivating for pupils to write.
6. Written so that all can be involved in this activity. The best writers alone should not be the sole writers. Each pupil should have contributions to make.
7. Fascinating for learner participation in order that roles may be chosen which harmonize with the learner's optimal chances of achievement.
8. Written so that further interest in literature pertaining to diverse academic areas is an end result.
9. Practiced by involved individuals until they feel comfortable for this presentation in front of different classrooms and smaller groups.
10. Stimulating sot hat increased effort in reading is in evidence.

Roles for the different parts should be assigned or can be volunteered for. Each person in a specific role reading the assigned play part should use appropriate stress, pitch and juncture. Voice inflection and proper enunciation is important for each participant in formal dramatics. Co-operation is needed in writing the parts as well as in the actual role play experience. The formal dramatization should be presented in front of other learners in the school setting.

Using Puppets

Pupils with teacher leadership may make puppets that relate to content read in reading, literature and the social studies, among other curriculum areas. The completed puppets might then be used to role play a given character or situation. Selected puppets are easy to make such as the sack puppet. Here, the learner may use a large paper sack and cut out eyes, nose and mouth. Ears may be drawn or pasted on to the sack puppet. Other forms of puppets are much more time consuming in their making such as a sock puppet. A sock might be used here to make this kind of puppet. The learner might sew on two buttons for eyes, two pieces of felt for the ears, as well as other needed features. Since a sock puppet takes much more time to make as compared to a sack puppet, the teacher might wish to evaluate the desired time that should go into the making of any form of puppet. If artistic endeavours are strongly emphasized by the teacher, then pupils may make sock puppets. There are numerous art objectives to be attained in the making of sock puppets including sequential progress in eye hand coordination and harmonizing specific features such as ears sewed on to the original shape and size of the sock. The sack puppet can be made more quickly and serves an equally purposeful function in its role play use. There are numerous other kinds of puppets that can be made including stick and paper mache' puppets. Regardless of the kind of puppet made, the puppets should be:

1. made neatly and accurately. Creativity can be emphasized as the need arises and is a salient objective for learner attainment.
2. functional according to their purposeful use.
3. related in their making to goals to be attained in the art curriculum.
4. interesting to make in order to obtain learner interest.
5. developed according to their needs to portray definite roles in the curriculum.

Creative dramatics, formal dramatizations and puppetry have specific goals for learner attainment. These activities are not implemented for the sake of doing so but to achieve educational purposes. What are these purposes?

1. To make inherent subject matter more understandable. A pupil may not understand that which has been read but the involved content becomes clear in creative and formal dramatizations as well as in the use of puppetry. Role play experiences tends to breathe life into an ongoing activity.
2. To diagnose what pupils do not understand from reading and discussion of ideas, facts, conclusions and summaries. The diagnosis may be made by the learner in that he/she realizes that what was previously assumed to be understood is vague and needs additional information. The need for additional information was discovered during the creative or formal dramatization, or in the learning opportunity involving puppets.
3. To achieve interest in learning subject matter. The writer has observed numerous times in classrooms how learners have become fascinated in attaining subject matter when role play is being used as a teaching device.
4. To perceive transfer values in learning. There are pupils who perceive that role play experiences can be used in numerous academic areas. What is learned then in role play activities in literature may be used in social studies units of study. An increase in integration of subject matter might then be an end result. The integration of literature and social studies provides situations whereby other academic disciplines might also become a part of the previously two mentioned areas of integrated content.
5. To perceive reasons for using what has been learned. Pupils might not understand reasons for using what has been learned until the inherent subject matter is emphasized in role play experiences. Thus, subject matter learned is used in creative and formal dramatics as well as in puppetry. Use of acquired knowledge, skills and attitudes must be in evidence or pupils will tend to forget previously attained objectives.

Debate in the Classroom

Too frequently, it is believed that debate is for the university level of education, largely or only. The writer believes that early primary grade pupils should have ample opportunities to experience debate on their understanding levels. Thus these pupils need to experience sequential activities in debate which will assist learners to realized that there are opposing points of view on issues. Sometimes within a teacher lead discussion, pupils tend to vigorously discuss both sides of a coin on an issue. The tremendous interest that pupils have on a specific issue propels learners to put forth much effort into discussing the inherent pros and cons. In a debate there are individuals who take a position as well as those who are opposed to that position taken. To be a good debater requires that individuals have much knowledge pertaining to what is being debated. The knowledge is acquired through reading and research. To be a good debater too, requires a clear speaking voice. One here also needs to be influential in presenting ideas. Background information is of utmost importance. A good debater is able to use acquired knowledge to score a victory over the opposition in the debate. How far the teacher wants to stress the rules of a typical debate in the elementary school years is open to analysis. However, the spirit of a debate can bee emphasized in any classroom starting with the kindergarten years. To be sure, early primary grade pupils are young and will lack information, skills and inclinations to debate the way juniors and seniors in high school and beyond can perform. However, young children can be guided to attain well in their consideration of a variety of view points, be it pros or con.

There are definite criteria which should be stressed for elementary pupils in the debate arena. These are the following:

1. Stay on the topic being debated.
2. Be well informed on content and subject matter pursued.
3. Present ideas with clarity and confidence.
4. Maintain quality eye contact when presenting information.
5. Look for additional content when needed to substantiate ideas presented.
6. Justify content presented if asked to do so.

7. Evaluate content presented by others in terms of accuracy, appropriate logic and thought.
8. Ask questions of a presenter of ideas if vagueness is in evidence.
9. Practice using appropriate stress, pitch and juncture when debating ideas with others. A tape recorder or a video-cassette recorder can provide much feedback to the speaker in terms of using language effectively in a debate as well as non-verbal facets of communication.
10. Put forth much effort in becoming a good debater who can use background information to advantage.

No one pupil can achieve all of the above named standards. Each learner, however, should attain as abilities and interests permit. Continuous progress is important for pupils on an individual basis.

If on the intermediate grade levels, a more formal debate between and among learners is desired, the following guidelines need to be followed:

1. Develop a topic for debate involving pupils with teacher assistance.
2. State the topic in debate form such as—Resolved that welfare recipients should not receive any federal assistance after two years of time.
3. Each side in the debate can then prepare content necessary for a quality debate to ensue. Much research is then needed.
4. Ultimately, the debate can be presented in front of the classroom or a larger audience. Each side has a time limit to present ideas to support a point of view.
5. A time for rebuttal by opponents is then necessary. Thus side A rebuts what side B has said and vice-versa. Questions can also come from the floor.

The debate should challenge each side to prepare well for the event. A challenging debate can certainly make for much learning and motivation for either side of the debate. The topic chosen for the debate should be of interest to the debaters. If interest is inherent, then effort will go in to studying for the debate. The teacher will need to assist each side to locate and use appropriate reference sources. Listeners to the debate should have excellent questions they wish to ask debate participants following the presentation and rebuttal. These questions could provide a further springboard for participants to find needed answers and enrich personal knowledge of the side taken for the debate.

Leisure Time Communication

Being able to visit with others in a recreational setting is certainly a valuable asset to the participant. One can learn much from others in informal conversation settings. Conversing should be an enjoyable experience. The topics to be discussed are endless. A topic selected should be pleasing and interesting for involved persons. Interest seems to keep a conversation going. An interesting conversationalist has much to offer to others. People seem to follow those who converse effectively. Generally, a good conversationalist has much background information and is able to use ideas in a fascinating manner. These individuals are relaxed when conversing and enjoy the company of people. A good conversationalist then is person centered, rather than having sole interest in objects and things en toto. He/she is able to develop and maintain a quality conversation. These individuals are generally admired by others and tend to be popular. Each pupil should have ample opportunities to become a person who converses well with others. The teacher should be a model and guide here. Creativity rather than direct standards are needed to be able to converse well with others. Classroom time may be given to assist pupils in the art of conversation. This can be time well spent since conversation is the most frequent kind of speaking activity for [illegible]s. The teacher then needs to:

1. assist learners to become relaxed individuals when engaging in conversation.
2. reward pupils with praise for genuine improvement in conversing with others. The praise is given to reward, not

retard abilities in oral communication. The focal point is upon helping learners to relax and wishing to engage spontaneously in conversation.

3. work worth pupils so that there is no ridicule of what others are saying. Rather each pupil assists the others to participate actively in conversation.
4. plan a wholesome classroom environment in which there are a variety of rich learning activities so that pupils achieve skill to have content to converse about.
5. have materials, objects and re-alia in the classroom whereby pupils can learn from these items in an incidental manner. Learning on one's own certainly should build background information within pupils so that improved conversation is a salient end result.
6. develop positive attitudes of each pupil toward the self and toward others. An adequate self-concept is necessary to be a good conversationalist.
7. achieve within the learner feelings of wanting to converse with others.
8. study each pupil carefully to ascertain what would assist each learner in attaining more effectively in conversation.
9. have pupils achieve positive attitudes toward conversation as a valuable speaking activity.
10. continue to work with all pupils in developing sequential conversation skills.

In Closing

There are numerous speaking activities which learners need to achieve skill in. Life in school and in society demands that individuals be quality communicators. The teacher of language arts then must establish goals of excellence in oral communication. These objectives should stress knowledge, skills and attitudinal ends. A balance among these three kinds of objectives should be an end result. Learning opportunities to attain these objectives should provide for individual differences so each pupil may attain optimally in oral communication. The learning opportunities should be of interest, meaningful, purposeful and challenging to the individual learner. The world of work needs individuals who communicate well. Personal enrichment also stresses that each person be able to communicate effectively.

Reference

Bhaskara Rao, Digumarti (1987). *Audio Visual Teaching Aids.* Guntur: Nagarjuna Publishers (in Telugu language).

18
Principles of Learning and the Teaching of Reading

Reading teachers need to use as guidelines emphasizing principles of learning that educational psychologists recommend in teaching and learning situations. By using these principles of learning in teaching reading, pupils should achieve more optimally. Thus, teachers of reading need to have these criteria well in mind and use them to create a positive learning environment for reading instruction.

Pupils Need to Perceive that Reading is Enjoyable

When it is time for reading instruction, pupils should fee that this is a time for enjoying content read. It should not be considered by pupils as a time for drill and more drill on phonics and other word recognition techniques. Negative attitudes toward reading should never be reinforced. The very first day of reading instruction in school should emphasize that literature is enjoyable in its many manifestations. We consider reading to be the most valuable skill possessed. We do much reading and find that new ideas obtained provide challenge and interest. Why should pupils not feel the same way ? Seemingly, we thirst for time and more time for reading. We have observed early primary grade pupils who can't wait for story time to come whereby the teacher reads enthusiastically and has eye contact with the involved learners. This is a good model for pupils to emulate—the enjoyment of reading at a young age and then build on this foundation throughout one's life-time.

To enjoy literature, pupils need to have ample opportunities to choose what is of personal interest. A variety of library books with different genres is a must so that pupils may select what is perceived as interesting and valuable. These library books must also be written on diverse reading levels. Individuals need to read library books that are on his/her reading levels. Thus, books chosen sequentially are on the reading level of the involved learners and are then understandable.

Pupils Need to Read in All Curriculum Areas

Too frequently, pupils perceive reading as involving the literature curriculum only. Reading then is not seen as an essential part of all curriculum areas in the school setting. A perception of holism is needed so that each pupil realizes that reading is done in the social studies, mathematics, science, language arts, art, music and physical education.

What is stressed in the literature curriculum is also useful in reading in the content areas. There should be no division among these curriculum areas when it comes to reading. Individuals read to obtain information. When reading to obtain information, the content needs to be understood, not merely memorized. We see no reason why reading in the content areas should also not be enjoyable. In all situations involving reading, effort must be put forth. Thus, the act of reading well cannot be given to the pupils but must be earned through effort. Each lesson and unit of study is important to pupils. Wasting time by the learner or teaching what is irrelevant by the teacher is lost time and must be made up in future lessons. While the make-up occurs, new content instead should have been learned by the pupil.

Each curriculum area has its own vocabulary and subject matter. Sequentially, pupils need to attain vital objectives in literature and the other subject matter fields.

Pupils Should Experience Quality Sequence

A vital principle of learning is that pupils experience an appropriate sequence in the reading curriculum. If the sequence is not appropriate, a pupil might well experience failure if the goals are not achievable. Should the objectives of instruction be too easy, the involved learner might well become bored and feel unmotivated. It is difficult for any teacher to determine the preset achievement level of a pupil and then have that learner achieve at an optimal level. However, the reading teacher needs to do the best possible with a roomful of pupils to assist each pupil to do the best possible in reading.

As much as is feasible, pupils individually should select their own reading materials. Generally, pupils select what to read which is challenging. Within a small group, the teacher may guide pupils to work collaboratively in content read. Pupils might then encourage and challenge each other to do well in the committee or small group endeavour. Those who find the content too difficult may then be assisted by the other committee members in word attack skills as well as in comprehension. A good reader in an atmosphere of respect may read to the less able. Pupils in working collaboratively may take turns reading the selection within the committee setting.

For the class as a whole with its many levels of reading instruction, the pupils together with the teacher might read the selection orally with all involved. Thus, all may read orally or follow along in their readers or from the Big Book used on the primary grade level. The sequence must be such that pupils individually learn as much as possible in reading literature and across the content fields.

Pupils Need to Perceive the Integrated Curriculum

Too frequently, reading of content has been separated from the other language arts areas such as listening, speaking and writing. Good standards for listening need to be stressed when discussing ideas pupils have gleaned from reading. There needs to be evaluation of pupil achievement in realizing the goals of good listening. Different levels of complexity in listening goals may be emphasized in the reading curriculum. As pupils discuss ideas gleaned from reading, the speaking vocabulary of pupils should increasingly emphasize more complex objectives. With a richer background of experiences through sequential learning, the speaking vocabulary of pupils should increase to discuss higher cognitive level subject matter objectives. Pupils should be able to communicate clearly, accurately and positively with other learners.

The writing vocabulary correlates well with reading. There are so many diverse projects and activities that pupils may use writing to express ideas. Pupils may choose which writing experiences to participate in as well as determine what to write about. Journal writing has been quite popular as an activity that correlates well with reading. Thus the individual pupil may choose what to write about in the journal in terms of content related to the selection read. A pupil may write about the setting of the literary selection. The learner may describe the setting, create a new setting and/or react to the author's established setting.

Pupils Need to Become Life-long Learners

Pupils with teacher assistance need to enjoy reading so that it can become an experience that lasts throughout one's life-time. Processes in reading can continually be improved upon. Comprehension may also become increasingly proficient. It appears that "there is nothing beyond more education", a statement attributed to John Dewey (1859–1952). Individuals need to read and study throughout their unique life spans.

The home setting is an ideal place to start as soon as the child is born. At that beginning point, parents need to talk to the child in a pleasant manner. Humming and singing to the new born is also very important. Experiences such as these help the infant to use language and its meanings. At a very early age, the infant, as soon as he/she can sit on the parent(s) lap should look at large illustrations, lasting as long as the attention span of the infant allows. The parents should point to objects an items and say the related words. For example, parents should say "milk" when pointing to milk as it is being drunk by the infant. As soon as the child can listen to oral reading of short stories written for young children, this should be done. One of us have noticed a parent reading "The Little Red Hen" to a three year old. The three year old was very receptive to the oral reading. Parents need to watch that a reading activity does not go beyond what a child can pay attention to. Forcing children to sit still during oral reading may invite unwholesome feelings toward reading by the child. Looking at library books and their illustrations as well as reading orally to pupils should be enjoyable experiences.

Pupils Learn to Read in Different Ways

There are many procedures which may be used to teach reading. A procedure may be a fad and come and go such as the initial Teaching Alphabet (ITA) of the early 1960s. ITA had forty-four symbols (graphemes) to represent forty-four different sounds (phonemes). Too many graphemes were greatly different as compared to our traditional symbols which made it difficult for pupils to make the transfer from ITA to traditional symbols. For example, the five long vowel sounds with the traditional letters of a, e, i, o and u were written as each having an attached lower case "e" letter. Thus, the "ae" grapheme always stood for the long 'a" sound. Or the ITA "oe" always stood for the long "o" sound. Later on, in sequence, the pupil would need to learn using traditional symbols since this is emphasized in the societal arena.

ITA then was a fad of short duration. Other plans have stood the test of time even though new procedures are used in their teaching. Presently, there are holistic approaches such as individualized reading and analytic procedures such as those stressing phonics in varying degrees. It appears that many other procedures of teaching reading are variations of these two procedures. Sometimes, there are educators who will say that all pupils should experience sequential lessons with heavy emphasis upon phonics instruction. The difficulty with this statement is that not all learn to read well with phonics instruction. Nor do all learn to read well with the whole language approach. Pupils differ from each other in learning styles and the teacher needs to pay attention to an individual style that a pupil possesses.

Pupils Need to Attach Meaning to What is Being Read

Learning involves pupils attaching meaning to what is being read or experienced. The criticisms which may be given to memorization work is that pupils do not understand much of what has been memorized. When pupils read, orally or silently, they need to say in their very own words what has been read. Comprehension of ideas read is very important. We have watched word callers many times during reading. These pupils may identify many words correctly, but cannot say what has been read. Correct identification of words being read is important if pupils individually also understand inherent content. In other words, what has been read must make sense to the reader. The reader must secure the meaning as presented by the author of the reading selection as well as comprehend contents in the reading selection.

Pupils Need to Realize Complexity in the Act of Reading

Pupils should learn the names of the individual letters of the alphabet so that learners know what is being talked about if references are made to certain graphemes such as the consonant "m". Otherwise we cannot communicate with each other.

Reading as one factor consists of seeing the graphemes in the reading selection. Appropriate vision is necessary to see these abstract symbols. In the English language, pupils also need to read from left to right. In Arabic, one reads from right to left instead. What we say is the back of the book is the front of the book in reading Arabic. There are units of meaning that pupils read and learn sequentially. These units of meaning include prefixes, suffixes and syllables.

There are selected patterns of word order called syntax. A very common order to words read is the pattern of subject, predicate and direct object e.g. "She caught the ball". Semantics is also involved in any language. Semantics answers the questions, "What is meant when saying words in a sentence or an idiom is used in communicating ideas?" Use of stress, pitch and juncture pertains to making a sentence meaningful by a speaker or communicator. Thus, even the same words used in a sentence can alter the meaning much from one time to the next when stress, pitch and juncture are changed.

When pupils read, they relate what is read to their own experiences. Thus, ideas gleaned from reading become one with the personal dimension of the individual.

Pupils Need Adequate Background Information

A major reason that pupils fail in reading is they lack background information in order to understand the new ideas encountered. If pupils have adequate background information pertaining to the new selection to be read, they will comprehend better. Thus, the new ideas to be read will have selected ideas that are needed by pupils in order that comprehension can come about. Sometimes, pupils engage in word calling and do not comprehend what is contained in the act of reading. Pupils will tend to lack in identification of unknown words due to not having the necessary information pertaining to the reading selection being pursued. It behooves the teacher to have pupils pursue adequate background information that relates to the new reading selection before it is being pursued.

Pupils Need Purposes for Reading

Very often, pupils read poorly in oral or silent reading because they perceive no or little value in reading a given selection. Pupils need to feel reasons exist for reading a story or it will not be read meaningfully. The pupil, if forced to, may react in a way that indicates the contents are being read. Here, in reality, the pupil is faking the reading process. The reading teacher rather should assist pupils to perceive purpose for reading. Thus the teacher may state purposes for reading by telling why a given selection is important enough to be read. A deductive procedure is then being used. The reasons given by the teacher are valid and logical. An inductive procedure might also be used in that the teacher asks questions of pupils as to why content pertaining to a specific story needs to be read. Pupils then need to respond as to why the contents in the story are important enough to be read. Thus, purposes for reading are involved. A third procedure for pupils to perceive purpose in learning is for the teacher to provide pupils with inexpensive prizes if they achieve at a specific level in the act of oral/silent reading or in comprehension. The teacher then needs to announce ahead of time what awards are to be given and for what kinds of achievement so that individual pupils know what to learn to obtain an award. The work performed by pupils here should be challenging. Pupil purpose is to obtain an award in reading, but effort must be put forth by the learner to secure the prize. The ultimate goal in using award is to assist pupils to become better readers.

Computers in the Reading Curriculum

There are diverse programs of reading instruction that sound favourable involving computers. A software package then may emphasize a tutorial approach. In a tutorial approach, the tendency is for the programmer to stress pupils reading a short selection, perhaps three or four sentences. The learner, after reading these sentences, responds to a multiple choice item to check comprehension. Usually, four responses are in the multiple choice item. If the learner chooses the correct response, he/she may move on to the next sequential item. Should the pupil have responded incorrectly, he/she may be given another chance to respond to the correct item. Or by seeing the correct response on the monitory, the involved learner may also respond to the next sequential item for reading using the tutorial package. This approach of "read, respond and check" may be stressed over and over again in the computerized program until completion. On the monitor, it will also show the per cent of correct items for the pupil doing the responding. The programmer has built into the program the objectives the learning opportunities and the evaluation procedures. Tutorial programs should be used to guide sequential pupil achievement in reading and not for the sake of using computer services.

A second type of software package is drill and practice. These need to be used only if the involved pupil has difficulties in learning to read with specific emphasis placed upon diagnosing that which needs remediation. Thus, there is a specific problem the learner faces in reading and that problem might be solved by participating in the drill and practice software program. For example, if a pupil has difficulties with the long and short vowels "a" and 'e", the software program of drill and practice should assist the learner to overcome this difficulty. Drill and practice programs should not be given for learner participation for the sake of doing so, but rather to guide the pupil to solve specific problems encountered in reading.

A third type of software package is simulation. These are more life-like and real as compared to the previous two discussed above. With simulation, the learner encounters a problem which relates to reality in a literature based setting. Thus, the pupil reads a paragraph and responds to a multiple choice item. The multiple choice item emphasizes what the pupil would do in solving a problem. Based on the learner's response, the pupil then reads another short paragraph and again selects an option of action from among four in a multiple choice setting. Related to the response, the pupil is presented another dilemma to solve with a paragraph to read. Four courses of action are provided from which the pupil makes a selection. The selection is a course of action. The same approach is presented again and again—read content pertaining to a setting with problem involvement; respond to a course of action represented by a multiple choice item. Based on the response made by the pupil. He/she faces a new dilemma in which decisions need to be made. The teacher needs to have a purpose involved when a pupil or a committee uses a stimulated program. Too frequently, the software package is in the school library and the teacher feels he/she must use it in teaching pupils, rather than it being an integral part of the curriculum.

Should pupils work alone or collaboratively when engaged in responding to a computer package such as tutorial, drill and practice and/or simulation? The answer depends on the following factors:

1. Which is the preferred learning style of these pupils, to work alone or with others ?
2. Which type of computerized program do pupils need ? If tutorial is needed, at what point does the particular child need sequential assistance ?
3. Which sequential program does a pupil need ? If drill and practice is needed, is there a program that will guide the learner individually or in a group to make progress sequentially ?
4. Which simulation program is on the reading and comprehension level of the pupil and will the learner be helped in learning problem solving procedures ?
5. Which other procedure, if any, might assist the pupil to make greater progress than a computerized package ?

The reading teacher has complex decisions to make in teaching and learning situations. There are many materials of instruction, including computer use. The teacher also needs to consider other materials, including the basal and related workbooks. It is important to remember that the objectives of instruction in reading need to be achieved. The objectives should be chosen very carefully and choices made are to make proficient readers out of learners.

Another type of computer program to consider in reading instruction is gaming. There are selected games in reading which should assist pupils to improve the quality of their reading. For example, pupils may work individually or collectively on a spelling game which has tremendous implications for the teaching of reading. Thus, in one program, pupils are to choose which word is spelled incorrectly from three others. The four words for the first presentation on the monitor were carefully selected such as : four, for, foer, and fore. Several children chose the wrong response by selecting "fore". Why was this choice made ? These pupils responded with the following : "Fore" is a prefix and is used in words such as "forearm". They were unable to say why "foer", in their thinking, was correctly spelled. Any way, the game continued with pupils choosing the incorrectly spelled word. There are very interesting discussions when a committee of pupils is at work on a game. The disagreements can be given in a very healthy way and also lead to higher levels of cognition. Pupils can learn much from mistakes made such as believing "fore" is a prefix only. Here, pupils learn meanings of new words as well as learn to use prefixes more effectively. Too frequently, it is felt that making mistakes in reading is evil and wrong. Reading teachers need to feel that mistakes pupils make in reading can provide building blocks for future learning.

There are so many uses the reading teacher can make of computer technology. Many pupils on the third grade level have used internet and World-Wide Web in the home setting. Good readers can be guided to make wise use of computer technology at a very young age, such as grade three or sooner depending upon the maturity level of reading. Teachers always need to appraise where the pupil is achieving presently before making judgements of when a pupil may be ready to use internet and

World-Wide Web. Information from these sources work well in the problem solving arena. Thus, a pupil may read from internet on how to solve a problem, involving reading. Or, the pupil may test an hypothesis by reading data from internet. New problems may also be chosen when surfing the internet.

E-mail messages may be sent to friends; hopefully responses will be forthcoming. Sending of E-mail involves writing and reading. Many times, an innovation such as E-mail spurs pupils on to greater energy level to accomplish in reading. CD ROMS can provide a learner with much information in the problem solving arena. Thus, a pupil may locate a problem when reading information from a CD ROM. The CD ROM might provide information after the problem has been identified. Evaluating of the hypotheses may be done by the pupil in reading additional information from the CD ROM. Additional data sources may be used other than technology sources. Thus, basals, textbooks, video tapes, workbooks, slides, filmstrips and illustrations, among others, may be used as data sources. Materials of instruction used to teach reading should be on the reader's level of reading, not frustrational nor the recreational reading level. The materials of instruction should be challenging and make it possible for the pupil to achieve objectives.

Plans of Reading Instruction

Use of computer and other means in technology are ways of guiding pupils in learning. Thus, they may also be considered as plans of reading instruction. We will now concentrate on the non-technological plans of teaching reading.

Individualized reading has had a rather long history of teaching reading. In the later 1890s, when my late father attend a rural one teacher school, pupils could checkout and read library books on their very own from the classroom library. There were no requirements in terms of how many books to read from the classroom library in a month or year.

With children today, there are many distractions that interrupt learning to read well or even learning to read at all. Children at a young age do love to watch TV programs; many of these are sheer entertainment and have little value in terms of recalling what has been listened to. One of us have talked to adults about TV programs they say were watched very recently, perhaps yesterday and yet almost nothing can be recalled in terms of what had been learned.

Individualized reading then can pertain to reading sequential library books of one's own choice and thus involve intrinsic motivation. Individualized reading can have more structure than what has been discussed so far. In addition to selecting a library book to read, the pupil may have a conference with the teacher after the completion in reading of the chosen book. Here, the reading teacher needs to appraise comprehension of content by the pupil in the conference setting. The pupil as well as the teacher may raise questions for discussion. The pupil may read a short selection orally to the teacher so that the latter may appraise if the learner needs assistance, for example, in phonics and contextual clue use. It is very important for the reading teacher to evaluate attitudes and feelings that the pupil has toward reading.

Individualized reading programs require a large number of library books written on diverse topics and on different reading levels so that individual interests and reading levels are provided for adequately. A whole language approach is being used here in that the pupil reads the entire book after it has been chosen. The pupil does the choosing, not the teacher, unless the learner cannot settle down with the reading of a library book. The interests of the pupil, in individualized reading, should hurdle problems that a pupil might have in reading. After the conference, the learner may choose another library book to read. Ediger (1996) wrote:

One approach in emphasizing sequence is to have pupils choose the order of experiences within a flexible environment. Thus, for example, in individualized reading, a learner selects which library book to read sequentially. After reading a book, the pupil has a conference with the teacher to appraise progress. After the completion of each conference with the teacher, the learner is ready to select the next library book to read. The teacher intervenes in library book selection if the student is unable to choose and complete the reading of a book.

In situations involving individualized reading, the pupil orders his/her own experiences. Sequence, it is felt, resides within the involved learner. Others, the teacher included, cannot select the order of goals for a learner to attain. The student in individualized reading must also do the processing of content. A teacher determined reading curriculum does not work, according to advocates of individualized reading. Humanism, a psychology of learning, strongly advocates concepts such as the following:

1. student-teacher planning of the curriculum.
2. learners choosing from among diverse objectives which to achieve and which to omit.
3. learning centers from which pupils may select or omit learning opportunities.
4. students being involved in determining evaluation procedures.

Individualized reading is strong on emphasizing the interests of pupils in its implementation. There needs to be a considerable number of library books in a quality individualized reading program. The library books need to be on different topics and titles, as well as on different reading levels. With diverse topics and titles, pupils may choose a book to read that is personally interesting and has perceived purpose. The library books, too, need to be on different achievement levels in reading so that the slow, average and fast readers may choose reading materials to read that are on their understanding level, not the frustration nor the too easy level of reading in which boredom sets in on the part of the pupil.... (Ediger, 1996).

Another whole language approach to use in reading instruction is the experience chart for primary grade pupils. Although this approach may actually be used for any grade level. With the experience chart, pupils need to have quality experiences from which to present ideas for the teacher to record. Thus, after pupils have viewed objects at an interest center, the pupils may, for example, present the following ideas on trees for the reading teacher to record on the chalkboard or on a monitor with computer use:

Acorns come from oak trees.
Walnuts come from walnut trees.
Pin oaks have very pointed leaves.
The mock orange is a bush, not a tree.

By looking at the contents in the above experience chart, one can tell what the teacher placed on the interest center to stimulate pupil interest in providing ideas for the experience chart. Ideas for the experience chart come from pupils, not the teacher. The contents tend to be holistic and come from personal experiences of pupils. The reading plan stresses a pupil, not adult centered concept of instruction. Pertaining to experience charts, Ediger (1986) wrote the following:

> Early primary grade pupils can have interesting, realistic experiences through the taking of excursions with teacher leadership. Depending upon the unit being taught, an excursion can be taken to a farm, dairy, fire station, zoo, museum, or on the school grounds. After the excursion has been completed, the pupils may present their ideas to the teacher about their experiences. The teacher writes ideas given by learners on the chalkboard using neat manuscript letters, large enough for all to see. The recorded experiences may be four to ten lines in length depending upon the developmental level of the children. Pictures may be drawn or collected and placed above the recorded written experiences. Pupils with teacher aid could read individually or collectively what has been written. In this learning activity, pupils had a life-like experience which was the field trip. The experience was recorded. Pupils then engaged in reading what had been written. Thus, early primary grade pupils were reading content...
>
> Too frequently, it is assumed that experience charts...would be used only on the early primary grade levels in reading readiness programs. Throughout the elementary school years, pupils can develop experience charts. Once a pupil has developed his/her own writing vocabulary so that ideas can be expressed effectively on paper, the involved learner should develop his/her own experience charts. For example, intermediate grade pupils having visited an assembly line can record their own experiences in writing. This learning activity should

not be used excessively; it should be used alongwith other experiences. Excursions are not the only basis for writing experience charts. Content for experience charts may come from what has been read in library/textbooks or from what was observed in the school or classroom.

Literature Based Curricula

There is a strong emphasis placed upon holism in the reading curriculum presently. It appears that the holistic reading approach and analytic procedures, such as phonics, are continually at the center of a debate. Holism certainly does have its backing among reading specialists.

Several themes seem to characterize the curriculum plans found in schools today : (1) an emphasis upon greater integration of reading and writing instruction; (2) increased use of unedited, authentic children's literature as the base of curricular planning; (3) developing reading and writing skills and strategies in the context of an actual reading and writing activity; and (4) attempting to provide all learners with access to the same high—quality curriculum. Each of these themes differs from the central tenets of traditional skills-mastery curriculum planning, where reading and writing were taught through different curricula, usually using specially constructed texts and tasks that focused upon practicing skills in isolation from actual reading and writing and where differential curriculum goals and experiences were deemed appropriate for learners of different aptitudes...

Our interest in the impact of curriculum plans and experiences on children's literary learning emerged about twenty years ago with a report of the substantial differences in the reading lessons experienced by higher-and lower achieving readers....(Allington, et al, in Graves, Van Den Brock and Taylor, Editors, 1996).

Holism in reading emphasizes integrating an increased number of curriculum areas. Writing, in particular, is receiving major stress upon being an integral part of reading. When practicing writing as it relates directly to reading, pupils are actually looking at words, word parts and hearing sounds, among other items and this increases pupils abilities in learning to read effectively. If writing is separated from reading, pupils may not perceive the relationship between the two curriculum areas. But when pupils perceive that the writing activity engaged in integrates with reading then the two curriculum areas become one and each reinforces the other. Thus, what is read can be written about and what is written about can be read. The act of reading then assists pupils to write and the act of writing helps learners to do more reading. Personal journals written by pupils is one way of stressing the relationship between reading and writing. Here, the pupil may write about his/her (1) reactions to the reading experience, (2) thoughts on how the story might be modified, (3) ideas on what to write to the author pertaining to his/her writing, (4) reflections about major generalizations to include in journal writing.

Reading and writing are interrelated : What is learned in one area makes it easier to learn in the other. Children are quite willing to take small detours—learning words and how they work, hearing and recording sounds while constructing messages, or analyzing words while reading—if these activities are in the service of real reading and writing (Fountas and Pinnell, 1996).

Processes are built up and broken down in both reading and writing, but the concept may be easier for children to understand in writing. During early writing experiences, children naturally and purposefully attend to the details of print....

Writing involves a complex set of actions. Children have to think of a message and hold it in the mind. Then they have to think of the first word and to start it, remember each letter form and its features and manually reproduce the word letter by letter. Having written the first word (or an approximation), the child must go back to the whole message, retrieve it and think of the next word. Through writing, children are manipulating and using symbols and in the process learning how written language works (Fountas and Pinnell, 1996).

Pupils need to experience a variety of genre in literature. Life-like experiences that individuals have need to be included in a holistic program of literature. These authentic experiences can provide models for pupils to consider in emulation. In life, people experience the good things, tragedy, happiness, ill health, handicaps, unemployment, a lack of opportunity, poverty, being disadvantaged, hostility, anger, disappointments and the positive in life's encounters. Uncertainties in life are a part of the human condition. The life of a family can change much in a matter of minutes from having a mother who was very concerned about my welfare at age eleven to one who needed detailed care. This is human condition, an everyday occurrence, but not nearly to the extreme mentioned.

Using real literature for reading instruction is the fifth critical cornerstone of the integrated literacy approach that we encourage for the classroom (the others were focusing on construction of meaning, learning in context, building upon children's developmental patterns in literacy, respecting and encouraging diversity). A teacher's ultimate aim will be to structure a classroom in which literature and instructional content intertwine. The term *Real Literature* refers to books that are written for children by writers who know children and have a sense of children's perceptions, understandings, interests and dreams. "Real" literature is not necessarily materials, written according to formula, in simple words using simpler sentences, based on a type of "baby talk" for beginning reading that doesn't ring true with the language and the world of kids. (Have you ever actually heard anyone who talks in the language of some materials that ae intended for children? e.g. "The dog is up. The dog is down". "I like to play. I like to run". While we will explore commendable "simple" reading books later on, those are simple in the way that they balance children's interests with meaningful support for the text through effective language, illustrations and story line—they are real literature. Real literature, both fictional and informational, is at the core of our literacy experiences throughout the primary and intermediate grades (Templeton, 1995).

While the move toward literature based classrooms has clearly encouraged teachers to involve children in writing responses to real books, those books continue to be narrative in nature. The use of information trade books in the classroom can help teachers meet the challenge of increasing student use of expository materials at the same time that they capitalize on children's fascination with facts. Moreover, inviting children to write in response to such books can help develop the problem solving and critical thinking skills essential to students survival in the Information Age. By involving children in reading and writing about information trade books, teachers can help to ensure that today's children are prepared for literacy demands of the world of tomorrow (Moss, Leone and Dipillo, 1997).

This still leaves time in the literature curriculum for other genres of literature which provide rich and varied experiences for leaners. In a print rich classroom, pupils have opportunities to read literature on a variety of topics to provide for the needs of individuals. Pupils also may choose books on their very own personal levels of reading. Books selected by pupils need to be on their individual reading levels. Reading and writing are encouraged and promoted in diverse ways such as in bulletin board displays, seminars, collaborative endeavours, committee work, murals, dioramas, dramatic activities, posters, reading and writing slogans and story telling, among others.

Conclusion

Pupils need to experience a quality literature and reading program. Following tenets of the principles of learning from educational psychology assists teachers to provide more adequately for individual differences such as the fast, average and slower readers in the classroom setting. Teachers need to study each pupil and attempt to ascertain which reading program will guide learners to achieve more optimally. Pupils individually have a starting point which indicates their present level of reading achievement. This is the place where reading and literature instruction needs to begin. After than point, pupil need to progress sequentially. With good sequence, continual optimal progress is an ideal for pupils to attain in ongoing reading lessons and units of study.

There are numerous plans of reading instruction which may assist learners to achieve as much as individual abilities make possible. Reading instruction needs to be challenging and demanding, but not to the point of learners no being able to meet goals. Nor should the literature and reading program be at a too easy level of instruction whereby motivation to learn decreases.

A combination of instruction programs in reading may be used so that a varied approach results in which pupil interests are fostered. Each pupil has a favourite style and procedure of learning. The reading teacher needs to analyze each pupil's style and make necessary provisions. The goal of all reading instruction is to have pupils become proficient readers. Reading needs to be enjoyable so that an inward desire to read is an end result.

References

Allington, et al, in Graves, Michael F., Paul Van Der Brock and Barbara M. Taylor, Editors, (1996), *The First R. Every Child's Right to Read.* New York : Teachers College, Columbia University, 73.

Bhaskara Rao, Digumarti, Editor (1998), *Reforming School Education.* New Delhi : Discovery Publishing House.

Ediger, Marlow (1997), Slogans in Society, *Journal of Instructional Psychology*, 24(1), 65–68.

Ediger, Marlow (1996), *Elementary Education.* Kirksville, Missouri : Simpson Publishing Company, 39.

Fountas, Irene C. and Gay Su Pinnell (1996), *Guided Reading.* Portsmouth, New Hampshire : Heinemann, 13, 15.

Moss, et al, (1997), Exploring the Literature of Fact : Linking Reading and Writing through Information Trade Books, *The Language Arts*, 78(6), 428.

Templeton, Shane (1995), *Children's Literacy.* Boston : Houghton Mifflin Company, 24.

19
Computer Literacy in the Public Schools

The use of computers is rapidly increasing in the societal arena. Banks, supermarkets, hardware stores, car dealership, and the business world in general, are using computers to store and retrieve data. The school setting is attempting to catch up with the use of computers. Schools are a non-profit organisation and depend upon tax moneys to pay for computers. As there is an increased amount of money in the school budget for technology purchases, more pupils are experiencing computer services than ever before.

In school districts throughout the country, computer literacy is considered a top educational goal. But too few administrators, teachers and parents understand what the term really means. What passes for computer literacy in many schools is a shadow of the real thing. To understand why, we need to look at the two roles the computer plays in most schools: information resource and self-contained teaching machine.

As an information resource, the computer can complement books, magazines videos and other media. For example, a fourth grade teacher might augment a unit on animals with an article from a multi-media encyclopedia or other software-based resources. The advent of the CD ROM, with its large storage capacity, has made such information-based software readily available.

But most educational software is designed to turn computers into teaching machines. A class of programs called integrated learning systems enables a computer to act like a personal tutor in subjects as diverse as reading, writing, mathematics and foreign languages. Students go through such programs at their own pace, with the software providing lessons, quick feedback, infinite patience and detailed achievement records (German, 1997).

School administrators need to understand and value technological use in the classroom. School administrators should perceive the necessity of implementing technological use in the classroom so that pupils may achieve more optimally. No doubt, there are school administrators who lack quality experiences with technology and therefore do not see the need for pupils experiencing learning activities involving technology. Each principal and supervisor should avail themselves in learning more about technology and how to integrate its use into the school curriculum. Talking to and learning from classroom teachers, as well as teachers learning from principals, should assist the school in realizing the importance of technology in a modern curriculum. Staff development programs in using technology in the curriculum should be in the offing. Teachers and administrators need to realize the importance of an updated curriculum. The school of today and the work place of tomorrow should not be in isolation from each other, but rather integrated entities. Definite goals in in-service education using technology are musts! These goals and experiences for participants need to be carefully chosen. Relevance and importance are two concepts that need careful consideration when in-service education programs are developed and implemented. The goals of the workshop should be clearly stated and cooperatively developed by workshop participants... (Ediger, 1997).

Computer software has different purposes in its use. Drill and practice programs began as basic instruction on such topics as multiplication tables, for example. Over the years their power, sophistication and subject coverage have grown....

Tutorial software offers the best hope.... for computer based individualized learning. The software, often with multimedia attributes like full motion video and sound, is written to tutor slow to fast students. Usually these programs offer teachers with some breakdown on student progress...

Simulation software artificially creates a real life experience and this artificial real life can be extremely interesting and effective. The approach is anything but rote, but (especially for scientific and technical subjects) draws on and augments the knowledge of participants. It can be used for single or large group players. The number of commercially available simulation programs is burgeoning. As the image resolution and full page display capabilities of computer monitors improve, the realness, if you will, of simulations will further improve...

Problem solving software tests critical thinking and judgment, often without looking for a "right answer". One product, for example, centers upon the accidental breaking of a teacher's vase by two students who had wanted to hide her two pencils. The player is first prompted to select (on the computer) four goals in order of importance. The goals are : 1. always be honest and tell the truth; 2. maintain good relations with peers; 3. protect yourself; 4. be well liked by your peers. Then repeated throughout the play, the player is prompted to select an option. For example, 1) tell the teacher you didn't break the vase; 2) say that you didn't see who broke it; 3) say the other boy broke it; and 4) say nothing. Then at the end of the program, a player is graded by the computer on how well his or her answers accorded with the goal selection. The program also allows a group of students to play with each student representing a separate "goal". The user manual states that the goal of the product is to represent the player with the consequences of his or her actions (Cosmann, 1996).

Schools of Thought in Computer Use

There are different schools of thought in terms of how computer use is to be stressed. The first school of thought emphasizes that precise, measurably stated objectives be written prior to instruction. These objectives might be state mandated or locally written. Care must be taken to write objectives that are relevant and important for pupils to achieve. Much time needs to be given in writing precise objectives that have worth, not trivia nor the unimportant.

Once the objectives have been agreed upon, they provide guidance to the teacher in stressing content to be taught.

Computer programs should then emphasize, as learning activities, that which is contained in these precise objectives. Thus, drill and practice, tutorial, simulation and games may provide necessary subject matter in order that each pupil might achieve the predetermined measurably stated objectives. In multimedia technology procedures, CD ROMs, and internet may offer further learning opportunities to pupils in achieving these precise objectives.

After instruction, the teacher needs to measure if pupils have/have not achieved the stated objectives. If objectives have been achieved, the pupil may move on to increasingly more complex objectives within the learning sequence. Those pupils not mastering what is in the stated objective(s) need other teaching strategies involving technology in its diverse forms.

A second school of thought in assisting teaches to guide pupil achievement is to stress problem solving. Within a unit of study, pupils identify a problem. The problem needs to be clearly stated so that pupils understand what will be achieved. After problem selection, pupils may gather data or information to solve the open-ended problem. Diverse reference sources using technology might then be used as information sources. A hypothesis is obtained from the information acquired to solve the problem. The hypothesis is tested with the use of additional technology sources of information.

A third school of thought in teaching pupils is an idea centered technology curriculum. Thus, in an ongoing unit of study the teacher has general objectives for pupils to achieve. These objectives are more open-ended as compared to the teacher who desires measurably stated objectives as compared to the teacher who desires measurably stated objectives in teaching and learning situations. Pupils with teacher guidance use a variety of technology to secure information pertaining to the sequential open-ended objectives as stated in the curriculum. Whatever the topic being studied, the teacher guides pupils through technology use to secure information in depth. The teacher observes how well pupils are realizing the general objectives. Subject matter achieved by pupils may or may not emphasize problem solving. Basic, essential subject matter may be obtained by pupils that is relevant and guides in attaining the general objectives.

A fourth school of thought in using a technology centered curriculum is to emphasize pupil/teacher planning of objectives, learning opportunities and evaluation procedures. The planning is done after pupils have been orientated to the new unit of study. Thus, pupils plan with the teacher what they wish to learn. The means of learning are also planned cooperatively in that information sources need locating. Cooperative evaluation is a further ingredient of teacher/pupil planning school of thought in the curriculum.

An additional procedure here is for the teacher to develop learning stations, perhaps seven to eight stations per classroom. Tasks on a card are listed at each center. The pupil then may determine what he/she wishes to learn as well as what to omit. There are an ample number of tasks so that the individual pupil may select what to learn an what to omit. A variety of technology is available to guide pupils in the learning process (Ediger, 1995).

Psychology in Computer Use

Psychologists in education tend to agree that learning activities involving technology use should be :

1. meaningful in that pupils understand what is being presented via technology. With meaning, pupils understand that which has been presented inductively or deductively.
2. interesting in that content and skills capture pupil attention. The use of technology provides time whereby pupils are thoroughly involved in the ongoing experiences.
3. purposeful whereby pupils perceive reasons for learning. Pupil purpose is a tremendously salient factor in guiding pupil learning. Intrinsically, pupils should develop a need for learning in ongoing units and lessons.
4. integrative among three kinds of objectives. Thus, relevant knowledge needs to be obtained by pupils. Skills that guide in using the obtained knowledge also need to be developed. Quality altitudes are beneficial in that an increased amount of knowledge and skills may be developed.

5. sequential in that pupils perceive new learnings secured as being related to those previously obtained. The relationship of the new and the previously secured subject matter should guide pupils to perceive the relationship of ideas (Ediger, 1994).

Based on learning opportunities being meaningful, interesting, purposeful, integrated and sequential, there are selected specific psychologies that merit attention in technology use.

There are teachers who desire that objectives be precisely stated. These specific objectives then provide direction in selecting learning opportunities. The chosen objectives emphasized by the teacher assists pupils to achieve the precise ends. After instruction, it can be measured if pupils have been successful in goal attainment.

A second psychology of learning stresses that open-ended, general objectives be used in teaching. These objectives are clearly stated, but do not possess the measurable component. More leeway is then given the teacher in planning sequential learning opportunities for pupils. Thus, pupils with teacher in planning sequential learning opportunities for pupils. Thus, pupils with teacher guidance are orientated to the new unit of study using technology, but the sequence now resides largely within pupils in planning cooperatively what to learn. Learners may then wish to work in committees to complete planned experiences. The teacher is a guide and assists pupils to stay on task with the use of technology. Evaluation consists of pupils with teacher guidance appraising that which has been learned, using quality criteria.

A third psychology of learning stresses a project method. Here, within an ongoing unit of study, pupils perceive a need or purpose. The need/purpose involves a problem area. The purpose is clarified so that meaningful learning accrues. After establishing purpose, pupils plan what needs to be done to obtain knowledge/skills to solve the problem. Technology needs to be surveyed and chosen for problem solving. Following planning, the involved pupils carry out the plans. Quality procedures need to be used here. Responsibility rests with pupils and teacher assistance. Criteria need to be developed to appraise the completed project in order to evaluate its worth or value.

A fourth psychology of learning emphasizes that pupils choose from among alternatives that which is to be selected as activities and experiences. The teacher might then develop learning centers pertaining to the unit of study being taught. The individual pupil chooses which center and which station to work at. The chosen tasks may be individual or committee work. The pupil does the sequencing in a psychological curriculum. He/she determines what comes first, second and third in terms of activities and experiences. Sequence resides within the pupil, not the teacher nor within teaching materials. If the activities do not meet personal needs of a pupil, he/she may plan with the teacher an alternative route of learning (Ediger, 1996).

A fifth psychology of instruction empathizes that pupils possess many intelligences and ways of presenting information acquired. A pupil then may well have a preferred approach to learning and revealing learnings such as verbal/linguistic, logical/mathematical, visual/spatial, musical, bodily/kinesthetic, interpersonal, scientific, humanistic and intra-personal procedures (Gardner, 1993).

Pupils should then have a greater say in how to indicate what has been learned. For example, a pupil may prefer to work with others or work individually in ongoing activities and also prefer to show what has been achieved in one of the two appraoches—interpersonal or intrapersonal. Or, a pupil in a history class may wish to show learnings acquired through musical experiences. Much history has been recorded in musical form with both lyrics and musical scores. There are numerous ways for pupils to show what has been learned to others. There are multiple intelligences to indicate these learnings. Through technology, one may indicate to others the breadth and depth of experiences and achievements.

National Standards in Education

Presently, much emphasis is being placed on national and state trends to motivate pupils to achieve more and at a more complex level. This includes the area of technology and computers. Our concerns when developing national and state standards are the following :

1. that the standards are realistic and achievable by learners. If the standards are too difficult, there may be many pupils failing in school. Pupils should achieve optimally to be sure. But, the standard setters need to avoid becoming overly ambitious in establishing goals not attainable.
2. that pupils and the teacher locally also have input into the curriculum. Having standards set by those outside the local school district, removes the teacher's chances of becoming very knowledgeable about each pupil's talents and abilities. It is more difficult to provide for individual differences when the standard setters are for removed from home base.
3. that pupils may not feel motivated to learn when the objectives chosen have little or no relevance for the learner. Standard setters are human beings like the rest of us are. They have their biases and preferences also. To be sure, there will be some common agreement about objectives that pupils need to achieve.
4. that too much forcing will be emphasized in a hierarchy from the standard setters to teachers and pupils in the classroom.

For computer literacy to occur, pupils need to understand hardware components and how systems such as Microsoft Windows and Mac OS works. Learners need to be able to switch between multiple programs through a menu structure and change fonts. Pupils also need to be able to develop a spreadsheet formula. There are many tools for software use and committee endeavours in writing. These include CAI programs, CD ROMS, drafting, spelling checkers, analyses to text, calculators, graphics, word processing and online databases. Pupils should be creative in determining what to do when certainty is not there in computer use. Asking for assistance is one approach, but becoming a problem solver is more important. Life consists of problems to be solved.

Feasible national and state standards are needed in the

technology/computer curriculum. Technologies as conduits to new knowledge, resources and higher order thinking skills have entered classrooms and schools nationwide. Personal computers, CD-ROMs, online services, the World-Wide Webb and other innovative technologies have enriched curricular resources and altered the types of instruction available. The new Office of Technology Assessment (OTA) reports 5.8 million computers are available in school for instruction—about one computer for every nine students. Approximately 35% if schools can access on-line services, 30% have CD ROMS and nearly all have TVs and VCRs. Most of these technologies are used for traditional instruction, such as presenting information, basic skills practice, word processing and developing computer literacy. Teachers are however, beginning to use more innovative applications—using desktop publishing, developing mathematical and scientific reasoning with computer simulations, gathering information using on line services and CD ROM databases and communicating via E-mail (Hartley, 1997).

Computer literacy is also for pupils with special needs, Hoge and Rogers (1996) wrote:

Why would a speech language teacher need technology to work with children with special needs? Studies of augmentative and alternative communication suggested options, but did they apply to the realities of my students?

Assigned to work with children with serious communication disorders, we soon saw the difference that technology can make. Technology is a motivating tool. The other trapezists and we learned that technology unleashes potential and creates opportunities for social interaction.

We began with simple application of technology—a big round switch and a tape recorder. Suddenly, a child would demonstrate that she knew what would happen when she pressed a switch—music played.

In another classroom, the special day class teacher and I applied for a small grant to get software and switches that special—needs could use to play with regular education peers on the classroom computer. They found they could race each other, play jokes and trade comments. Disabilities were less a factor that they had been without technology. Pressing a key too play a game involves less muscle coordination than many other more physical games....

Children with special needs deserve a way to interact socially with others. Sometimes physical limitations eliminate normal playground activities. Sometimes communication limitations interfere with normal requests, comments and conversation so integral to a child's world. Technology provides alternatives. Accessing technology can be as simple as depressing a switch with a finger or an arm. Even chins and feet work if necessary. Muscles used in pointing are far simpler than the complex ones required for many other kinds of interactions.

In Closing

School and society should be integrated, not separate entities. In the societal arena, much use is made of technology. The school setting also needs to have pupils become proficient in computer literacy. For example, all pupils should learn to use the word processor. The typewriter of the past is a museum piece.

In writing about the future pertaining to technology, Mehlinger (1996) wrote:

Finally, technology will have greater intelligence. This intelligence will be displayed in several ways. First, the technology will have more features and greater capacity. Second, it will have the capability to learn from the user, so that it can customize its services to fit the user's learning and interest. Future technology will provide not only data bases but knowledge bases. And technology will be able to stay abreast of that information most valued to the user and alert him or her to its availability. Integration, interaction and intelligence. These are the three features we can expect of technology in the future. And they will change the way technology is employed in schools.

References

Cosmann, Richard (1996), "The Evolution of Educational Computer Software", *Education*, 116(4), 621.

Ediger, Marlow (1997), *Teaching Reading and the Language Arts in the Elementary School*. Kirksville, Missouri : Simpson Publishing Company, 269–70.

Ediger, Marlow (1995), *Philosophy in Curriculum Development*. Kirksville, Missouri: Simpson Publishing Company, 1–15.

Ediger, Marlow (1994), "Early Field Experiences in Teacher Education", *College Student Journal*, 28(3), 302–03.

Ediger, Marlow (1996), *Elementary Education*. Kirksville, Missouri: Simpson Publishing Company, 172–84.

Gardner, Howard (1993), *Multiple Intelligences : The Theory in Practice*. New York : The Basic books.

German, Mark, "Computer Literacy : Teaching for the Read World", *The Principal*, 76(4), 46.

Haertel, Geneva D., "Creating School and Classroom Cultures that Value Learning: The Role of National Standards", *Educational Horizons*, 75(3), 144.

Hoge, Suzi and Sharon Rogers (1996), "Two Perspectives for Children with Special Needs", *The Delta Kappa Gamma Bulletin*, 63 (1), 12–13.

20
Supervision in the Reading Curriculum

The role of the supervisor in improving the reading curriculum is more demanding than formerly. The supervisor needs to be well versed in trends and issues in the teaching of reading. He/she must be highly knowledgeable about measurement instruments and devises used in determining pupil progress in reading. The lay public and specifically the business world, is wanting higher standards of achievement from pupils. Criticisms toward education and the achievement of pupils continue to abound, right or wrong. We do not believe that public school education has any more weaknesses than the medical or legal profession. People we talk to mention the weaknesses of diagnosis and prescription procedures of medical doctors and these are not complementary in many cases. The legal profession can easily be criticized for wrong outcomes in court cases and frivolous lawsuits.

The teaching profession needs to make do with what there is in the public schools, be it class size, equipment, materials of instruction and a hostile learning environment in the school setting. Whatever the present situation in any profession, improvements need to be made. We as teachers need to change teaching procedures to something better than exists presently so that pupils become better readers and increase achievement in all curriculum areas. A feeling of professionalism needs to be in evidence in the school setting. The supervisor of instruction must assist with instructional problems in the classroom. A quality environment for reading instruction needs to be in the offing.

The Reading Supervisor and Human Relations

We doubt very much if changes and improvement in reading instruction can come about unless there is good human relations between teachers and the supervisor. Quality human relations involves a feeling and an attitude of trust among co-workers. Trust is built up over a period of time. Since assistance and help given to teachers will go a long way in fostering good human relations, a caring supervisor needs to be in evidence. Here, care is shown for the welfare of teachers as well as for pupils. There are at least two dimensions involved in the concept of care and caring. The reading supervisor needs to realize that teachers have personal lives to live with its many attending tasks. Then too, there are the institutional demands of the school that should receive adequate attention. Too many in-service education programs might well sight time from the personal lives of teacher. Too little time for teacher growth and development may hinder quality instruction to come about. The supervisor then needs to look at both dimensions—the personal lives of teachers and their professional growth in reading instruction—needing adequate stress. We doubt very much if the personal and professional lives of teachers and supervisors can be separated. The reading supervisor needs to realize, however, that the personal relations of individuals in the home setting is important and not to place strain upon concerns and wants of teachers. Teachers are human beings and like to be recognized for achievement and growth in personal and professional living. Thus, a teacher who receives an award from a civic or religious institution should receive recognition from faculty members and from the reading supervisor. Meeting recognition needs is of utmost importance.

We will now focus upon the professional needs to reading teachers. Reading teachers should make their needs known to the supervisor in order to strengthen the classroom environment. What if discipline problems in the classroom hinder the teacher from doing a good job of teacher? A teacher in most cases cannot select which pupils will be in his/her classroom. A well known teacher known for quality teaching was ready to quit in the middle of the school year due to two pupils who kept the entire classroom in an uproar. She mentioned all the approaches that were tried to discipline pupils in a humane manner. These included assertive discipline problems. She achieved the greatest success by varying learning opportunities for pupils, establishing set before the major parts of the lesson were to be presented and attempting to provide for individual differences. However, in degrees, the problem was not solved to the extent desired so that all pupils in the classroom could achieve more optimally in reading. Much research and experimentation will need to be done so that individuals who reveal discipline problems can have their energies channeled into positive directions in reading. We recommend here that reading teachers and supervisors study diverse procedures pertaining to disciplining pupils and use that approach which meets individual needs.

Second, the supervisor needs to be a good listener to problems in reading instruction as expressed by teachers. A reading teacher may expressed by teachers. A reading teacher may express a problem of a pupil calling words read orally and yet not comprehending content read. For example, I, Ediger, taught a pupil fitting this description in my early years as an elementary school teacher. This pupil, called Larry and not his real name, read very loudly and haltingly so that pupils in another classroom across the hallway could almost hear him. Larry was very tense when reading aloud and knew he was struggling alongwith his slow methodical way of reading without comprehending what was read. I first had to have Larry realize that merely being able to read aloud does not make for knowing what has been read. I asked Larry again and again after he had read both silently and aloud which ideas he had gotten from the reading activity. It took time for Lorry to realize that he had to say in his own words what had been read. Once he understood this, the next task was to have Larry obtain meaning from reading that which was completed. Merely understanding that he had to say aloud ideas gotten from reading was one item of Larry's achievement as compared to actually doing it. There were numerous word recognition problems that hindered comprehension of content. I had Larry keep a special notebook on words listed that he did not know how to pronounce. Larry was given practice on saying these word correctly by classmates and by myself. The extra help made it possible that he recognised about fifty per cent of the words from the list and used approximately one-half of these in oral and silent reading correctly. At the beginning, Larry would recognise these listed words in his notebook, but not in the basal reader. With extra help, Larry's case and solutions tried out. Seemingly, Larry made slow progress throughout the remainder of the school year. After the school year ended, Larry and his family moved away and I lost contact with him. I have discussed Larry's problem with reading supervisors in the public schools and most indicate that word calling but not comprehending content read is a perennial problem among selected pupils. Reading supervisors need to be able identify and assist in solving problems pertaining to pupil reading.

Third, reading supervisors need to be approachable. Teachers need to feel that they can truly go to the supervisor and talk over problems experienced in the classroom. There is then an open door to the supervisor's office. The reading supervisor welcomes teachers to identify reading problems faced in the classroom. He/she is very willing to come to the classroom to help with problems in reading. A kind, knowledgeable and caring reading supervisor is wanted by teachers to assist in securing better methods of teaching and learning. If teachers avoid meeting the supervisor, valuable contacts are lost and assistance is not available.

Fourth, the reading supervisor realizes that the community has expectations in that pupils become better readers. Parents should have opportunities to meet with both teacher and supervisor (Burns, Roe and Ross). Too frequently, parents meet with the child's teacher in parent/teacher conferences, but not with the reading supervisor. The reading supervisor needs to realize that parents have valuable information to present of their offspring which will truly be of value to improve reading instruction. The reading supervisor, the teacher and parents need to work together for the good of the child.

Fifth, the reading supervisor may be chairperson and organizer of in-service education, workshops and faculty meetings involving reading instruction. Here, the supervisor recognizes the responsibilities of having in-service education that is goal centered. There are definite approaches and experiences for participants to attain the stated goals of in-service education in reading instruction. Ultimately, it needs to be evaluated if the goals have been met. The reading supervisor needs to be a leader in guiding teachers to change from what is to what should be in reading instruction.

The reading supervisor then is a good organizer of people to further the goals of the institution of quality reading instruction, in particular, within the public school system. Thus, he/she is a people centered person and yet highly knowledgeable about how to improve teaching and learning in reading. These areas are two sides of the same coin. Improving reading instruction within the framework of good human relations are musts! The chances are little will get done unless human relations and knowledge/skills in reading are in evidence.

Democracy within the Reading Curriculum

The reading supervisor needs to be a strong believer in democracy as a way of life in school and in society, with an integration between the two domains. Supervisors and teachers of reading need to guide pupils in developing an attitude of respect toward themselves and others. Discussions pertaining to comprehension of content from reading assignments and voluntary reading will fare better if pupils accept each other as persons having much intrinsic worth. Discipline problems will then be more minimal and learning becomes increasingly positive. People are unique and possess differences in interests, talents and abilities and yet there are common needs possessed such as physiological, safety, belonging, esteem and self-actualization. Likenesses and differences need to be accepted by others. Individuals need to be accepted regardless of race, creed and religious beliefs. Discrimination among individuals has no place in a democratic society. The reading curriculum then must possess a multi-cultural emphasis. Subject matter, content and ideas read need to emphasize respect for all. Each cultural group should have its fair share of emphasis in terms of minority participation in pictures, study prints and print discourse concepts and generalizations within materials read. Being left out of literary content hinders pupils from identifying with and being a part of the ongoing learning opportunities. Basal readers, library books and other reading materials must stress a multi-cultural emphasis. Pupils with diverse perceptions and beliefs must be included in the literature curriculum.

Pupils should have ample opportunities to work with others of different cultures when participating in discussions and collaborative endeavours. Committee work to discuss content read in an ongoing lesson or unit of study must follow tenets of democracy in order that quality human interactions occur. Each pupil needs to participate actively. All should participate in an engaged plan of participation. No one should be minimized or ridiculed for ideas presented. Content presented needs to circulate among committee members so that main ideas and conclusions are increasingly valid in the discussion. Thus, discussions pertaining to characterization, setting, sequence, plot, theme and point of view need a depth emphasis during the ongoing discussion. Sharing of ideas is one way of stressing depth probing of the author's writings. Too frequently, survey approaches with a single correct response to a question is stressed. However, meaningful learnings in reading emphasize critical and creative thing procedures. With critical thought, ideas presented are compared and contrasted as pupils contribute to the discussion. Creative thinking emphasizes learners coming up with unique ways of thinking about subject matter, such as in brain storming. There are excellent ideas that can come from pupils with an environment that encourages originality in thinking. Thus, pupils may brain storm descriptions pertaining to the main character in the story or reading selection. Here, pupils might realize diversity of thinking on the part of participants. Learners might also wish to brain storm the many alternate kinds of main characters that would fit within the content read. A further activity involving brain storming might well stress problem solving. In the problem presented in the story, what other ways may have been used to solve the problem(s) than those actually used ? Problem solving as a skill is important now as well as in the future for all pupils. Ideas presented during the discussion need to be respected and new ideas generated as the endeavour continues.

Democratic living and learning in the reading curriculum might well provide pupils with a set of values to consider in adopting. Content read presents a variety of value to live by.

Most of these values are very transitory. New values being considered may come from a literature based curriculum (Templeton, 1997). Thus, if pupils are considering point of view from a reading selection, how does this differ from their very own thinking ? A critical analysis may assist pupils to compare and contrast their values with that given in the point of view. Each person needs to ultimately develop a philosophy of life pertaining to the following dilemmas with its pros and cons: capitol punishment, abortion, competition versus cooperation, collectivism versus personal endeavours in society and to what degree, amount of aid provided by the government to the poor and the role of government in society as well as its right to tax people adequately for roads, bridges and other public works.

The supervisor has an important task then in guiding teachers to implement democracy as a vital tenet in the teaching of reading. Pupils will tend to achieve at a higher level if a relaxed classroom environment is in the offing. Perhaps, the heart of democracy is teacher/pupil planning of the reading curriculum. Certainly, pupils should have a voice in selecting objectives, learning opportunities and evaluation procedures in ongoing lessons and units of study. How can teacher/pupil planning be implemented in reading instruction ? Let us go back to discussing structural ideas in the ongoing literature curriculum. If pupils are studying the setting of a reading selection, pupils could make suggestions as to what they would like to emphasize and study. The following are possibilities that pupils may wish to pursue:

1. Provide a different setting than the one stated by the author.
2. Elaborate on the setting provided by the author.
3. Give as many alternative settings as possible within a given time period.
4. Develop a setting whereby an earlier century is being emphasized.
5. State a setting that provides severe conflict with the main characters of the reading selection (Ediger, 1997).

Tenets of democracy in the teaching of reading do not stress;

1. Pupils doing as they choose. This would amount to anarchy. Rather, pupils are working on tasks that are relevant to the objectives of instruction in the classroom and for the school. Continuing with structural ideas in literature, pupils might plan with the teacher a different plot for the reading selection being considered.

2. Little direction or guidance given by the teacher. Instead, the role of the teacher is important in democratic settings in that he/she is a leader, a guide and encourages pupils to achieve and learn. The teacher then has an active role in obtaining pupils' interests, purposes and meet needs to learners.

3. A highly competitive environment for learning. Democracy as a way of life stresses collaborative endeavours by pupils. Inter-personal endeavours mean that pupils need to plan together, work in the direction of achieving the plans, as well as evaluate the quality of the involved processes and products. For example, in reading a given selection, pupils in a committee, with teacher assistance, may develop a different point of view, other than that presented by the author. Achieving this goal requires knowledge of the literary selection, making comparisons when diverse points of view are presented by pupils and appraising the worth of each. Learning can be fascinating and exciting when these comparisons are being made. Competitive endeavours may be contrasted with intra-personal achievements whereby the learner works on a project independently. The achievement here stresses the involved pupil comparing his/her present level of progress with that of an earlier time. Both collaborative and intrapersonal endeavours need to be emphasized.

4. Rigid rules and standards to follow. In contrast, democracy in the classroom emphasizes flexible standards that are reasonable and achievable by pupils. It is good procedure to involve pupils in planning these standards or rules of behaviour as well as in the evaluation process. Evaluation is always done in terms of stated objectives which are feasible for pupils to attain. For example, if pupils are to locate the main ideas of a story, it is possible, after

instruction, for pupils to do so. Or, if pupils are to locate supporting ideas for the main idea, learners possess the necessary pre-requisite skills to achieve this objective.

5. Pupils seated in rows and columns, facing the teacher. In comparison, flexible approaches to grouping pupils should be in evidence. There may be a few opportunities whereby pupils are seated in rows and columns, such as in large group instruction in team teaching. Other procedures too need to be emphasized such as pupils seated in a circle for small group discussion. Or, pupils working in carols for individual endeavours need to be emphasized. One of us observed a fascinating discussion on pupils working collaboratively in arranging sentence strip sequentially for a story. The discussion and debate was excellent as well as challenging. Each pupil on the committee listened intently and was engaged in the ongoing task.

6. Limits content read to basal textbooks and workbooks. Opposite of this approach is for pupils to read widely from diverse literary materials including various genres and reading levels of materials. The reading needs of individual pupils need to be provided for. Pupils need a variety of rich experiences in order to make better choices in the school/societal arenas. In reading library books, there should be an ample number on different categories of information as well as on diverse reading levels. Each pupil may then benefit from the many offerings of children's literature. Interest in reading is a powerful factor in helping pupils to achieve much in comprehending print discourse.

7. Exact answers are expected of pupils. When discussing content read. Rather, democracy stresses pupils engaging in higher levels of cognition. Why? Life in society emphasizes higher cognitive levels in order to solve personal and societal problems. Exact answers usually are factual, but much of life has to do with decision making which is complex and goes much beyond the memorizing and regurgitating of facts. Thus, facts need to be understood and placed in a meaningful context. Application of facts is very important. Otherwise knowledge for its own sake has little value. What is used needs to be analyzed into

component parts to separate the useful from the not useful as well as the accurate from the inaccurate. After, analysis, the learner should synthesize ideas that remain after the test of analyzing. Finally, evaluation of the process or product is important. The worth of the process/product needs to be determined (Ediger, 1988).

The reading supervisor then needs to assist teachers in moving toward democratic settings in the public schools. How can this difficult task be done? First, faculty members should be aided in perceiving purpose in studying democracy as a way of life in school and more specifically in the reading curriculum. Why? Teachers and pupils do better in the educational arena when there is respect, caring and accepting of others. Too frequently, we see good readers look down upon the less proficient readers. The slow reader may ridicule the sophisticated terminology used by gifted pupils in ongoing lessons and units of study in reading. In numerous situations, pupils "put down" ideas presented by others during a discussion. There are pupils who snicker at ideas presented by a pupil in the classroom setting. Democracy is an ideal whereby teachers and pupils move from where they are presently in the school environment to some reasonable ideal in teaching and learning.

Criteria should be developed and evaluated pertaining to the meaning of democracy in the school setting. This is ongoing and continuous. The criteria may change as evidence warrants making these changes. Objectives in reading instruction should be based on democratic tenets. Thus, in the area of phonics instruction, both the teacher and the pupil need acceptance, respect and a caring feeling. The teacher and the pupil will achieve more so if tenets of democracy are continuously planned and implemented within lessons and units of study. A relaxed learning environment should be an end result with more optimal learner achievement in reading.

The reading supervisor then needs to establish objectives emphasizing democracy with involved individuals in the school setting. These cooperatively developed objectives provide the framework for goals to be obtained by all involved directly or indirectly in reading instruction. Attempts at realizing the objectives will be ongoing and continuous. The objectives stress ideals for professionals to attain in teaching and learning situations. Ideals cannot be achieved once and for all. Rather continuous efforts in goal attainment need to be in evidence. Evaluation by all involved should be ongoing and continuous to ascertain if the objectives are being realized (Ediger, 1994).

The Democratic Supervisor and Technology

A major trend in teaching reading is to integrate technology into the reading curriculum. The supervisor needs to be well versed in different kinds of software as well as criteria to use in evaluating these products. Teachers need to be involved in choosing which software to adopt and purchase. Teachers need assistance in implementing quality software into ongoing lessons and units of study. Drill and practice, tutorial, diagnostic and remedial, simulation and games software should become an inherent part of the reading curriculum. Sending messages by E-mail and using internet for research purposes should be experienced by all pupils when ready to participate.

CD ROMs may provide pupils with numerous illustrations, subject matter content, as well as interesting experiences. The reading supervisor should assist teachers and pupils to use and emphasize modern technology within the reading curriculum. A major goal of technology is to assist pupils to become better readers and to enjoy reading as a life-long endeavour.

Conclusion

It is important for individuals to be able to work together harmoniously. This does not discredit creativity. Individuals need to be human relations orientated and this involves unique efforts being made toward becoming democratic in words and deeds. The reading supervisor and those teachers being supervised need to experience collaboration as a community of learners when processes and products of instruction are stressed. More can be accomplished in the teaching of reading if people involved are making headway toward respecting. Caring and helping other individuals. Pupils should achieve more optimally in reading if a democratic environment is in evidence. Pupils need to achieve relevant objectives in reading instruction. They must evaluate the self in order to achieve, grow and develop. Ample input from pupils should be in the offing so that relevance can be stressed directly in the reading curriculum.

As a final statement, we would recommend strongly that school/university cooperation be implemented whereby individuals may learn from each other in an atmosphere of respect. A planned series of meetings may be held which stresses university/school partnerships in improving reading instruction in terms of practicums and field endeavours for reading teachers/supervisors as well as for university personnel. Shared leadership in improving the reading curriculum is a must! (Ediger, 1994).

References

Bhaskara Rao, Digumarti, editor (1998). *Teacher Education in India*. New Delhi: Discovery Publishing House.

Burns, Paul C., et. al., (1996), *Teaching Reading in Today's Elementary School*. Boston: Houghton Mifflin Company, 609–14.

Ediger, Marlow (1997), *The Modern Elementary School*. Kirksville, Missouri, 192–206.

Ediger, Marlow (1988), *The Elementary Curriculum*, Second edition. Kirksville, Missouri : Simpson Printing Company, 123–26.

Ediger, Marlow (September, 1994), "Shared Leadership in the Curriculum", *The Education Magazine*, Doha, Qatar (Persian Gulf), Qatar National Commission for Education, 11–15.

Ediger, Marlow (December, 1994), "Grouping Pupils in the Elementary School", *The Education Magazine*. Doha, Qatar (Persian Gulf), Qatar National Commission for Education, 20–34.

Templeton, Shane (1997), *Teaching the Integrated Language Arts*, Second edition. Boston : Houghton Mifflin Company, 89–120.

21
Reading and the Pupil in a Challenging Curriculum

Pupils learn to read in different ways with the use of diverse procedures. Many approaches in teaching reading have been used in the last thirty years and are still widely used. These include:

a) basal reading approaches. Basal readers have had a rather long history of use in teaching pupils; according to Ediger (1997):

Most teachers use basal readers published by a reputable company to teach reading to pupils. Basal readers by themselves will not automatically do the job of providing for individual reading needs of pupils. The teacher needs to use supplementary readers or trade books to assist each pupil to achieve as optimally as possible in reading. Basal readers, however, can provide a quality framework for the teaching of reading. The teacher needs to emphasize readiness activities before pupils are to read a given selection from the basal reader. Thus, the teacher should introduce new words that pupils will meet, when reading silently or orally. These words should be printed in neat manuscript letters on the chalkboard or on a transparency. Each new word may be presented in isolation or within a given sentence. The writer prefers the latter since pupils may then see each new word in context. Generally, words are printed in context as one reads for a specific purpose. Learners need practice at the time of word introduction to be able to identify these words later when reading orally or silently. Being able to recognize the new words in print when reading is salient. Learners then have benefited from being introduced to the new words from the chalkboard or overhead projector.

Readiness activities also include pupils having adequate background information before reading from the basal as well as having one or more purposes, or questions to be answered, before beginning the reading of a selection.

b) individualized reading using library books. Pertaining to individualized reading, Ediger (1996) wrote:

In situations involving individualized reading, the pupil orders his/her experiences. Sequence, it is felt, resides within the involved learner. Others, the teacher included, cannot select the order to goals for a learner to attain. The student individually must do the processing of content. A teacher determined reading curriculum does not work, according to advocates of individualized reading. Humanism, as a psychology of learning, strongly advocates concepts such as the following:

1. student-teacher planning of the curriculum.
2. learners choosing from among diverse objectives which to achieve and which to omit.
3. learning centers from which students may sequence their own tasks.
4. students being involved in determining objectives within a contract system.

Veatch (1959), a strong advocates and writer in individualized reading programs, clarified this program of teaching reading when writing:

The difference lies in the instructional role of the teacher. For example, in recreational reading, we find the following:

A weekly or biweekly period
Little or no actual instruction
Teacher largely free or inactive once books are chosen
Little attention paid to skill development
Reading entirely silent

A quite different picture is found in the individualized approach, to wit:

A daily reading period
Continual instruction
Teacher active and in demand
Concern for skill development

Reading silent with frequent opportunities to read orally to the teacher and to the class.

As such it has certain prime characteristics that occur regardless of the variations in practice found throughout the country. There are: (1) self-selection of material by pupils for their own instruction, (2) individual conferences between each pupil and the teacher and (3) groups organized for other than reasons of ability or proficiency in reading.

Many teachers confuse an individualized approach and recreational reading because both entail self-selection of books.

c) strong phonics emphasis for young learners

Here, a commercially published textbook is generally used in teaching primary grade pupils and older learners, if needed, in experiencing sequential teacher directed lessons to guide pupils to associate sounds with symbols, decode consonant and vowel digraphs, as well as identify diphthongs. Relevant prefixes, suffixes and root words are also studied by pupils to identify unknown words in order to become proficient readers.

d) whole language approaches. As one approach in whole language teaching, Fayden (1997) recommends the following:

Shard reading is a whole language technique which emphasizes the acquisition of specific reading skills such as book concept awareness, return sweep, identifying words after frequent repetitions, vocabulary, prediction of story events, understanding of character motivation, grammatical skills, phoneme awareness and enjoyment of reading. The children's Shared Reading experiences consisted of learning these skills, using accepted techniques, as they read and explore one new Big Book every week....

The accepted definition of Shared Reading is that the teacher uses a Big Book-the reading is directed to a group of children who eventually learn, through repeated readings and other techniques, how to read the book independently. However, the phrase is also used in the literature to indicate the commonality of more than one person sharing the same reading method at the same time...

Pertaining to the use of quality literature in the reading curriculum, Tiedt (1983) wrote:

Literature has seldom been part of the reading program in the elementary school, for reading has been dominated by the basal reader series. What are the advantages of a literature based reading program over the traditional controlled-vocabulary anthology? The use of literature in a reading program for elementary school students offers quality content to a course of study which has concentrated solely on the teaching of skills. It is time that we acknowledge the value of provocative material in exciting the student about reading. Until this excitement is present in the reading lesson, we will not develop a nation of readers.

Many titles from children's literature can be and are being, used as reading text material. The advantages.... over the familiar basal reader are overwhelming:

1. Excellent writing—imagery, use of words, story-telling ability.
2. Continuity of a longer story—plot development, characterization.
3. Greater interest value—intrigue, atmosphere, entertainment.
4. Integration of literature, language and composition studies.

e) Experience charts. Pupils need to have concrete experiences as a basis for developing experience charts. Lee (1981) noted the following essentials in forming an experience chart:

1) An experience common to the group—field trip, story read, an experiment, film, classroom incident, topics introduced by the teacher, a picture.

2) Class discussions with sentences recorded by the teacher, aide, or students.

3) Reading the composed story aloud, discussion of words:

4) Duplicated copy of the story used in individual and group reading experiences.

5) Follow-up activities—varied reading opportunities, dictation of individual sentences according to ability, small group work to extend abilities, language study, listening to literature, extension of vocabularies.

There are approaches used in the last thirty years that are probably not in evidence presently. These include;

a) the initial Teaching Alphabet

b) linguistic procedures with a strong word and sentence patterns emphasis.

c) programmed reading in book form.

There are selected basic ideas that survive and are important in new procedures advocated in the teaching of reading. First, pupils need adequate background information to benefit from an ongoing reading lesson. The background information assists pupils to attach meaning to what is being read. The learner while reading relates the new content read with that which was already possessed in the repertoire of the involved pupil. It behooves the teacher in any content area to provide pupils with necessary background information in order to understand more meaningfully that which was read. A variety of audio-visual materials may be used by the teacher to guide more optimal reading comprehension of the learner. Effective readers (Billmeyer, 1996) actively pursue meaning and carry a mental dialogue with the writer. An ideal reader's mind, or mental disposition, is alive with questions :

* What is this text about?
* How does that fit with what I already know?
* What is the author trying to say?
* What is going to happen next?

* What does the author mean?

Pertaining to background knowledge for readers, Barton (197) wrote:

Prior knowledge plays a crucial role in text comprehension. Strategic readers bring to the task enough accurate background knowledge to make sense of what they read. Prior knowledge acts as a framework through which the reader filters new information and attempts to make sense of what is read.. It also acts as a mind of mental velcro to which the reader can attach new information....

Students bring a variety of experience and prior knowledge to class. Therefore, content area teachers should employ an array of pre-teaching strategies that will help them activate, assess and extend each student's level of prior knowledge.

Another feature of past programs of reading instruction stresses the importance of pupils understanding vocabulary concepts to be read. There are concepts that have similar meaning no matter which academic area is being read. Then too, there are vocabulary terms that are unique to a discipline such as in geography—meridians, parallels, longitude, latitude, among others. Vocabulary terms that might be new to pupils in reading content need to be identified and made meaningful. Objects and pictures that relate to these terms can be shown and discussed with pupils in ongoing reading activities. The act of reading becomes easier for pupils if there is enough background information as well as adequate knowledge about new vocabulary terms that will be contained in the selection to be read. If pupils receive instruction on seeing new words in print on the chalkboard, prior to the actual act of reading, comprehension should increase due to receiving practice in recognizing each new word. Thus, when pupils reed silently or orally, they will recognize the "unknown words" sooner in print. With fluent reading, comprehension of content also increases as compared to the one who reads slowly in a laborious manner. Ediger (1988) wrote the following pertaining to the development of fluent readers using basal reader use:

Basal readers have been misused by classroom teachers. Certainly, teachers must apply basic principles of learning involving the use of basal readers. These principles include:

a) providing for individual differences.

b) attaching meaning to what has been read.

c) stimulating learners in desiring to learn.

d) praising pupils for improved performance regardless of past achievement.

e) diagnosing pupil difficulties and working toward remediation.

f) having learners achieve at their own optimum unique rates of achievement.

g) selecting interesting learning activities.

h) having pupils sense for participating in ongoing learning activities.

i) providing sequential learnings for pupils.

j) having pupils voice their concerns and interests in selecting reading materials.

k) maintaining balance among objectives pertaining to learning word recognition techniques, reading for a variety of purposes and reading for enjoyment.

Newer plans of reading instruction based on sound educational thinking reflecting an appropriate philosophy and psychology of learning will now be analyzed.

Evaluating Diverse Reading Curriculum Plans

A) Reading Recovery (RR) originated in New Zealand through the work of Marie Clay. This plan of reading instruction is based on a one tutor per child emphasis. Generally, young pupils are placed into the RR program to avoid failure. Thirty minutes instruction time per day is given each child in reading for a period of twelve to sixteen weeks in a highly structured program. The lesson starts with the pupil being guided by the teacher in reading a book already read the previous day. The teacher observes how well the child does in reading the abstract words. A running record is kept of how well the child did in word recognition and pronunciation. The teacher then writes a sentence in which meaning to content read well as to the sue of syntactic and visual clues might be demonstrated by the reader. The sentence written by the teacher is cut apart for reassembling by the pupil. Here, the pupil is to see word order or syntax and understanding of content when arranging the sequence of words. A new book is then introduced to the pupil for reading. In-service education for teachers is ongoing and rather continuous. A lead teacher works with other teachers to help in maximizing a pupil's strategies in becoming a better reader.

The RR pupil is taught in a separate room from other pupils. The focal point in instruction is upon the pupil. Generally, the at-risk pupil is in RR. These pupils may come from low income areas and have experienced an environment not conducive in learning to read and not experiencing success in school.

Critics of RR believe that little is done with the emphasis of this program in stressing school reform. The thinking here is that too many minority pupils become members of RR instruction. These critics believe that school reform should not discriminate among pupils in reading and other curriculum areas. Thus, the individual pupil is pulled out of the regular classroom and taught in one on as if he/she has failed rather than school or society. A further criticism is that RR pupils, after instruction, need to return to the regular classroom where appropriate sequence in reading instruction is not in evidence. Critics further believe that pupils in RR do not experience democratic living in a regular classroom. Rather they experience separation from other learners. Gee (1990) wrote the following about school based discourses:

Privilege us who have mastered them and do significant harm to others. They involve us in foolish views about other human beings and their discourse. They foreshorten our view of human nature, human diversity and the capacities for human changes and development. They render us complicity with a denial of "goods", including full human worth, to others humans, including many children. They imply that some children—including many black, Chicano, native American and other children disproportionately fall in school—mean less than other children.

Dudley–Marling and Murphy (1997) wrote the following for trying to counter, in part, their criticism of RR:

> RR teachers might work with classroom teachers to adapt classroom reading instruction on the basis of what can be learned from research on Reading Recovery... Therefore, it makes sense to use research on RR as a basis for encouraging classroom teachers to increase the amount of time for sustained reading and writing within the regular classroom.

Classroom teachers might also determine ways of assisting all pupils individually to learn to read with adequate attention given to each learner's style of learning. Pupils should have opportunities to read library books just as is done in RR. Teachers should evaluate how their teaching favours higher socio-economic level pupils in the classroom. They need to accommodate diverse cultures in the classroom setting. Dudley-Marland and Murphy (1997) continue with writing the following:

> Finally, the evidence suggests that the efforts of RR teachers have improved the prospects of many students and demonstrates that given the right individual support and direction, all children can master the technical act of reading. RR teachers must ask, however, whether the students with whom they work have really learned to read, whether the worlds of school reading deny their worlds, whether their mastery of the technical aspects of reading works so well that these readers become implicated in their own subjugation. These questions suggest that RR teachers must find ways to challenge the discourse of schooling, to fit less well within existing structures of schools. Working to improve the reading of individual students may make a difference in the short term, but long term change requires the exploration of ways to challenge racist, classiest, sexist, homophonic and ablest structures of schooling that produced so much failure in the first place, structures that disproportionate numbers of students from marginalized groups will achieve little economic or social success no matter how literate they become.

Our feelings on RR are the following:

1) One teacher and one pupil has long been advocated in providing for individual differences among pupils. Ediger (1986) wrote the following :

The Puritans felt that infants were born in sin, John Locke and Johann Friedrich Herbart felt that individual were born neither good nor bad. Human beings were neutral due to the mind initially being as a blank shee. Toward the other end of the continuum, Jean Jacques Rousseau (1712–1778) felt that infants were born as good individuals. The infant must be nurtured as a gardener would take care of plants. Rousseau believed in using real-life experiences through which pupils would learn....Learning through the senses was of utmost importance; nature always determines what is best for individuals, according to Rousseau.

Rousseau advocated one tutor teach one child. One teacher then would accompany one pupil in ongoing learning activities.

There have been numerous programs of reading instruction which have emphasized pupils working individually in reading. These have included individualized reading stressed in the 1950s and still popular today as well as Science Research Associates (SRA) Reading Program, a commercially published plan of teaching reading which also has popularity presently. Both of these programs of reading instruction can emphasize pupils being in the same classroom regardless of reading abilities. Or learners might be grouped homogeneously. With mainstreaming of pupils in full inclusion, classrooms are becoming more heterogeneously grouped for teaching and learning.

2) RR stresses pupil pullout for a period of 12 to 16 weeks to assist at-risk and other pupils in this program to catch up with learners in the regular classroom. On task behaviour is very strong during the thirty minutes period of structured time devoted to RR for each pupil.

3) The short term goals of RR is to assist pupils to increase

reading skills where the rate of success has not been that great in previous attempts in teaching reading. There is an attempt in RR to increase proficiency in reading for individual pupils who have experienced failure previously. This short term goal should harmonize with long term objectives of participants in RR whereby a better self-concept should accompany increased proficiency in reading.

4) Selected pupils need assistance if given in the regular classroom or in pullout programs. There probably is less interference in reading in a quiet area for RR instruction. Labels should never be given to pupils regardless of the plan of reading instruction being followed. Labelling in terms of race, socio-economic levels, or any other forms of elitism needs to be avoided.

We believe that much of learning emphasizes a one on one approach. Pupils differ much in their interests, talents and abilities. For example, Clark (1985) stresses that each pupil has a different process in writing and teachers then emphasize a one on one approach in teaching writing. Howard Garner (1995) is well known for his advocating the multiple intelligence theory. One of the seven intelligence, the pupil is able to do well on tasks by himself or herself, as compared to being a member of a group. According to our thinking, reading is so individualized, perhaps a one on one approach needs to be emphasized more often than in generally the case in the curriculum.

5) Pupils in RR can be integrated into the regular classroom after instruction has been completed on a one to one basis. These pupils should not feel embarrassed when reading orally in situations where highly proficient pupils read well. No matter what plan of teaching is used, there will be loopholes. It appears that to "every action, there is an opposite and equal reaction" also holds true in education as well as in physics.

Reading teachers should always evaluate present programs of reading instruction and make necessary modifications in moving away from *what is* to *what should be.*

B) There is a substantial body of research that advocates using inter-disciplinary/integrative approaches in teaching. People tend to perceive knowledge as being related and not in component parts as do many academicians. Whatever knowledge is needed at a given time is used in problem solving. It does not matter here which discipline(s) are involved. Rarely does an individual ask which academic discipline is involved when engaging in problem solving. Dinsmore (1997) wrote:

At this point, it is appropriate to re-examine the terms interdisciplinary and integrative studies. While traditional definitions of inter-disciplinary focus on, amongst other things, the relationships among the disciplines, a new approach could focus attention to the process of inter-weaving and blending knowledge derived in formal and informal environments. Integration also encompasses the assimilation of experiential, essentially practical learning, with theoretical, conceptual (and essentially abstract) learning. Viewed from these perspectives, it is proposed that inter-disciplinary and integration are not necessarily inter-changeable terms. Interdisciplinary takes place in the broader macro arenas between and among disciplinary remains, by etymology, primarily in the real of formal education, integrative education is not so constrained. In the context of ...education, with its capacity to embrace informally derived experiential learning, it is helpful to recognize both integrative as well as the inter-disciplinary ones.

Dinsmore (1997) believes that formal (generally in classrooms) and informal education (in society) compliment each other in providing background information to pupils. Both provide background information to pupils when, for example, they read. This background information helps pupils much when reading, because new content is always built upon what has been learned previously. The new content then sounds more familiar to the pupil doing the reading. Then too, when pupils perceive that knowledge from the academic disciplines is related, they have a broader base of information to draw upon when recalling the old and relating it to the new just being read. Our recommendations for an inter-disciplinary/integrative reading curriculum are the following:

1) A strong argument can then be made for an inter-disci-

plinary, integrative reading curriculum which guides pupils in obtaining background information to understand the new subject matter to be read. Knowledge perceived as being related may be recalled sooner than if viewed as being isolated content from each academic discipline. One idea possessed by the learner will then trigger the recall of other information.

2) Adequate time in reading instruction needs to be given in assisting pupils to perceive knowledge as being related so that the act of reading becomes easier due to possibilities of learners possessing enough background information. Better understanding of what has been read and improved content retention should be an end result.

3) A multi-cultural approach in teaching reading should be in evidence. Interacting with pupils of other cultures and reading about these cultures relates knowledge and should assist learners to read more effectively, not only in the reading curriculum, but also in the social studies.

4) Reading to solve problems needs adequate emphasis since problem solving tends to stress the relationship of knowledge. Whatever knowledge is needed, regardless of academic disciplines inherent, is then used in problem solving.

5) Reading becomes more life-like and utilitarian when it becomes important in solving personal and social problems. Knowledge that is put to use appears to have retention values.

C) What about pupils rereading stories if this is done in remedial reading classes or for learners in the regular classroom ? We believe as children, each one of us had our favourite stories. There are educators who recommend pupils individually collecting their favourite stories and/or poems. The stories and poems collected represent what is of interest to the learner. Then too, these stories and poems are enjoyable to the involved pupil.

Performing in front of others has many values such as developing confidence and poise. We strongly recommend that each pupil have opportunities to be in front of diverse groups to speak, sing, play a musical instrument and dance, among other approaches, to develop wholesome self-concepts and attitudes.

We agree also with Howard Garner's theory of multiple intelligences (1995) in that each person should have opportunities to reveal what has been learned and different intelligences may be used to show these learnings; music is a dimension of multiple intelligences. In addition to the identification by Gardner of intrapersonal and music intelligences mentioned above, the others are inter-personal, spatial, bodily-kinesthetic, logical-mathematical and verbal/linguistic. Verbal/linguistic includes the reading arena. Reading at a proficient level is so necessary for all ! We have a neighbour in our rural area who can read *very* little. He is very proficient in repairing automobiles, but is so limited when a manual is needed to read on specific repairs that need to be made on a certain model, let alone listing out on the many enjoyments that can come from recreational and other forms of practical reading.

Reading educators continually need to study, analyze and think of procedures which assist pupils to improve reading quality and achievement. Could re-reading of content assist pupils to become better readers? There needs to be relevant purposes for choosing to re-read a story or poem that appeals to the learner. Samuels (1997) wrote the following:

The method consists of re-reading a short, meaningful passage several times until a satisfactory level of fluency is reached. Thus, the procedure is repeated with a new passage.

For example, in one of our earlier studies, children who had been experiencing great difficulties in learning to read were instructed to select easy stories which were of interest to them. Then, depending on the reading skill of the student, short selections (50–200 words) from these stories were marked off for practice.

The student read the short-selection to an assistant, who recorded the reading speed and number of word recognition errors in a paragraph....

Repeated readings can be done either with or without

audio support. If audio support is used, the student reads the passage silently while listening to the tape recorded narration over earphones. After a number of re-readings, the audio support is no longer necessary and the student reads the story without help....

There are additional factors to consider regarding use of repeated readings. So that students will understand why repeated reading is done, we have involved them in a discussion of how athletes develop skill at their sports. This discussion brings out the fact that athletes spend considerably more time practicing basic skills until they develop speed and smoothness in this activity. Repeated readings uses this same approach.

Teachers may wonder what role comprehension plays in the re-reading method. Repeated reading is a meaningful task in that the students are reading interesting material in context. Comprehension may be poor with the first reading of the text, but with each additional re-reading, the student is better able to comprehend because the decoding barrier to comprehension is gradually overcome. As less attention is required for decoding, more attention becomes available for comprehension. One additional technique for building comprehension is to ask the student a different comprehension question with each re-reading of the story.

Our evaluation of re-reading philosophy of instruction stresses the following:

1) There are pupils who do not benefit from re-reading diverse materials. Perhaps, there is a style of learning involved whereby selected learners do benefit and others are bored with re-reading due to comprehending contents well the first time.

2) There are pupils who have favourite stories or poems that they like to re-read and develop a personal collection. This needs to be encouraged.

3) Re-reading of subject matter could minimize the need for phonics instruction which can be quite laborious for pupils, if over done. With re-reading, individual pupils recognize an increased number of words. Holism in reading instruc-

tion is then emphasized rather than segmenting words into phonetic elements..

4) As adults, we do re-read what was not understood the first time when reading content. Metacognition philosophy advocates that individuals monitor their very own reading to determine comprehension of content.

5) Learners individually may place in their portfolios favourite reading selections that have been mastered in terms of reading skills developed.

D) Higher levels of pupil cognition are continually being emphasized in the reading curriculum. Thus, pupils are not to stop with rote learning or memory items but go much beyond these levels in thought when engaged in reading. Benjamin Bloom (1956) came out with six levels of thinking in the cognitive domain. Pupils should achieve at the highest level possible so that thinking becomes a major goal in reading instruction. Bloom's six levels or taxonomy of educational objectives are the following:

1) *Recall.* Here, pupils after reading a given selection are asked questions covering content read. The questions raised require pupils to merely given memorized items as responses.

2) *Understanding.* Pupils are asked to say in their own words what has been read. Using textbook wording does not suffice as being on the understanding levels of cognition.

3) *Application.* Pupils, on this level of cognition, are to use what has been read in a new situation. Pupils then need to recall and understand what has been read and then use the information in a practical situation.

4) *Analysis.* With analysis, pupils are asked to separate facts from opinions, fantasy from reality and accuracy from inaccurate statements. A considerable amount of background information is needed to work on the analysis level of pupil cognition.

5) *Synthesis.* Pupils then relate content that has been analyzed. Being able to perceive wholeness after dividing

subject matter into component parts is a high level of cognition for pupils to work on in reading.

6) *Evaluation.* Here pupils judge the worth of what has been read using quality criteria. Pupils with teacher judgement need to work on statements whereby these may be used to appraise content read.

Sternberg (1997) worte the following:

A Yale study, based on the premise that intelligence has analytical, creative and practical aspects, shows that if schools start valuing all three, they may find that thousands of kids are smarter than they think. In viewing the language arts, Sternberg (1997) has provided an example of what it means to teach for four abilities. These are the following:

Language Arts

Memory

Remember what a gerund is or what the name of Tom Sawyer's aunt was.

Analysis

Compare the function of a gerund to that of a participle, or compare the personality of Tom Sayer to that of huckleberry Finn.

Creativity

Invent a sentence that effectively uses a gerund or write a very short story with Tom Sawyer as a character.

Practicality

Find gerunds in a newspaper or magazine article and describe how they are used, or say what general lesson about persuasion can be learned from Tom Sawyer's way of persuading his friends to whitewash Aunt Polly's fence.

In Closing

There are numerous plans in the teaching of reading. Each plan needs to be appraised in terms of following tenets of the psychology of education. The reading plan used must provide for the needs to individual pupils. A caring, conscientious teacher must have the pupil in mind when implementing a quality literature and reading program. Ediger (1997) wrote:

> Students need ample opportunities to select materials for reading. The teacher should display trade books covering variety in topics so that each learner may locate one that has personal interest, meaning and purpose. The student, however, is the chooser of what to read. Trade books for learner selection to read should also be on a variety of reading levels to provide for individual differences.....
>
> The...student chooses his/her very own books to read. Books selected should be challenging to read. Ideas must be of interest to make for further wishes to read. Interest is a powerful factor in stimulating students in wanting to do more reading.

Psychological factors of interest, meaning and purpose are important in emphasizing a quality reading curriculum. The following are additional factors to consider in providing for individual differences among pupils:

1) How much structure a reading program needs to have to guide optimal pupil learning.
2) The amount of direct teacher involvement in teaching reading.
3) The pupil/teacher ratio necessary in emphasizing a quality reading program.
4) The degree to which high expectations by the teacher has on pupil achievement in reading.
5) The kinds of background experiences learners bring to the selection to be read.

References

Barton, Mary Lee (1997). "Addressing the Literacy Crisis : Teaching Reading in the Content Areas", *National Association Secondary School Principal's Bulletin*. 81,587: page 24.

Bhaskara Rao, Digumarti, editor (2000). *International Encyclopaedia of Science and Technology Education*, II Vols. New Delhi: Discovery Publishing House.

Billmeyer. B. (1996). "Teaching Reading in the Content Areas: If Not Me, Then Who ?" Aurora, Colorado: Mid-continent Regional Educational Laboratory.

Bloom, Benjamin (1956), *Taxonomy of Educational Objectives. Cognitive Domain*. New York: David Mc Kay Company.

Clark, B. L. (1985), *Talking about Writing : A Guide for Tutor and Teacher Conferences*. Ann Arbor, Michigan: University of Michigan Press.

Dinsmore, Ian (1997), "Multi-disciplinary and integrative Learning: An Imperative for Adult Education, *Education*. Vol. 117, No. 3: pages 452–67.

Dudley-Marland, Curt and Sharon Murphy (1997), "A political critique of remedial reading programs : The example of Reading Recovery", *The Reading Teacher*. Vol. 50, No. 6, pages 460–67.

Ediger, Marlow (1988). *Language Arts Curriculum in the Elementary*. Kirksville, Missouri: Simpson Publishing Company, page 22.

Ediger, Marlow (1986). *Social Studies Curriculum in the Elementary School*. Kirksville, Missouri : Simpson Publishing Company, page 4.

Ediger, Marlow (1996). *Elementary Education, A Collection of Essays*. Kirksville, Missouri: Simpson Publishing Company, page 39.

Ediger, Marlow (1997), *The Modern Elementary School*. Kirksville, Missouri: Simpson Publishing Company, page 194.

Ediger, Marlow (1997), "Transcends, Classroom Interaction and Reading", *Reading Improvement* 34, 1; 31–36.

Ediger, Marlow and Digumarti Bhaskara Rao (1997), *Science Curriculum*. New Delhi : Discovery Publishing House.

Fayden, Teresa (1997), "What is the Effect of Shared Reading on Rural Native American and Hispanic Kindergarten Children?" *Reading Improvement*, 34, 1: 22–30.

Gardner, Howard (1995), "Reflections on Multiple Intelligences: Myths and Messages, *Phi Delta Kappan*, 77, 3: 200–03 and 206–09.

Gee, James (1990). *Social Linguistics and Literacies: Ideology in Discourses*. Philadelphia : The Falmer Press, page 191.

Lee, Doris (1981), "Reading, Writing and Responsibility", Speech at the National Conference on Language Arts in the Elementary School, Portland, Oregon, April 10.

Samuels, S. Jay, "The method of repeated readings, *The Reading Teacher*. 50,5: pp. 376–81.

Sternberg, Robert J. (1997), "What Does it Mean to be Smart?" *Educational Leadership*, 54, 6: 19–22.

Tiedt, Iris M. *The Language Arts Handbook*. Englewood Cliffs, New Jersey: Prentice Hall Inc., page 313.

Veatch, Jeanette (1959). *Individualizing Your Reading Program*. New York: G.P. Putnams Sons, pages IV and X.

22
Grouping for Instruction in Reading

There are numerous plans in grouping pupils for instruction. It seems as if there are pros and cons for any approach mentioned. Whichever procedure is implemented should assist individual pupils to achieve as much as possible in reading. The self-contained classroom is a rather popular way of grouping pupils for instruction. Most elementary schools group learners in terms of being in a self-contained classroom. Thus, the teacher teaches a single set of pupils in a classroom for most of the school day, except, perhaps, for music, art and physical education. The teacher has numerous opportunities to get to know pupils well in a self-contained classroom. The teacher then should be able to provide for individual learners so that each may achieve as much as possible. Teachers here should be able to provide for diverse learning styles of pupils. We believe that teachers in a self-contained classroom can plan objectives, learning opportunities and evaluation procedures well due to observing the same set of pupils frequently in the classroom setting. There are ample opportunities to understand each pupil so that he/she might learn as much as possible. Pupils, too, can get to develop selected expectancies of teachers due to having seen them teach each sequential days of teaching. We fell that pupils develop feelings of security when they know what to expect of teachers. Should there be a conflict which hinders a pupil to benefit from a teacher's instruction, he/she could be transferred to another classroom and teacher. Further advantages of the self-contained classroom include the following:

1. The teacher can relate subject matter from several different curriculum areas effectively.
2. The teacher may use knowledge acquired from each pupil to more adequately provide for individual differences among learners.
3. The teacher might communicate with parents more effectively by knowing more about each parent and child due to the self-contained classroom (Ediger, 1997).

Limitations of the self-contained classroom (Shepherd and Ragan, 1982) are the following:

1. The need for increased achievement in a basic subject calls for greater depth of preparation on the part of the teacher than teaches in a self-contained classroom generally have.
2. Critics of the self-contained classroom maintain that pupils need experiences with many teachers.
3. Teachers not well prepared in all areas may neglect the areas in which they lack competence. This leads to an imbalance in the school program.
4. Teachers in self-contained classroom tend to become isolated from other teachers, rather than working as members of a team.

In addition, we will present a brief explanation of other plans and then analyze each in terms of strengths and weaknesses pertaining to specific programs of reading instruction. We need to think through each plan with a critical eye and then attempt to come up with a whole or synthesis which is then usable in the teaching of reading.

The reading teacher has a challenge indeed to guide pupils individually to attain as much as possible. This is not easy since pupils differ so much from each other in many ways. Teachers need to have much information of each child in reading so that the best approach possible may be implemented in reading instruction.

What then should a teacher know about each pupils to do a professional job of grouping pupils for instruction? We believe teachers need to look at standardized test results to notice where a pupils stands in comparison to others. Here, we are attempting to obtain as much data as possible pertaining to the learner. The information from the standardized test may be presented as a grade equivalent, percentile and/or a standard deviation. Results for standardized tests are not held as sacred as they were a decade or more ago. Standardized tests are developed in a certain way with the major intent being to spread out scores from high to low such as the first to the ninety-ninth percentile or a pattern following the bell shaped curve.

If available, we would look at the criterion referenced tests (CRT) score of the pupil. The CRT does not attempt to provide a built in range of scores from high to low, but rather measures if pupils have/have not achieved needed objectives of reading instruction. Many states have state mandated testing emphasizing CRTs. On the state level, the precise objectives are developed for teachers to use. The teacher then provides learning opportunities for pupils to achieve. After an interval of time, determined by the state, schools measure if pupils have/have not achieved the stated objectives. Hopefully, pupils will do well on the CRT and the spread of scores will then be minimal. Third, we would like to hear pupils read orally to ascertain where they are in achievement in reading. Questions can be asked of the learner to notice comprehension of subject matter read. It is important to notice if a pupil enjoys reading of library books in spare time. We think it is very important to notice the kinds of errors a pupil makes while reading such as not being able to pronounce words, reading in a halting manner, or providing an incorrect word while reading. In order to do a good job of grouping pupils for instruction, the teacher needs to possess ample information pertaining to each child. Grouping should be flexible and not rigid. Thus, if a pupil needs to be changed to be in a different group for instruction in reading, this should be done.

Team Teaching in Reading

Team teaching has been in evidence since 1957 and has been effectively used in the school setting. Here, two or more teachers plan together the objectives, learning opportunities and appraisal procedures for sequential lessons and units of study. Critical analysis of each plan needs to be in the offing. With interaction among team members, the best approach in the teaching of reading should in evidence. Teachers on a team have ample opportunities to learn from each other in planning sessions. There is built in in-service education in each planning session. Hopefully, the best objectives, learning opportunities and appraisal procedures will be used to teach pupils in reading.

Generally, there are three levels of instruction. First, there is large group instruction with the total class of pupils taught. There can be interaction of team members while teaching or team members may take turns in large group construction. The strongest teacher at any given time should do the large group teaching. Next in sequence, team members work with small numbers in a group or committee in reading. Here in collaborative endeavours, the pupils supervised by a team teaching members analyze ideas presented in large group instruction. The third level of teaching is the individual endeavour. Here, a pupil generally works on a project or task directly related to the large group or committee endeavour in reading.

What are the strengths of team teaching? We think the strongest point is that in-service education can occur directly as teachers interact with each other in planning for reading instruction. Here are opportunities for teachers to learn from each other in an informal way. Second, we believe that more than one mind can be better than one mind when discussing teaching procedures and methodology. In a democratic environment for planning, a teaching team should do well in obtaining the best in learning experiences possible for pupils.

We believe to that having large groups, small group or committee endeavours, as well as individual study, provide variety in terms of grouping of pupils.

There seemingly are disadvantages in stressing team teaching as a way of grouping and as a means of instruction. If teachers on a team do not get along with each other, the chances are it will be an unpleasant school year. Pupils might then not achieve well in reading. Large group instruction may provide problems in providing for individual differences. There are then too many pupils in one group to give individual assistance.

There can be an inter-disciplinary team as well as team members emphasizing a separate academic area domain. The former would be more typical of elementary school teachers in which the concept of the self-contained classroom has been stressed in teacher education training at a college or university. Thus, most elementary school teachers have not majored in a single academic areas such as history or biology, but they have experienced a general education curriculum plus professional course work and student teaching in becoming a licensed teacher. If an elementary teacher was educated at a college/ university school of education with a double major such as history and elementary education, then a team of teachers with similar training may teach social studies in a departmentalized plan. An inter-disciplinary team could also comprise of team members having majors in the social sciences/elementary education; English/elementary education; and biology/elementary education. These teachers would then plan the objectives, learning activities and evaluation procedures for teaching a given set of learners in large group instruction, committee endeavours and individual tasks. Relationship of diverse academic disciplines would then be in evidence (Ediger, 1997).

Heterogeneous Grouping in Reading

The prevailing attitude of educators is that heterogeneous grouping should be emphasized in the teaching of reading. Thus, mixed achievement levels of pupils should be in evidence in any classroom. Pupils of different ability levels may then learn from each other. A more democratic atmosphere should be prevalent when pupils interact with others of different ability levels. Teachers need to look at diverse levels of reading achievement to be a blessing in a classroom. Pupils may work together in peer groups to assist each other in reading for a variety of purposes. Pupil then will differ from each other in many ways which include:

1. intelligence and achievement.
2. interest and motivation.
3. parental backing and help.

4. socio-economic levels.
5. degree to which pupils are able to process information.

Even though pupils differ from each other in many ways in a heterogeneously grouped classroom, they still may be taught with professional teacher assistance to achieve optimally in reading.

There are numerous advantages in emphasizing heterogeneous grouping of pupils in a classroom. Pupils may then work and play with other in a democratic manner. In society, people interact with each other regardless of ability levels; pupils in school too should have the opportunities to interact with individuals who are different from others. The differences occur in different ways. The school setting might then become a miniature society. Learning to work together presently is important regardless of the kinds of differences that exist among members since the work place will, in the future, also stress diversity in terms of who is employed there.

Disadvantages given for grouping heterogeneously in the classroom include the teacher having to provide for the wide range of ability and achievement levels in reading in the classroom. Planning and implementing for instruction in reading becomes much more difficult in heterogeneously grouped classroom of children. The range of differences in reading achievement may be wide indeed. Then too, pupils who achieve very well in reading may be held back by slow learners if heterogeneous grouping is being stressed in committees and collaborative endeavours.

Homogeneous Grouping in Reading

Homogeneous grouping has been advocated in the past and still has its advocates presently. Here, there is uniformity of reading achievement among class-mates. Heterogeneous grouping has a wide range of pupil achievement in reading whereas homogeneously grouped pupils tend to have as narrow a range as possible in reading within a classroom of pupils.

There are advantages in homogeneous grouping of pupils in reading instruction. There is less of a range of learner achievement and the teacher tends to find it easier to provide for pupils when learner achievement is more uniform in the classroom. Pupils are challenged more by good readers in a homogeneous group as compared to having slow learners who might hold a group back in reading achievement.

In addition, homogeneous grouping advocates stress the following:

1. Pupils who possess more of homogeneous characteristics can do a better job of challenging each other, especially the more talented learners.
2. The teacher can do a better job of providing for individual differences in a homogeneous grouping setting due to a smaller range of pupil achievement in a classroom.
3. Each pupil can do more of his/her fair share of work when committee endeavour are emphasized.
4. Less looking down upon slow learners should be in evidence when pupils are quite similar in achievement within a classroom.
5. There can be numerous opportunities to stress heterogeneous grouping when pupils are in physical education, art and music classes (Ediger, 1997, p. 224).

Disadvantages occur when teachers teach the homogeneously grouped class as if these learners are all alike in reading achievement. The reading teacher still needs to provide for pupils of diverse achievement levels.

The Non-graded School

The non-graded school has a philosophy of not stressing grade levels in teaching. Pupils just do not fit into a grade level with its uniform recommended standards of achievement in reading. The non-graded advocates realize that pupils are different from each other and are on different levels of reading achievement. To say that a pupil is in grade five is ridiculous. That is an artificial standard of achievement. The non-graded people rather say that pupils are reading on certain levels and hopefully these levels will make for continuous progress. What pupils have achieved on one level of instruction in reading provides readiness for continuing to the nest level. There is no break or gap in the levels, but rather pupils gradually go on to the next more sequential complex level of reading instruction. Ideally, there are no failures in the non-graded school since each lesson is always based on the previous one, but is one that learners individually may be successful in.

Continuous progress as a concept is different than a pupil having completed grade four, for example and now is in grade five. Thus, the grade levels philosophy of reading instruction states that pupils having completed the basal and other reading materials for grade four and then fifth grade materials of reading instruction follow. There may be no or little sequential progress between the two grades and continuous progress is not possible.

The concept of continuous progress is quite different than pupils going through different grade levels with using first grade materials in reading for the first grade and second grade materials with the second grade, followed by materials equivalent to other grade levels, such as grade three, grade four, grade five and grade six. With continuous progress, teachers attempt to determine an entry point for each pupil in terms of present actual reading level. If a pupil is starting school as a kindergartner, he/she may experience a traditional readiness program or be guided in using a Big Book approach in reading the contents together orally with the teacher. The traditional readiness program or be guided in using a Big Book approach in reading the contents together orally with the teacher. The traditional readiness approach may consist of a play center, a creative dramatics center, an objects center, a toy center, a listening center and audio visual aids center and a speaking center, among others. These activities provided background information to the learner as well as a basic sight vocabulary for formal reading instruction. The basic sight words for reading might come from children experiencing an experience chart approach in learning to read.

Advocates of the Big Book whole language approach stress pupils reading at a much earlier level as compared to traditional procedures. The traditional procedures had their advantages and many of these approaches have been incorporated by the Big Book advocates. The Big Book is large enough for all pupils to see and the contents are read orally by the teacher first and then by the pupils together with the teacher in class. Pupils achieve a basic sight vocabulary of words as they read and re-read the contents from the Big Book and other reading materials. The traditional approach in readiness can also be stressed alongwith the Big Book philosophy of teaching. Phonics can be brought into either the traditional or Big Book approach in teaching. A games approach may be used such as the teacher may ask, "who can give me a word that starts like *bird* does?" Or, "Who can give me a word that rhymes with "*man*"? These are example of the kinds of activities a teacher may devise creatively. There are also advocates of a strong program in scope and sequence in phonics. Their thinking is that pupils through phonics instruction will become proficient in oral and silent reading. We recommend the game approach whereby in context of the lesson, a teacher thinks of enjoyable and stimulating experiences for pupils in analyzing words such as in phonics. Phonics instruction should be made as contextual as possible so that a direct relationship exists between what is stressed in word analysis and reading.

In the non-graded continuous progress continuous progress plan of instruction, the teacher's role is to see that each pupil progresses sequentially, from one age level to the next. Grade levels are not mentioned. Why? Again, what transpires on one grade level may be unrelated to the next when using basal texts. If a pupil has done poorly in reading from a grade two basal reader and then is promoted the next year to read from a grade three basal reader, he/she falls further and further behind. The following year, an unsuccessful pupil in reading in third grade materials is then to read fourth grade materials. In grade four, the pupil gets further and further behind. Continuous progress is completely lacking. Good sequence is definitely not in evidence.

Good records need to be kept of each pupil in terms of progress in reading. For each lesson taught, the teacher then knows where to begin the next day and that is where instruction ended for the previous day.

What are the advantages of the non-graded school? Continuous optimal progress in reading is a very noble goal for all teachers to implement. Pupils should achieve as much as they can on an individual basis in reading. This does not rule out collaborative endeavours whereby peer learning is in evidence. The plan ideally rules out failure for pupils in that achievement in terms of levels are being emphasized regardless of the age of the child. Continuous progress, not age or grade levels, are in vogue in the non-graded plan of reading instruction.

What are the disadvantages of the non-graded plan in teaching reading? Parents as well as selected educators have problems in thinking about schooling without referring to grade levels. I have heard people say that without grade levels, there are no standards for pupils to achieve. My answer to that statement is that age and grade levels have very little to do with where a pupil is achieving presently in reading. A continuous progress plan operates so that pupils individually should not fail. There are parents who believe that whatever grade level a child is in, he/she should be reading from that designated basal reader. For example, a pupil is in the third grade and therefore must read form a third grade reader. These parents would feel it is bad if a third grader would be reading second grade materials, even though that is the present reading level of that child.

Individualized Reading and the Pupil

We will describe one plan of individualized reading, although there are several approaches. In individualized reading, there must be an ample supply of library books to read. Library books are used instead of basal readers. The books are on diverse genres and on different reading levels. Why ? Each child needs to choose a library book to read that is of personal interest and on his/her own reading level. The learner picks which book to read. The teacher does the choosing if a pupil cannot settle down to read a book. This pupil is unable to select and complete the reading of a library book.

After the library book has been completed in reading, the pupil needs to have a conference with the teacher. Here, the teacher discusses the content with the pupil of the completed library book. Here are ample opportunities for the teacher to evaluate comprehension of content of the learner. Stimulating questions covering content in the library book may be raised by both pupil and teacher. The teacher also should evaluate reading skills of the involved pupils by having him/her choose a selection to read orally. The teacher may then notice deficiencies that a pupil has in reading.

Individualized reading does away with the issue of homogeneous versus heterogeneous grouping. Pupils read on their very own and have individual conferences with the teacher.

What are the advantages of individualized reading? Pupils may read materials based on their own individual interests and ability levels. Pupils choose what to read. Thus, individual differences are being provided for. If pupils choose sequential library books to read, they also should perceive purpose for reading. Thus, individualized reading is a child centered procedure in emphasizing reading instruction.

Disadvantages of individualized reading include a lack of emphasis on social development of pupils. Pupils need to have ample time to work together. We believe this can be implemented in individualized reading. For example, a committee of pupils could read the same paper-back and have a peer discussion of its content with teacher guidance. There are pupils who need more assistance with word analysis and phonics instruction than do others. Individualized reading does not provide for a systematic period of time for phonics and other means of word analysis such as syllabication.

Constructivism Versus Behaviourism

Constructivism as a philosophy of instruction has come in rather strong in the educational arena. Constructivism stresses that knowledge is subjective and pupils individually and in committees create their very own knowledge. It is the learner that does the creating of knowledge in terms of what is read and discussed. The child's past experiences and values enter into these subjective experiences. Within context of a lesson, the pupil interprets and makes knowledge.

Opposite of constructivism is behaviourism with its specific measurably stated objectives written prior to instruction. The teacher teaches toward having pupils achieve the precise objectives. If successful, the pupil has achieved the measurably stated objectives. If not, the teacher needs to find a new teaching strategy so that each pupil has achieved the precise objective(s). Here, knowledge is perceived as being objective. Independent of the learner, the knowledge is true or false. The pupil does not create knowledge but receives through instruction that which is objective information.

These are two schools of thought in teaching and learning. We believe it is definitely true that human beings create much knowledge. It has always been held to be the case that in creative endeavours, pupils make, develop and send oral/written original content. Here, uniqueness, novelty and newness is in evidence. On the other hand, on lower levels of cognition or mental endeavours, there are answers to questions that leave no room for interpretation. If, for example, pupils are to write the traditional eight parts of speech, seemingly there is only one correct response—nouns, pronouns, adjectives, adverbs, prepositions, verbs, conjunctions and interjections. If pupils are to write a sentence containing a compound sentence with two dependent clauses, there are many unique responses that can be made. Higher order thinking will tend to stress more of constructivism whereas lower cognitive levels emphasizes more of factual knowledge whereby one answer is correct. We wholeheartedly subscribe to pupils working and thinking on the higher cognitive level. Why ? There are many decisions that need to be made by pupils presently and at the work place later in life. These decisions will tend to demand higher levels of cognition. Tried and true answers tend not to work since situations differ from one time to the next.

What are the advantages of using constructivism as a psychology of learning? Much knowledge is subject to interpretation and to originality of thought. Thus, creativity is necessary and there will be no "correct" answers. For example, when pupils suggest different settings, characterizations, plots, than that written, creativity will be there or should be. In writing of poetry that goes alongwith the lesson or story being discussed, creativity endeavours are wanted. Many decisions made in life stress that which works satisfactorily for the self and for others. Major decisions, in particular, have no ready made answers. These examples are situational, that is, solutions are offered in context by learners in ongoing experiences, be it in school or in society.

Disadvantages for constructivism include the idea that anarchy is involved in knowledge development. This should definitely not be the case. For example, in brainstorming sessions pertaining to suggesting a different setting of a story than that contained in the text, the ideas provided by learners still need to fit the topic. It is true that there will be no absolute answers, but much of life does not possess rightness or wrongness. We believe that many want right answers to problems. It might be a desire to have the knowledge beforehand to make correct decisions, but the crystal ball is just not there. We have to do the best we can with the background knowledge and information available to make rational decisions. John Dewey (1859–1952) wrote about certainty not existing in life's situations (Dewey, 1915). His philosophy of experimentalism indicate a problem solving strategy whereby in context or within a learning activity, pupils identified a problem, clarified the problem, gathered information directly related to the problem, developed an hypothesis, checked the feasibility of the hypothesis and modified or changed, after evaluation, what needs revision. Experimentalists believe that we work in a contextual situation and objective knowledge is not possible. We can only know experiences and these do not provide exact information.

The dominance in education of reductive research practices—which have at their heart a belief in the possibility of clear, certain, universal descriptions of teaching and learning—leads to the enactment of narrow, prescriptive curricula that deny the complexity of the human experience. In a discourse that values certainty, it is possible for state lawmakers to legislate daily phonics drills, for example, as an antidote to poverty. (Presumable, a heavy dose of phonics will cure illiteracy, which will in turn, eliminate poverty, as if poor reading scores among the poor is the cause of grinding poverty). Belief in certainty leaves no role for taking up the role of context in learning, the complications of multi-culturalism, or even individual differences. The "tyranny of certainty" focuses the attention of educational researchers, policy makers and teachers on technical aspects of teaching and put them at risk of losing track of why and how children learn. Our reading of the educational research literature indicates that most educational researchers focus on the technical aspects of teaching (e.g., whole language versus phonics) that take for granted that questions about why and how children learn have been settled. This certainty leaves no room for to wonder or to question...(Dudley-Marling and Murphy, 1998).

Constructivism can be stressed on an individual basis in grouping for instruction such as a pupil writing a legend; the legend is appraised, pupil with teacher guidance, in terms of quality criteria. Within a dyad setting of two pupils, each may share his/her talents in the written product. The teacher in context encourages, assists and evaluates the written product of students. A committee may also write the legend and harmonize their endeavours. The class as a whole may receive introductory experiences in readiness and background in order to write individually, in dyads, and in committees. The teacher is facilitator and helper for pupils to be successful in ongoing writing endeavours.

With behaviourism, pupils individually may achieve each sequential objective as abilities permit. The teacher may also wish to have pupils work in groups and committees to achieve stated objective in sequence. Thus, individual and committee work as means of grouping for instruction work well to achieve behaviourally stated objectives in reading instruction.

A first cousin of the behaviourally stated objectives movement is programmed reading. I, Ediger, supervised student teachers in Ottumwa, Iowa up to the middle 1980s when programed textbooks were used. Each person worked individually in the programmed text and could achieve as rapidly as possible. It would not matter then if heterogeneous or homogeneous grouping of pupils was used since each pupil worked individually from the programmed text. In the text, the fourth grade pupil, for example, would read a few sentences or a paragraph in the programmed book. Next a response was made in the answer booklet. The response was in answer to a multiple choice item covering the few sentences or paragraph read. Then the pupil checks his/her answer with that given by the programmer or writer of the text. If correct, the pupil was rewarded. If incorrect, the pupil now saw the correct answer and was still ready for the next sequential item to read. Read, respond and check was stressed again and again in programmed reading. Response meant reading a pair of sentences or a paragraph before checking to see if the response from the multiple choice item was correct. The pupil is either right or wrong when responding. Thus, it can be measured if a pupil responded correctly or incorrectly to a programmed item. Behaviourism as a psychology of learning is certainty in evidence here with its emphasis upon specificity of objectives in programmed learning with correctness and incorrectness of answers.

There are software packages in reading that are based on principles of behaviourism. Tutorial programs may stress the read, respond, and check approach as was true of programmed texts discussed above.

There are some excellent games that software packages stress. Here, pupils in teams may compete in a wholesome manner against each other. One software game stresses which word of four is spelled incorrectly. Here are numerous lists of four words in a set. For each set, the team that spots the incorrect word in a set of four soonest wins that time. We have observed pupils on teams play this game and they appear to truly enjoy playing with healthy competitive feelings. The software package emphasizes building a larger sight vocabulary, if these are new words for involved pupils. Even if these are not new words in a set, pupils do have opportunities to review what has been learned previously. Pupils then may be working on computer packages involving tutorials, drill and practice, gaming and simulation individually or collaboratively within a team/committee approach in grouping for instruction.

In the information age in which we live, literacy is essential to enable groups, individuals and societies access to the best information in the shortest time so as to identify and solve the most important problems and communicate this information to others. Information access, problem solving and communication are essential to success in the information age in which we live.

It is no secret that the internet has appeared at this time. The internet is currently the most efficient way to store, access and communicate large amounts of information to vast number of people interested in identifying and solving important problems. To prepare our students for the challenge of their tomorrows, the internet and future technologies will be central to our mission (Lieu, 1997).

Linguistic Approaches in Reading Instruction

We will be discussing a linguistic approach in reading instruction from the point of view of Leonard Bloomfield (1961), a pioneer researcher in the area of linguistics. Grouping procedures will also be discussed. Bloomfield advocated a patterns approach in having pupils learn to read. The patterns approach is not a phonics procedure of instruction. Thus, Bloomfield emphasized that pupils in early reading instruction study word families as patterns. These word families to be sure stressed consistency between symbol and sound, but were presented as a more holistic pattern in learning to read. The following words pattern well : *man, can, ban, fan, tan, Dan, Nan, Jan, pan, ran, van* and *an*. It is very difficult, however, to write meaningful sentences using words that pattern. For example, the following sentence could be written : Tan man can fan Dan. This is a meaningful sentence having a subject and predicate that stand by themselves. But, there are so few sentences with meaning that can be written using word patterns. The following words also follow a common spelling and rhyming pattern : *bat, cat, fat, hat, mat, pat, rat* and *sat*. And yet, it is very complex to write even one sentence to show a pattern : "Fat cat bat hat".

How then can one make use of a linguistic approach in reading instruction ? We would suggest pupils providing rhyming words for a work in context from the basal reader or a library book. Thus, pupils may brainstorm rhyming words for "base", as an example. Learners may well be an end result also. The entire class may participate in this activity. A more limited approach might also be used in sentence writing in which some of the words pattern, but not all such as in the following sentence : The *cat* caught the *rat* and then *sat* down. Certainly, noticing how words pattern can be a way of recognizing known and unknown words. Here, pupils may work in small groups of four members or in dyads or pairs.

Disadvantages in using a linguistic approach in thinking about reading instruction includes a lack of meaningful sentences that can be written. Thus, it is difficult to write sentences whereby words need to pattern continuously in early reading instruction. No one speaks or writes in that manner. Facets of the patterns approach can be used to teach pupils in reading. Thus, pupils may realize that there are likenesses and differences in words in terms of pronunciation and spelling. We have noticed pupils who took much interest in noticing words that rhyme and have the patterned spelling such as had, pad, sad and lad. These pupils were also fascinated with words that rhyme but the spelling pattern is not there. These words include the following : blue, to, too, dew, lieu, Lou and two. Locating words that rhyme can be very challenging, when ready, for pupils on an individual basis. Thus, large group, small group and individual endeavours may be used in grouping in stressing linguistic patterns in reading instruction.

Conclusion

There are numerous ways of grouping pupils for instruction. Whatever approach is used, pupils should benefit as much as possible from reading instruction. Team teaching stresses large, small and individual methods of grouping for instructional purposes. I would not favour more than one classroom of twenty pupils taught data a single time in large group instruction. If twenty pupils make for one classroom of pupils in large group instruction, then it would also be good to teach fewer at a one time, such as having committee or individual work in reading. We think flexibility is a key concept when thinking of grouping pupils for instruction. Rigidity and dogmatic thought is not good when thinking of how to group pupils for reading instruction.

Many educators recommend pupils be grouped heterogeneously with mixed achievement levels in a classroom so that learners from all ability groups may learn from each other. Thus, when content is discussed from a reading assignment, each pupil may participate fully regardless of ability levels.

We believe that there should also be homogeneous grouping whereby there is more uniformity within a group as compared to heterogeneous grouping. For example, three reading groups within a classroom has served well for many teachers to provide for three achievement levels in the use of basal readers. Here again, flexibility can be a key concept in moving children from group to group when evidence warrants.

With individualized reading using library books, there are few problems in grouping since the pupil chooses sequential library books to read. If two to four pupils have read the same library book, they may be in committees to have a conference with the teacher covering the content of the completed reading of the book.

Constructivism is a contextual approach in evaluating pupil achievement in reading. The teacher observes and assists pupils in reading when situations arise. Learners construct their own knowledge within a given selection being read. In contrast, behaviourists believe that knowledge is objective and external to the learner. Pupils may achieve the behaviourally stated objectives as quickly as individual abilities permit. Pupils might also desire to work cooperatively in a reading activity. The sharing of ideas in a committee to achieve behaviourally stated objectives can be an excellent way of grouping for instruction, if pupils work harmoniously within the committee. Pupils need ample experiences in learning to work together effectively.

Linguistic procedures may stress individual endeavours such as one person reading a library book. Dyads may involve two pupils reading the same library book. Large groups may be in evidence to provide background information and provide directions for all pupils who sequentially will be working individually and in committees.

Technology has made tremendous strides in assisting pupils to achieve in reading using software packages, CD ROMs, and the internet, among other procedures. New approaches will need to be implemented to guide pupils to achieve well in large group, small groups and individual work. Much of reading instruction continually, we believe, will stress the use of the latest in proven technology. The information coming forth will include improved methods of grouping pupils for reading instruction. Here, we would suggest that teachers use Reading online, an electric journal of the international Reading Association, particularly the Electronic Classroom section. The Electronic Classroom section highlights teacher applications of technology important to reading and the language arts. They also report on technology important to reading and the language arts. They also report on technology based programs and projects of interest to educators. This is a valuable resource to teachers in particular. Reading online is published electronically through World Wide Web (w w w. readingonline.org).

Reading teachers need to study diverse procedures in grouping pupils for instruction in reading and then guide each learner to achieve as much as possible in reading.

References

Bhaskara Rao, Digumarti and Pushpa Latha, Digumarti, editors (1998). *International Encylopaedia of Women*, 5 Vols. New Delhi: Discovery Publishing House.

Bloomfield, Leonard and Clarence Barnhart (1061), *Let's Read. A Linguistic Approach*. Detroit: Wayne State University, page 2.

Dewey, John (1915), *Democracy and Education*. New York: The MacMillan Company.

Dudley-Marling, Curt and Sharon Murphy (9198), "Editors' Pages", *The Language Arts*, 78(2), 88–89.

Ediger, Marlow (9197), *Teaching Reading and the Language Arts in the Elementary School*. Kirksville, Missouri: Simposon Publishing Company, 224.

Ediger, Marlow (1997), *The Modern Elementary School*. Kirksville, Missouri: Simpson Publishing Company, 26.

Ediger, Marlow (1997), *Teaching Reading and the Language Arts in the Elementary School*. Kirksville, Missouri: Simpson Publishing Company, 228–29.

Lieu, Donald J., Jr., Exploring Literacy on the Internet, The *Reading Teacher*. 51(1), 63.

Shepherd Gene D., William B. Ragan (1982), *The Modern Elementary Curriculum*. New York: Holt, Rinehart and Winston, 50.

23
Staff Development and Reading

Much is being emphasized in staff development in the area of reading instruction. Elementary school are studying where they are presently in the teaching of reading and then thinking of moving toward some kind of ideal. Change from where the school is presently in reading instruction toward moving in a different direction is quite obvious. Life itself seemingly consists of change and modification. Stability and the routine seemingly are not there. Society changes much and, therefore, the school setting in the teaching of reading is also subject to considerable change. That is why diverse procedures in staff development are important. Better approaches in reading instruction need to be in the offing. Pupils need to read at an improved rate and at a higher quality level of comprehension. The business world and personal development of the individual makes for a necessity in having better readers.

When we attended the public schools, an illiterate person was one who could not read at all or sign his/her name. Presently, my guess would be that if an adult reads below the ninth grade level, he/she is illiterate. Being able to read on the eighth grade level is quite good for many people. Thus, if an eighth grade reader is viewed, the contents are quite complex and many purposes in reading could be stressed at that reading level, be it in the vocational or in the personal dimension areas. As professionals in the teaching reading, we must always strive for better means of teaching reading. Teaching stresses continuous learning. A teacher never completes the learning process. New ideas keep coming up and higher quality of instruction is in evidence. There are numerous journal articles and teacher education textbooks that stress improving the reading curriculum. Teacher education conventions in reading instruction as well as videotapes that are out stressing improving the reading instruction as well as videotapes that are out stressing improving the reading curriculum behooves us to keep up with modern trends in teaching and learning in reading. This is not to say that a reading teacher should jump on the bandwagon with every when and every new idea that comes out. Sometimes a "new" idea is merely using a different term for the very same approach in the teaching of reading, such as cooperative learning is now being substituted for the previous concepts of committee work. It is very important for each teacher to study and think reflectively about what can be done to improve the reading curriculum (Ediger, 1997).

The Workshop

One procedure in improving the reading curriculum is to stress a quality workshop. The workshop should be based upon the needs of teachers in reading instruction. We recommend that the contents of the workshop be based upon what teachers of reading deem to be salient. A valid and reliable questionnaire could be sent around to determine what teachers feel is important in a workshop. Relevance is a very important concept in conducting a workshop. Time cannot be wasted here because teachers have their very own personal lives to live and to relax after a difficult day to teaching. If at all possible, the workshop should be held during the school week with teachers receiving reimbursement for attending.

The theme of the workshop should be decided with heavy teacher involvement (Ediger, 1988). The school principal also should be actively involved in assisting with workshop planning and attending. Principals need to provide leadership and guidance in developing a quality workshop. It is unfortunate if a principal wishes to dominate plans for what goes into a workshop or if he/she stays aloof and does not back and assist in having a quality workshop. Leadership from teachers and school administrators is so necessary in improving instruction.

Once the theme has been decided upon and the meetings planned in terms of time, necessary furniture, consultant assistance and materials to use, the large or general session should be conducted to decide upon problem areas that need to be covered during the workshop. Members participating in the workshop and being involved in the general session should probably be no more that twenty in number. The general session participants need to be small enough in number so that all may participate actively.

From the questionnaire results obtained prior to the workshop and the decisions made in the general session, participants should then have some good ideas as to the direction the workshop should be taking. Hopefully, needs of reading teachers will be met as a result of having participated in the workshop. Several models may be developed on staff development of teachers and school administrators.

During the general session, participants choose problem areas. A democratic atmosphere needs to prevail so that creative thinking on the part of participants is in evidence. Thus, there is a feeling that wide participation, but not domination, is wanted. Chairpersons for the general session may be elected by participants. There also needs to be opportunities for individuals to volunteer for leadership positions. Certainly, good leadership may come from volunteering from the professional staff. The following criteria should be followed by participants during the general session:

1. All should participate in decision making as to problem areas to be covered during the workshop.
2. No participant should dominate the general session deliberations.
3. Respect for the thinking of others is a prime consideration in interactions that occur among individuals at the workshop.
4. Quality human relations and acceptance of others are very important throughout the workshop.
5. Each participant should contribute knowledge and talents possessed.
6. Participants should stay on the topic being pursued and not digress to something unrelated. Time is wasted if a participant digresses from the ongoing topic being discussed.

7. Critical and creative thinking skills as well as problem identification and solving are welcomed.
8. Care for participants is at the heart of any endeavour that emphasizes change and progress.
9. Ideas should circulate within a group or committee rather then moving from one person to the chairperson and then to another person and back to the chairperson indicating a pattern. When ideas circulate among individuals within a circle, a more open ended discussion will be an end result.
10. Should ideas not be clear, it is the responsibility of the person who needs answers to ask for clarification in a polite manner.

Within the general session, problems are identified and clarified. Participants need to be clear in terms of what consists inherent content in each question. We will outline here selected questions raised by participants in a reading workshop. These were the following :

1. How can a rational balance exist between phonics instruction and holistic approaches in the teaching of reading?
2. Should phonics be taught as a sequential set of learnings for pupils or should phonics be taught in context as the need arises?
3. How can I best determine reading levels of my pupils at the beginning of a new school year, when having twenty-five pupils at the beginning of a new school year, when having twenty-five pupils in my classroom?
4. What can I do to develop a good reading portfolio that is valid and reliable for each of my pupils?
5. What role does diagnosis play in a whole language approach in the teaching of reading?
6. How can I individualize instruction when there are so many behavioural problems of children in the classroom?
7. What role should testing of pupils and constructivism play in evaluating pupil achievement in reading?

8. How should I group pupils for reading instruction when the differences in achievement are so great among children in the classroom and yet educators are calling more and more for heterogeneous grouping of learners for instruction?
9. How can Sustained Silent Reading (SSR) be implemented in my school?
10. How can a mentor teacher approach in the teaching reading be started in my school?

These ten questions are vital in any workshop devoted to improving the reading curriculum. Each problem area identified in the general session needs thorough discussion since important and relevant problem need to be solved. A reference library is needed for participants engaged in problem solving. Consultant assistance is there when a committee needs guidance. Depth discussion and learning is wanted and teachers may try out in their classrooms ideas gleaned from the workshop. Committee members should also report to other committees at work so information is shared by all.

Teachers might then volunteer to serve on a committee for one of the ten identified problems areas above. Choices made by teachers should indicate a need to improve the quality of teaching. Four to five teachers, as a maximum, should be on a committee. With the use of reference materials and consultant assistance, there is a good chance of reaching census within the committee. How successful the committee part of the workshop is depends upon purpose that is seen by participants in the problem to be solved. The attitudes of participants within the committee is also important. If an attitude of wanting to achieve is inherent, the chances are better for success in the ongoing endeavour. Quality human relations are a must! Individuals should learn to work harmoniously and learn to know each other better. The talents and abilities of each person are valuable here in order to come up with good solutions to problem areas. Thus, if interested teachers are working on problem one above on some kind of balance between whole language and phonics procedures in the teaching of reading, hopefully the deliberations within the committee will come up with a rational answer. The area of whole language and phonics has been debated for some time and probably will endure as a problem. However, by researching, using consultant assistance and considerations given for problem solving, the chances are good in finding information on how to stress, for example, both phonics and whole language approaches in the teaching of reading. Teachers also need to look at needs of pupils in the classroom. After looking a diverse reference sources and using consultant assistance, the teacher needs to design a curriculum in reading which harmonizes with the individual pupils needs. A few pupils will need more phonics as compared to others. Phonics learnings may need to be presented in context so that the pupil perceives a need for what is necessary at a given time. Then too with research results, even with a carefully controlled design for the study, there are always pupils who do not do as well in the experimental group even though this group did better, for example, at the .05 level than the control group. Thus, if the experimental group, using innovative teaching methods in reading, did better than the control group at the .05 level of confidence, within that experimental group, selected pupils did not do as well as they might have in the control group which usually has more traditional methods of teaching. The results, of individuals who did not do well in the experimental group, may be examined to notice diagnosis, even though the others in the experimental group did better than the control group.

Committee reports to indicate progress may be shared with other committees at designated intervals. Quality communication is essential in the workshop sessions. Teachers on committees should try out in the classroom that which has been learned when working collaboratively with others. Feedback to the general session of how the new idea worked in teaching should be reported to the community of learners at the workshop, meaning the participants at the workshop.

In addition to the general sessions as well as committee endeavours, a third level of the workshop emphasizes individual projects and activities. Each teacher has a unique problem to solve in the teaching of reading. Diverse resources may be used here as was true of committee work. The problem areas chosen by teachers are unique to the individual. We have noticed teachers working on an individual basis on the following problems, as an example:

1. How does one engaging first graders in reading when The Big Book is used with the class as a whole?
2. What are selected good ways to assist pupils in identifying unknown words in oral and silent reading?
3. How can I have conferences on a one of one basis at the same time other pupils supposedly are reading a library book silently?
4. What is the role of standardized tests in diagnosing and reporting pupils progress?
5. How should the results of learners be analyzed after taking norm referenced as well as criterion referenced tests?
6. How can pupils be engaged to read from and achieve when basal texts are used?
7. What can be done to have a good parent/teacher conference so that the child does better in reading?
8. How can I assist my kindergarten/first grade pupils to develop a functional basic sight vocabulary?
9. Which are good rewards to use to motivate individuals to do more reading of library books?
10. How can I encourage pupils to do more journal writing as well as other kinds of purposeful writing in which the literature curriculum and written discourse is related?

Much effort and time needs to be put into the solving of any one of these problem areas. It would be good to try out in actual teaching of reading situations, solutions arrived at for any one problem area. Lines of communication need to be kept open among committee members so that all can learn from each other in a learning community.

Faculty meetings may also be emphasized in improving the reading curriculum. Too frequently, faculty meetings have emphasized the mundane and the unimportant. When routine information is presented to teachers, these can be placed on the bulletin board or notices may be placed in each teacher's mail box. With faculty meetings, we recommend that an adequate number deal with improving the reading curriculum. We have noticed school whereby faculty meetings for one calender school year stress improving reading. The other curriculum areas also need to receive time, from the entire faculty, to update and change in terms of quality modern trends. Reading well on the part of pupils is relevant in any curriculum area in the elementary school (Ediger, 1997). Teachers and supervisors need to watch that a bandwagon approach is not used in evaluating new ideas in the thing of reading. Too frequently, many jump on board when a new idea is being presented from educational literature. We would like to present a plan for conducting faculty meetings pertaining to improving the reading curriculum. There needs to be an agenda, ready for faculty members, two days before each meeting. Thus, teachers and the principal have time to think about what should be recommended at the faculty meeting. The items listed sequentially should be clear and focused. Vagueness should be eliminated. Faculty members should place items pertaining to reading instruction on the agenda. The school principal also should be involved in agenda development. An elected leader should be in charge of obtaining ideas from teachers and the principal for the agenda. Leadership may rotate so more faculty members have the opportunity of placing and arranging items on the agenda. Participants at the faculty meeting may add items for the agenda in an orderly way.

Relevant, important items need to be on the agenda for depth discussion. We would recommend that refreshments be served prior to the faculty meeting which generally follows a demanding day of instruction for pupils. Rotation of participants in the faculty meeting is important when deciding upon a committee to be in charge of refreshments in an informal setting. It is good to have time for relaxation in a social setting with refreshments. Here, teachers and the principal can interact in a social manner and get to know each other as human beings who can work together to solve problems of instruction.

There should be ample materials of instruction and instructional assistance at the faculty meeting. Thus, video-tapes, teacher education texts on reading instruction, cassette tapes, handouts and computer services, among others, should be available for participants. Faculty meetings need to have appropriate sequence so that teachers may grow and develop in the teaching of reading in the elementary school. Resources at faculty meetings need to be relevant for teachers and the principal to study and evaluate problems in reading instruction. I have observed whereby teachers demonstrate innovative teaching strategies using six or seven pupils from the elementary school setting. The teaching may be video-taped and played and played back to the involved teacher and others. A thorough analysis of teaching needs to be in evidence so the participants learn and develop pertaining to the teaching of reading.

After thorough discussion of problems and possible solutions to these problem areas, it is good for teachers to try out new ideas gleaned from the faculty meeting(s). These ideas can be tried out the next day by individual teachers in their respective classrooms. Perhaps, these teachers may send a bulletin to other teachers in the school stating what happened in trying out innovative ideas in the teaching of reading. If the feedback is presented at the next faculty meeting, there can be a discussion and solving of problems pertaining to new concepts in the teaching of reading being emphasized.

Content in video-tapes might be excellent to use in which model teachers teach reading. The contents may be analyzed using quality criteria, cooperatively developed. Models presented on video-tape can be quite helpful to teachers in using innovative procedures in teaching reading. Whole language approaches might then be observed with a Big Book emphasis for young children. Re-reading and echoic reading may be used after the teacher has orally read the contents with pupils are doing in learning to read after instruction has occurred.

Visiting Innovative Classrooms

There are teachers who speak highly of visiting innovative classrooms where new approaches in reading instruction have been tried out with success in helping pupils learn to read. New ideas in their repertoire are then a part of the visiting teachers in guiding pupils in reading achievement within the classroom setting. We maintain that a newsletter in the school setting should be circulated by teachers telling of approaches used in reading instruction. The methodology might then be open to many teachers in improving the reading curriculum.

To visit innovative reading instruction programs, faculty members need to identify who those teachers are within a building locally as well as other nearby schools. Inquiries need to be made pertaining to making observational visits. Professional teachers do need to share their expertise. Arrangements need to be made for local teachers to visit these places where innovative teaching procedures are taking place. Ample time should be at the place of visitation to notice the objectives, learning activities and evaluation procedures of reading instruction. Discussions with the innovative reading teacher of methodology used are musts! New approaches in sharing ideas in reading need to be in the offing. E-Mail has been an excellent way for teachers to learn from each other with the sharing of innovative approaches in reading instruction. Videotapes should be available, from the school's professional library, to take home to study and analyze new procedures in the teaching of reading. Hopefully, teachers will feel renewed energy in teaching with the presentation of new ideas by visiting innovative classrooms and/or by assessing teaching episodes on video-tape.

There needs to be ways for teachers to report to others in the school setting about innovative procedures viewed in the teaching of reading, such as at workshops, faculty meetings, in school bulietins, sharing sessions with other teachers and in frequent teacher interaction following along in the Big Book with its print discourse. Pupils might wish to re-read he contents several times and thus obtain a larger sight vocabulary.

To vary approaches in the teaching of reading, a videotape on model teachers using behaviourism as a psychology of learning may be shown and critiqued. Here, the teacher uses behaviourally stated objectives in the reading lesson as standards to aim toward when teaching. Either a pupil does or does not achieve a precise objective as a result of teaching. The objectives are very specific indeed, and it can be measured if a pupil has or has not achieved a sequential behaviourally stated objective. If an objective has not been achieved, a different teaching strategy needs to be used. Diagnosis is in evidence here so that problems areas of pupils are identified and remediation following for each unachieved objective in reading.

With a small group of learners, a teacher may use behaviourism in the teaching of reading. Thus, the teacher plans a lesson with the accompanying pupils in mind. The teacher determines a set of behaviourally stated objectives for these learners to achieve. Learning activities for pupils to attain the stated objectives are selected. Evaluation techniques to notice if pupils have achieved the specific objectives become an important part of the lesson. The lesson plan is then applied and taught to the available pupils. Observers may notice the quality of teaching being presented. They may also notice if the objectives, stated in measurable terms, have been achieved by the involved pupils.

Faculty meetings can be exciting and interesting. They need not be dull nor irrelevant. Ideas gleaned from faculty meetings in the teaching or reading may be tried out in the regular classroom. Feedback to participants at the faculty meetings in the teaching of reading may be tried out in the regular classroom. Feedback to participants at the faculty meetings assists others to evaluate new ideas in helping pupils learn to read. Micro-teaching involving a small group of pupils may be taught at the faculty meeting. Evaluation is an important process for any teaching/learning situation involving innovative approaches in the teaching of reading. We do want to know how well in informal settings, such as in the school lounge.

The goals that teachers have in mind are very important when visiting schools to observe innovative teaching as well as when observing quality video-tapes involving actual classroom experiences in reading instruction. What might teachers look for in these in service opportunities?

1. How teachers work with pupils who do not use context clues to identify unknown words.

2. How new words are introduced to pupils in an ongoing lessons in reading instruction.
3. How pupil hesitations are handled when attempting to identify unknown words and yet the learner is able to ultimately say the correct words. Hesitations hinder comprehension in reading subject matter.
4. How teachers group pupils for instruction to optimize reading achievement.
5. How to determine the present reading achievement level of the pupil in the classroom.
6. How to optimize quality sequence for pupils in the reading curriculum.
7. How reading and writing are taught as being correlated and integrated with other curriculum areas.
8. How collaborative learning is stressed in the classroom?
9. How constructivism, as a philosophy of teaching, is emphasized in evaluating pupil progress.
10. How to use test results to improve the reading curriculum.

We believe very strongly that all teachers should be videotaped in teaching reading. This should be done once a month to notice what can be improved upon in reading instruction. Not only may the instructional facet of teaching reading be appraised, but also the physical dimension might also be scrutinized. The teaching and learning situations in reading may be appraised using the following criteria:

1. The teacher may notice if pupils are actively engaged and interested in reading.
2. The teacher may observe if pupils are achieving objectives in the reading curriculum.
3. The teacher may observe contextual progress of learners using constructivism as a philosophy of instruction.
4. The teacher may related different curriculum areas with that of reading instruction.

5. The teacher may notice and eliminate negative mannerisms from the act of teaching.
6. The teacher may use feedback from teaching and from test results to improve the reading curriculum.
7. The teacher may change setting arrangements for pupils so that more optimal achievement comes about.
8. The teacher may look at the kinds of errors made by pupils in reading aloud so that a meaningful reading curriculum may be developed. These errors may include pupils' abilities in recognizing sound/symbol relationships, syllabication skills and in using context clues to determine unknown words in reading. If child is on the first grade level, the teacher needs to emphasize learners using picture clues. Thus, if a pupil does not know a word, he/she may look at the picture and this may provide the child with the correct word for the unknown.

Errors diagnosed by the teacher may become objectives for pupils to achieve. To achieve these objectives, the teacher needs to provide appropriate learning activities. If a pupil does not use context clues/he/she should receive practice in using this valuable skill to unlock new words. Thus, the pupil should receive assistance in determining what word makes sense for the unknown, and yet if fits in meaningfully with the rest of the words in the sentence (Ediger, 1996). The teacher may need to explain this in many ways and in different contexts. If a pupil does not associate sounds with symbols in phonics, the teacher may need to play reading games with that pupil. Thus, to stress the letter "I" and its related sound, the child may pickup anything in the classroom that starts with the "I" sound. Some examples might be the following : lamp, lion (toy), lace, log, lamb (toy) and lock. Pupils in these activities are learning words that begin alike in sound/symbol relationships. Pictures may be used to show initial consonants such as pictures of the following stressing the "b" sound : boy, bat, bicycle, bone, baby, ball and beet. Learners need much practice in learning to associate sounds and symbols in phonics.

Using Cassettes to Improve Teaching

Many teachers that do not have videotape recording

services available may find cassette recording feasible. Here, the teacher may notice the following:

1. The kinds of errors pupils make in oral and silent reading, such as syllabication skills.
2. Errors made in blending consonants.
3. Attitudes in being passive recipients of reading, rather than being actively involved.
4. Behavioural problems in the classroom, such as bothering others in the classroom.
5. Inability to follow directions when reading assignments are being made.
6. Problems in locating more challenging reading materials for gifted and talented readers.
7. Several pupils reading in a hesitant manner and yet being able to identify words correctly.
8. A pupil engaged in word calling when reading orally, but not comprehending what has been read.
9. Selected learners not being interested in materials being read.
10. Two pupils being easily distracted from reading.

Evaluating why pupils are not achieving adequately in reading is difficult. There are so many factors that enter in to the skills of reading. We always recommend to teachers to assess background knowledge of the individual to notice if this makes for poor sequence whereby the pupil fails to achieve as adequately as possibly. We adults need to put ourselves into the shoes of listening to a technical paper by a scientist on space travel and feats; it would indeed be difficult for most teachers to comprehend the contents of the presentation. Why? We simply have not experienced the necessary background information. In other words, the sequence has been poor due to not having the needed subject matter and active involvement that the scientist has had that is presenting he paper (Ediger, 1997).

Observations Made by the Supervisor

Observational visits by the reading supervisor can be beneficial as a technique of in-service education. The better kinds of observational visits stress an invitational approach by the teacher. Thus, the teacher has a purpose in wanting the supervisor to observe the quality of reading instruction in emphasis. The following purposes may be involved:

1. Wanting the supervisor to notice achievement in reading by pupils since the last visitation.
2. Wanting the supervisor to notice how a new unit in reading is being introduced (Ediger, 1997).
3. Wanting to have the supervisor notice the culmination of a reading unit of study.
4. Wanting the supervisor to notice shared reading experiences of a specific committee in working collaboratively.
5. Wanting to have the supervisor to notice shared reading experiences of a specific committee in working collaboratively.

The supervisor of reading instruction needs to be actively involved in solving curricular problems in reading. He/she should possess much knowledge and skill in working with classroom teachers. Let us look briefly at these two dimensions, First, the supervisor needs to have much knowledge pertaining to the teaching of reading. Our thinking is the supervisor should be a thorough specialist in diagnosing and remediation in problem pertaining to the teaching of reading. Our thinking is the supervisor should be a thorough specialist in diagnosing and remediation in problem pertaining to the teaching of reading. The supervisor can be learned upon to be a problem solver in reading instruction with knowledge possessed pertaining to improving reading instruction. The second dimension is equally important and that is the supervisor must have a quality human relations repertoire. The supervisor is then able to work with teacher effectively in curricular problems involving pupil proficiency in reading. Getting along well with others is vital in the school settling. Each person needs to try to get along well with others. A community of learners can come about when teachers work collaboratively to identify and solve problems that pupils have in reading. There are many new ideas to try out to assist a pupil in becoming a better reader. Also, there are many innovative procedures that need to be identified to guide optimal pupil achievement in reading. The supervisor needs to possess human relations skills which assist classroom teachers to do a better job of teaching reading. Supervisors should also guide teachers to work together for the good of the child in the teaching of reading.

Should all observational visits by the supervisor be based upon teacher invitation only? We think not. We do believe, however, that inviting the supervisor to the classroom is the best kind of observational visit that can be made. The visit could be open ended in terms of what to look for when requested by the classroom teacher. There are times too when the supervisor is requested to come to the classroom when specific downhill in achievement at a given time. We also feel that teachers need to become used to having reading supervisors visit classrooms for the purpose of improving instruction. Supervisors should there to help teachers with instructional problems and must do this with good intentions. The supervisor then has a delicate task of observing teaching as a part of his/her responsibilities. Good rapport between supervisor and teacher is ongoing and must be continually cultivated and not left to chance. The supervisor then needs to schedule observational visits with classroom teachers. The observational visits must suit both teachers and the supervisor in terms of time and priorities being emphasized by the teacher in the classroom.

The observational visit should be as unobtrusive as possible. The supervisors wishes to observe pupils in a normal classroom situation. The supervision provided may be clinical in nature. Thus, the supervisor first observes the stated objectives of the teacher. These are evaluated and clarified. The learning opportunities to achieve these objectives are viewed in terms of feasibility and provision made for individual difference among pupils in reading achievement. Also, the evaluation procedures are appropriate in terms of validity and reliability. The approaches and techniques used must ascertain if the pupil has/has not achieved the stated objective of the lesson in reading instruction. The follow up conference then indicates what the pupil has achieved and what is left for additional goals to attain. Throughout the conference, the supervisor and the teacher work in an atmosphere of respect and acceptance. At the same time diagnosis is involved in determining what pupils have left to achieve to make progress in reading. Co-operation and collaboration are necessary so that pupils experience a quality reading curriculum.

Team Teaching and In-service Education

Teaching teams have built in in-service education. Two to three team members planning cooperatively the objectives, learning activities to achieve the objectives and evaluation procedures to ascertain if pupils have/have not attained the objectives, bring in ideas from more than one mind. With a team working together, there are many opportunities to learn from each other. The best ideas should be used in teaching and learning in reading. An essential ingredient in team teaching is that members work together in a mutual atmosphere of care and empathy (Ediger, 1994).

Generally, there are three levels of teaching such as large group, committee endeavours and individualized study by pupils. There are opportunities for teachers to observe each other teach in large group instruction since one teacher teaches the entire group of pupils on his level. The presentation may be critiqued and evaluated with the involved teacher. This should be done in an atmosphere of respect with the intent of improving reading instruction. Areas of evaluation of the teacher in large group instruction might well be the following:

1. Did the teacher secure the attention of the entire group of pupils?
2. Were pupils interested and motivated in the large group session?
3. Was the presentation clear and meaningful to all pupils?
4. Did pupils voluntarily raise relevant questions during the large group instruction session?

5. Did the teacher follow quality procedures in sequencing learning opportunities?
6. Were pupils encouraged to raise questions and identify problem areas?
7. Did the teacher establish purpose for pupils learning?
8. Were individual differences in achievement provided for among learners?
9. Were pupils respectful during and after instructional time?
10. Did pupils put forth effort during large group instructional time?

After large group instruction, pupils work in committees and individually on projects and activities. It is vital that teaching team members follow the following criteria when working at these two levels:

1. Observing pupil progress and achievement as continuously as possible in order to provide for the needs of learners.
2. Assisting pupils with learning activities as needs indicate.
3. Showing care and consideration in working among and with pupils.
4. Challenging pupils to achieve as optimally as possible.
5. Developing interest in learning on the part of pupils.

Team teaching members need to upgrade their teaching skills continuously and share worthwhile ideas with team members. There are built-in opportunities for in-service education for teachers when they are members of a team and provide learning opportunities for pupils. As team members discuss objectives, learning opportunities and evaluation techniques, the ideas circulate and provide in-service ideas in teacher education.

The Professional Library

Teachers need to have ample opportunities to browse through and read materials from the professional school library. Each school should subscribe to educational periodicals that benefit teachers to become increasingly professional in teaching and learning. The principal of the school as well as teachers should encourage each other to read educational journal articles and teacher education textbooks in the area of involved teaching. A community of learners might well be an end result. Sharing of ideas dealing with improving teaching performance is a must. A school bulletin might also be developed to call attention to leading articles in education. At teachers meetings, school faculty should share ideas on teaching and work toward an improved curriculum. At a public school meeting of faculty and administration, we observed teachers reporting on the following topics at sequential meetings:

1. How to teach the at risk pupil in reading.
2. How to plan instruction for the mobile pupil.
3. How to identify gifted readers for a special class.
4. How to plan instruction for first grade pupils who are not ready for a formal reading program.
5. How to uphold high expectations for pupils in sequential reading experiences.

When teachers have special needs and feel purpose in reading professional literature on the teaching of reading, there appears to be much motivation to grow, develop and achieve. We wholeheartedly subscribe to the idea of having a professional library for teachers and administrators to use in improving reading instruction. Reading instruction emphasizes reading across the curriculum. We would like to make the following recommendations in developing and using a professional library for educators in the public school setting:

1. The journal articles and teacher education textbooks assist teachers in doing a better job of teaching. There are indeed many good teachers out in the field and each can always achieve from where they are to where they might be as professionals in reading instruction.
2. Educational journals and teacher education textbooks need to be reputable and functional. Teachers should have access to "how to" literature as well as content on theories

of learning, psychology of education, as well as philosophy of education.

3. The professional library should be developed cooperatively by those involved in the teaching of reading.
4. The materials in reading instruction should be accessible and easy to use. With normal wear and use, the journals and teacher education textbooks will show the function they serve.
5. There should be comfortable facilities to check out and read professional content.
6. Time provided specifically for reading professional materials is time wisely given by the school.
7. Worthwhile ideas from the journals and teacher education textbooks on reading instruction should be tried out and feedback given to other teachers in the school setting.
8. As time goes on, the library holding should be increased to include video-tapes, cassette tapes, internet and CD ROMs, among other electronic media. Networking is a good idea to obtain ideas on reading instruction in assisting each pupil to achieve as well as possible (Ediger, 1991).

Parent and Teacher Conferences

An excellent way to improve the reading curriculum is to discuss a learner's progress during a parent/teacher conference. This is a good way for the teacher to receive input from parents as to how to guide the offspring to achieve more optimally. There is much that the teacher can learn about the child and his/her environment (Ediger, 1988). Among other items, the following comments may be made by the parent of the pupil:

1. The aspirations parents have for the child.
2. The amount of assistance parents provide in helping the child to improve in reading.
3. Attitudes that the pupil has toward reading materials.
4. Motivation that the learner has in wishing to improve in reading more fluently.

5. Kinds of errors the learner makes in reading.
6. Types of reading programs that guide the learner to make the most progress in reading instruction.
7. Kind of home life the pupil experiences.
8. The physical and emotional health that the pupil possesses.
9. Attitudes of parents to the offspring.
10. The positive adjustment the child has made toward the home and the school.

In Summary

There needs to be a variety of in-service education methods to guide teachers to do the best job possible in the teaching of reading. Teachers need to have access to diverse procedures in in-service education so that each pupil may be guided to achieve as much as possible in reading.

In-service education programs for reading teachers should be functional and useful to teachers. Teachers need to perceive purpose or reasons for participating in in-service education programs. Interest in improving instruction is a powerful approach in guiding teachers to pursue and achieve in improving reading instruction. Administrators need to be well versed in the teaching of reading and assist teachers to make needed changes in the area of reading instruction. Positive feeling toward each other helps teachers and administrators too in using different approaches to improve the teaching of reading.

References

Bhaskara Rao, Digumarti (1993). *Teaching of Science*. Guntur: Nagarjuna Publishers (in Telugu Language).

Bhaskara Rao, Digumarti (1997). *Teacher and Education*. Guntur: Nagarjuna Publishers (in Telugu Language).

Bhagya Lakshmi, L. and Digumarti Bhaskara Rao (1999), *Reading and Comprehension*. New Delhi: Discovery Publishing House.

Ediger, Marlow (1988), *The Elementary Curriculum*. Kirksville, Missouri: Simpson Publishing Company, 117–23.

Ediger, Marlow (1994), *Education Magazine*, Doha, Qatar. National Commission for Education (The Persian Gulf), 29–31.

Ediger, Marlow (1988), *Curriculum*. Kirksville, Missouri: Simpson Publishing Company, 297–307.

Ediger, Marlow (1997), *Teaching Reading and the Language Arts in the Elementary School.* Kirksville, Missouri : Simpson Publishing Company, 1–17.

Ediger Marlow (1997), "Transcents, Classroom Interaction and Reading. *Reading Improvement* (34), 4: 176–181.

Ediger, Marlow (1997), Recent Issues in Education, *Philippine Education Quarterly*, (26), 1: 1–6.

Ediger, Marlow (1996), "Reading in Science", *School Science*, (34), 3: 50–56.

Ediger, Marlow (1997), "Reading in Mathematics", *Teaching Mathematics in the Elementary School.* Kirksville, Missouri: Simpson Publishing Company, 161–186.

Ediger, Marlow (1991), *Relevancy in the Elementary School.* Second edition. Kirksville, Missouri : Simpson Publishing Company, 154–213.